Structure and Experience in Shakespeare's Romances

Structure and Experience in Shakespeare's Romances

J. Symonds

CYBER TECH PUBLICATIONS
4264/3, Ansari Road, Daryaganj, New Delhi-110002 (India)
Ph.: 011-23244078, 011-43559448 Fax: 011-23280028
E-Mail: cyberpublicationsdelhi@yahoo.com
Website: www.cybertechpublications.com

STRUCTURE AND EXPERIENCE IN SHAKESPEARE'S ROMANCES

J. Symonds

First Edition 2010

Published by :

G.S. Rawat for **Cyber Tech Publications**
4264/3, Ansari Road, Daryaganj, New Delhi-110002 (India)
Ph.: 011-23244078, 011-43559448 Fax: 011-23280028
E-Mail: cyberpublicationsdelhi@yahoo.com
Website: www.cybertechpublications.com

Preface

This comprehensive and well-informed study is also a work of detection and reappraisal. Each tragedy is considered both as a text and as a play to experience in performance. Shakespeare's engagement with this form of drama is followed step-by-step until its concluding years of intense activity. No theory of tragedy emerges, but rather an increasing ability to maintain and communicate a clear-eyed perception of a changing and often violent society in which action is stronger than words or conscious intention.

William Shakespeare, by universal consent the greatest author of England, if not of the world, occupies chronologically a central position in the Elizabethan drama. He was born in 1564 in the good-sized village of Stratford-on-Avon in Warwickshire, near the middle of England, where the level but beautiful country furnished full external stimulus for a poet's eye and heart.

In 1597, the Admiral's Men revived the play 'possibly in revised form, for a run of thirteen performances.' (Lukas Erne, Beyond 'The Spanish Tragedy':XVI) The play was printed in 1592, reprinted in 1594 and 1599. In his Diary, Henslowe recorded in 1601/2 a payment to Ben Jonson for additions to the play. In 1602 the play is printed with additions for the first time - 'probably not those by Jonson' concludes Lukas Erne in his Preface to Beyond 'The Spanish Tragedy':XVI. The play appeared in further editions in 1603, 1610, 1615, 1618, 1623, and 1633 - and probably continued to be performed. Last news on the early stage life of the play is that it was 'performed at the Nursery Theatre in Hatton (reported by Pepys)' in 1688. (Lukas Erne, Beyond 'The Spanish Tragedy':XVI).

— *Author*

CONTENTS

Preface

1. Introduction 1
2. Shakespeare's and Kinds of Drama 10
3. Romance of the Shakespeare's 104
4. Beyond Tragedy of the Britain King Lear's 143

Bibliography 261

Index 263

1

Introduction

Shakespeare is very much with us and has been for a long time. The language, the stories, the images, the very way of thinking saturate Euro-American culture and also reach beyond. Lovers speak (one on a balcony), a man holds a skull, a fat man argues for life against honor and death, a king speaks and the troops are roused to battle, a Roman asks for the ears of his friends and countrymen and they are roused to folly. And there is the language: "The quality of mercy is not strained," "Hath not a Jew eyes?" "Oh what fools these mortals be," "To be or not to be," "All the world is a stage." Don't complain about all the clichés: Shakespeare wrote them first; others repeat them. Shakespeare is part of our daily life. We play out the love stories, the power struggles, the tricks and we muddle through toward the sort of insight that hits suddenly as it does at the end of a comedy or a tragedy.

Shakespeare walks with me everywhere. It's not just that I see and have seen so many productions on stage and on film. It's not just that I teach his work and have studied it at every level of my schooling. His language permeates my thinking and speech. Most every day, sometimes every hour, I think about events and compare them to events in Shakespeare's plays. Sometimes it seems I am living in the plays and so are you and so are George W. Bush and Osama Bin Laden. Art does not imitate reality; it creates it.

For me, formal study of the plays happened in Junior and Senior High. At U.C.L.A. I had undergraduate classes on Shakespeare from

Richard Lanham (who focused on game theory, rhetoric and notions of personality), David Rodes (a humanist and close-reader with a keen eye for performance elements), Robert Maniquis (Marxist and psychoanalytic approaches), and audited classes by Jimmy Phillips (a vivid humanist teacher and author of a study of Shakespeare's Roman plays) and Paul Jorgenson (major critic of Shakespeare with focus on historical context). In graduate school at U.C.L.A., I took written exams in Shakespeare and the Renaissance, a tutorial with Stephen Bates and a seminar on The Tempest from George Guffey. I am also influenced by many friends from graduate school with whom I discussed and studied Shakespeare. Grace Ioppolo taught me much about the texts (her work is in a significant book). Out in Wyoming I have learned from Laramie colleagues Duncan Harris, Susan Frye and Peter Parolin, brilliant critics and teachers.

Performances have influenced my thinking immensely. In Los Angeles, where I grew up, I saw Shakespeare in small Hollywood theaters, at the Music Center, at U.C.L.A. and at the San Diego Shakespeare Festival. Peter Brooks' circus version of A Midsummer Night's Dream was the most memorable and Charlton Heston as Hamlet, the most forgettable. I saw lots of Shakespeare during a summer in London, England (where I was working on my Ph.D. dissertation on William Blake), most memorably As You Like It with Ralph Richardson. I never did visit Stratford-on-Avon and have not seen the rebuilt Globe Theater. Several years ago, I went to the Shakespeare Festival (there are a lot—including one in Boulder, Colorado) in Ashland, Oregon. They do fresh interpretations with a talented ensemble of actors during a nine-month run in three theaters, one a large outdoor recreation of the Globe. I have seen many plays in Boulder and at the Denver Center (Taming of the Shrew as a Western and an exciting and fast King Lear) and Twelfth Night as a 60's rock and roll drug fantasy at the Victorian Playhouse.

I have spent lots of time over the years in Washington D.C. have seen many plays at the big downtown Shakespeare Theatre plus the Folger Shakespeare Library, though none could surpass a local company's Macbeth, with the entire cast naked from start to finish.

There is Shakespeare in Casper—I have seen Romeo and Juliet done by Casper College, actors from London and the Wyoming Shakespeare company, two Tempest's, two Midsummer Night's Dream's (CC and Stage III, outside) and Taming of the Shrew done by Stage III and The Merry Wives of Windsor, a great Hamlet and a fresh take on As You Like It done by Casper College. The seldom-performed King John was at the Nicolaysen this summer. This semester we will see Casper College's production of King Lear.

Out of this mish-mash comes my approach to Shakespeare. I emphasize historical context, performance and current meaning. The plays do not just reflect the history of their times, but were active participants in shaping that history. We will pay a lot of attention to Shakespeare's world and what the plays have to say about it. Part of that world is the reality of producing plays in Elizabethan London and the history of performance. We will pay considerable attention to how the texts function as guides to a performance and how audiences would likely respond.

Recently, an eccentric church burned a variety of purportedly evil books including an edition of Shakespeare's plays. This act invited and received a very hostile response, in part, for reminding us of Hitler, but also for picking on Shakespeare who has come to represent the heart of Western culture and wisdom. The act also reminds us that the plays can be edgy and controversial (there is plenty of sex and violence and maybe some blasphemy) as the best art often is. We should also remember that Shakespeare was a working dramatist aiming "to please" and that if he is "universal" it is because the plays often do. Perhaps it seems an odd idea to seek for pleasure and delight in a college class, but I hope we find it in this one.

POLICIES OF SHAKESPEARE

1. Late papers are accepted with a penalty of half a grade for each day overdue.
2. Revised versions of graded assignments will be regraded. The final grade will be a ratio between the two grades with

the grade on the first version counting 2/3 and the grade on the revised version 1/3.

3. Plagiarized papers receive an "F" and the author is subject to disciplinary action. Students who plagiarize may receive an "F" for the entire course and, in appropriate cases, I will inform the owners of the plagiarized document so they can pursue legal action against the offender. According to the "Style Sheet" from the UCLA English Department, "plagiarism is the use of another's ideas or words as if they were one's own" (5). Be sure to acknowledge any borrowed ideas or quotations. If you have questions about difficult cases, see me.
4. Attendance is important and will be graded. I reserve the right to lower the course grade for anyone who misses more than one class.

THE PHILOSOPHY OF SHAKESPEARE

I subscribe to (pardon the clichés) a student-centered, active learning model. In my view, class sessions are collective enterprises that use argument, discussion, analysis, description and humor to create knowledge. I am willing to argue that knowledge is not some pre-existing construct available from, say, a textbook, a professional article or a lecture, but is part of an ongoing process to describe and explain the world. Textbooks, articles, lectures are part of a continuing conversation or argument among scholars, students, readers, writers, journalists, whomever to create, not discover, knowledge.

In this class I want you to learn how to participate in the conversation, how to be a part of the process of creating knowledge and how careful (and not so careful) thinkers reach judgments about cultural documents.

Members of a class ought not to be passive receptacles of one person's conclusions, but participants in the exercise of reaching conclusions. I hope you learn not what to think, but how thinking works, how to draw judgments, how to respond more fully to the world and the things in it. You will learn in this class that there are many, many ways to respond to cultural objects--because they are so complex, because they exist in so many contexts and because we readers are so complex and diverse.

I plan to run this class as a discussion-seminar with lots of writing and small group work. Lectures may break out, but they will usually be accidents or responses to immediate issues. The best research thus far shows that people LEARN ALMOST NOTHING from sustained lectures, but do much better with discussion and writing in a participant, experience-based educational environment.

We will use mostly discussion: talk, talk, talk, write, talk, talk, write, talk, draw, talk, write. Your notes should record the flow of conversation in the class and the judgments and arguments of the different class members. Views expressed during our sessions will form an important part of the final exam. Regularly, I will ask you to write a brief summary of the most important points made during the class. Keep a log of these. Listening carefully to others and reflecting on what they say are important skills in our enterprise.

Finally, I have become convinced that people learn to write best in groups. Writing, so often a lonely effort with one struggling soul and one ominous judge, needs to go public. Drafts, notes, ideas, texts all should pass through a stream of hands and receive a multitude of responses. In the "real" world of professions, papers are done by many, for many. Only in schools is it otherwise. (Fortunately, this is changing and changing fast!)

SOME USEFUL WORKS ON SHAKESPEARE

It is probably impossible in a lifetime to read what has been written on Shakespeare. Following are some books that I am reading or have read recently that I recommend. Shakespeare, William. Norton Critical Editions. Includes texts of the plays, notes, sources and backgrounds and critical essays. New ones of King Lear, Macbeth, Othello and The Tempest are especially good. Also see the Bedford

Shakespeare Series. The Texts and Contexts edition of Macbeth (edited by William C. Carroll) includes a full set of documents related to the play. Bevington, David. Shakespeare (1999). Fresh and thoughtful commentary.

Callaghan, Dympa, ed. A Feminist Companion to Shakespeare (2000). Rich, dense and lively essays argue that most Shakespeare studies are dominated by patriarchal thinking. Dobson, Michael and Stanley Wells, eds. The Oxford Companion to Shakespeare (2001). A lot of information in well-written, up-to-date entries. Garber, Majorie. Shakespeare and Modern Culture. (2008). Energetic discussion of Shakespeare as a stimulant and convener of modern cultural discourse.

Greenblatt, Stephen. Will in the World: How Shakespeare Became Shakespeare (2004). This best-seller combines strong discussion of the plays, rich and specific historical material and highly speculative ideas about Shakespeare's life. Gurr, Andrew. Playgoing in Shakespeare's London (2nd edition, 1996). Gurr focuses on the general audience for Shakespeare's plays. Kernan, Alvin. Shakespeare: The King's Playwright: Theater in the Stuart Court, 1603-1613. (1991). Kernan looks at Shakespeare's plays performed at the court of King James and discusses how they were a part of court politics.

Kermode, Frank. The Age of Shakespeare (2004). A short introduction to Shakespeare's time with comments on the plays. Nicholl, Charles. Shakespeare The Lodger: His Life on Silver Street (2007). Finds much meaning in the details of Shakespeare's life on Silver Street and involvement in a marriage dispute. Good information about London in Shakespeare's time and intriguing biographical detective work. Shapiro, James. A Year in the Life of William Shakespeare: 1599 (2005). Connects events of 1599 to four of Shakespeare's plays.

Thompson, Ann and Neli Taylor, The Arden Shakespeare Hamlet (2006) and The Arden Shakespeare Hamlet: The Texts of 1603 and 1623 (2006). The three versions of Hamlet, printed separately with extensive notes and commentary. The editors argue that there is not one, but three texts of Hamlet each with a claim on our attention. Wells, Stanley. The Cambridge Companion to Shakespeare Studies (1986). The essays here survey the history of performances and criticism of Shakespeare and present recent information of different topics related to his plays. Wells, Stanley. Shakespeare and Company (2007). Essays on the other dramatists with whom Shakespeare competed, collaborated and lived. Plays on DVD and CD. There are many recorded versions of the plays available at the Casper College Library and The Natrona County Public Library.

SHAKESPEARE'S ACTIVITY

The segment of a play we have read this semester of your choice with a group with everyone acting and one or more directing. Your segment should run about ten minutes. You may do the scene with hand-held scripts or memorized.

Provide a written commentary (five to ten pages) on the scene that discusses in detail its meaning, emotion, elements of character, and role in the themes and structure of the play.

You may divide this up among the group with each writer/actor taking on a different element.

You will be evaluated on the paper you write, not the acting, though it is important that you work hard and with others on your presentation of the scene since this will give you good information to write an outstanding paper.

Characters: overall character and motivation, motivations and goals in this particular scene, process of thinking in the scene and overall, techniques of persuasion at work, style of interaction with others, basic drives, style of speaking—characteristic metaphors and vocabulary. How does the character speak? How do they move? What do they wear?

Blocking: Where is everybody standing, how do they move, explain entrances and exits, how do they interact with the set, with each other, identify gestures and specific actions.

Set: Where are the events happening; what sort of space do you have; what kind of set and props do you envision? Is there music or other sounds?

Overall Concept: How does the scene fit into the main actions and ideas of the play? What fundamental relationships are there among the characters? What is the mood of the scene and the play as a whole?

When? Rehearse and discuss scenes on March 18. Present scenes and review drafts of your paper on March 25. Paper due April 3.

SOME TOPICS OF THE LITERATURE PAPERS BY SHAKESPEARE

1. Your paper needs a thesis, a statement that can be argued for or against, that demands evidence. "Shakespeare wrote about kings" would be a lousy thesis--there is nothing to say about it; it is non-falsifiable. Here's a better one: "In Hamlet Shakespeare seems to show a difference between playing a monarch and being one, though the example of Fortinbras shows that there is no fundamental difference--how you act is what you are." This makes a claim that can be proved or disproved by appeals to particular evidence. The second part of the sentence suggests a narrow focus that can be adequately developed in a short paper.
2. Each paragraph is a mini paper, starting with a claim or point that is developed in that paragraph. No one sentence paragraphs: give us some meat.
3. Use details to prove your arguments. Do not just quote for the sake of quoting, but use the language that makes your point and omit that which is irrelevant. You may wish to mention details without quoting, but do use details.
4. Quote accurately and make quotations part of your own sentence. Type verse quotations of longer than two lines as verse, separating them in block fashion from your text. Enclose shorter quotations in quotation marks and type

them as part of your consecutive text. Use a slash ("that is the question:/Whether 'tis") to indicate a change in lines. Provide the play, act, scene, and lines in a parenthetical note after the quotation (Hamlet, 3.1.56-7). You may omit the name of the play if it is clear from the context. If you use a secondary source, indicate it in a parenthetical note supported by a "Works Cited" page at the end of the paper. Omit the title of the work if the source is obvious. Follow standard MLA format for the list of books at the end.

5. Type the paper double-spaced with reasonable sized type and margins. Put page numbers in the upper right hand corner. Provide a title page with a title that describes your topic and your thesis (Not The Winter's Tale, but, say, "Pastoral Escapism in The Winter's Tale"). Staple together the final copy (no plastic folders). Make your instructor happy and do not justify the right margin.

6. *Do your paper in stages.* Take some notes as you read; jot down an idea in the margin; write down thoughts that come to you as you cross campus. There is no one right way to compose, but all writers follow some process. Give yourself some time to let the material germinate and use drafts to help you along. If writing is thinking or writing is learning then you would do well to write often. Make your work as public as possible. Talk to others; let them read what you are doing; invite honest responses. And certainly have a clear-eyed friend read the final draft to correct obvious errors.

7. *Have some fun. Writing is hard work.* I'm sweating right now--but can be a great joy. Beyond the pleasures of creation and discovery, there are great sensual delights in caressing a sonorously cadenced sentence or banging out an explosive joke. We'll be reading some wonderful poetry this semester; may its glories infect us all.

2

Shakespeare's and Kinds of Drama

INTRODUCTION

At the end of his career Shakespeare experimented with a new dramatic mode that we call romance. His efforts in this form include Pericles, Cymbeline, The Winter's Tale, and The Tempest, as well as the two collaborations written at the very end of his career with John Fletcher, The Two Noble Kinsmen and probably Cardenio. Never one to be bound by the Roman models to which some of his contemporaries were faithful, Shakespeare was by this time uncommonly adventurous in combining kinds and adapting into drama the various tales and narratives that appealed to him.

Many of his contemporaries were adventurous too, for by about 1608 the London stages offered audiences a range of choice: historical tragedy, domestic tragedy, imitations of classical tragedy, romantic comedy, city comedy, satire, prodigal-son plays, apprentice-makes-good stories, chronicle plays, and tragicomedy.

Francis Beaumont and John Fletcher, writing under the influence of Continental models, were gaining attention for their development of English tragicomedy in plays such as Philaster and A King and No King.

Shakespeare's last plays most resemble this kind of tragicomedy, which, as Fletcher's description makes clear threatens its audience with disaster or death and abruptly changes gears so that the action comes to a happy ending.

SCENE I.: THE PARK

Enter ARMADO and MOTH

ARMADO. Warble, child; make passionate my sense of hearing.

[MOTH sings Concolinel]

ARMADO. Sweet air! Go, tenderness of years, take this key, give enlargement to the swain, bring him festinately hither; I must employ him in a letter to my love.

MOTH. Master, will you win your love with a French brawl?

ARMADO. How meanest thou? Brawling in French?

MOTH. No, my complete master; but to jig off a tune at the tongue's end, canary to it with your feet, humour it with turning up your eyelids, sigh a note and sing a note, sometime through the throat, as if you swallowed love with singing love, sometime through the nose, as if you snuff'd up love by smelling love, with your hat penthouse-like o'er the shop of your eyes, with your arms cross'd on your thin-belly doublet, like a rabbit on a spit, or your hands in your pocket, like a man after the old painting; and keep not too long in one tune, but a snip and away.

These are complements, these are humours; these betray nice wenches, that would be betrayed without these; and make them men of note- do you note me?- that most are affected to these.

ARMADO. How hast thou purchased this experience?

MOTH. By my penny of observation.

ARMADO. But O- but O-

MOTH. The hobby-horse is forgot.

ARMADO. Call'st thou my love 'hobby-horse'?

MOTH. No, master; the hobby-horse is but a colt, and your love perhaps a hackney. But have you forgot your love?

ARMADO. Almost I had.

MOTH. Negligent student! learn her by heart.

ARMADO. By heart and in heart, boy.

MOTH. And out of heart, master; all those three I will prove.

ARMADO. What wilt thou prove?

MOTH. A man, if I live; and this, by, in, and without, upon the instant. By heart you love her, because your heart cannot come by her; in heart you love her, because your heart is in love with her; and out of heart you love her, being out of heart that you cannot enjoy her.

ARMADO. I am all these three.

MOTH. And three times as much more, and yet nothing at all.

ARMADO. Fetch hither the swain; he must carry me a letter.

MOTH. A message well sympathiz'd- a horse to be ambassador for an ass.

ARMADO. Ha, ha, what sayest thou?

MOTH. Marry, sir, you must send the ass upon the horse, for he is very slow-gaited. But I go.

ARMADO. The way is but short; away.

MOTH. As swift as lead, sir.

ARMADO. The meaning, pretty ingenious?

Is not lead a metal heavy, dull, and slow?

MOTH. Minime, honest master; or rather, master, no.

ARMADO. I say lead is slow.

MOTH. You are too swift, sir, to say so:

Is that lead slow which is fir'd from a gun?

ARMADO. Sweet smoke of rhetoric!

He reputes me a cannon; and the bullet, that's he;

I shoot thee at the swain.

MOTH. Thump, then, and I flee.

Exit

ARMADO. A most acute juvenal; volable and free of grace!

By thy favour, sweet welkin, I must sigh in thy face;
Most rude melancholy, valour gives thee place.
My herald is return'd.

Re-enter MOTH with COSTARD

MOTH. A wonder, master! here's a costard broken in a shin.

ARMADO. Some enigma, some riddle; come, thy l'envoy; begin.

COSTARD. No egma, no riddle, no l'envoy; no salve in the mail, sir.

O, sir, plantain, a plain plantain; no l'envoy, no l'envoy; no salve, sir, but a plantain!

ARMADO. By virtue thou enforcest laughter; thy silly thought, my spleen; the heaving of my lungs provokes me to ridiculous smiling. O, pardon me, my stars! Doth the inconsiderate take salve for l'envoy, and the word 'l'envoy' for a salve?

MOTH. Do the wise think them other? Is not l'envoy a salve?

ARMADO. No, page; it is an epilogue or discourse to make plain

Some obscure precedence that hath tofore been sain.
I will example it:
The fox, the ape, and the humble-bee,
Were still at odds, being but three.
There's the moral. Now the l'envoy.
MOTH. I will add the l'envoy. Say the moral again.
ARMADO. The fox, the ape, and the humble-bee,
Were still at odds, being but three.
MOTH. Until the goose came out of door,
And stay'd the odds by adding four.
Now will I begin your moral, and do you follow with my l'envoy.
The fox, the ape, and the humble-bee,
Were still at odds, being but three.
ARMADO. Until the goose came out of door,

Staying the odds by adding four.

MOTH. A good l'envoy, ending in the goose; would you desire more?

COSTARD. The boy hath sold him a bargain, a goose, that's flat.

Sir, your pennyworth is good, an your goose be fat.

To sell a bargain well is as cunning as fast and loose;

Let me see: a fat l'envoy; ay, that's a fat goose.

ARMADO. Come hither, come hither. How did this argument begin?

MOTH. By saying that a costard was broken in a shin.

Then call'd you for the l'envoy.

COSTARD. True, and I for a plantain. Thus came your argument in;

Then the boy's fat l'envoy, the goose that you bought;

And he ended the market.

ARMADO. But tell me: how was there a costard broken in a shin?

MOTH. I will tell you sensibly.

COSTARD. Thou hast no feeling of it, Moth; I will speak that l'envoy.

I, Costard, running out, that was safely within,

Fell over the threshold and broke my shin.

ARMADO. We will talk no more of this matter.

COSTARD. Till there be more matter in the shin.

ARMADO. Sirrah Costard. I will enfranchise thee.

COSTARD. O, Marry me to one Frances! I smell some l'envoy, some goose, in this.

ARMADO. By my sweet soul, I mean setting thee at liberty, enfreedoming thy person; thou wert immured, restrained, captivated, bound.

COSTARD. True, true; and now you will be my purgation, and let me loose.

ARMADO. I give thee thy liberty, set thee from durance; and, in lieu thereof, impose on thee nothing but this: bear this significant [giving a letter] to the country maid Jaquenetta; there is remuneration, for the best ward of mine honour is rewarding my dependents. Moth, follow.

Exit

MOTH. Like the sequel, I. Signior Costard, adieu.

COSTARD. My sweet ounce of man's flesh, my incony Jew!

Exit MOTH

Now will I look to his remuneration. Remuneration! O, that's the

Latin word for three farthings. Three farthings- remuneration.

'What's the price of this inkle?'- 'One penny.'- 'No, I'll give you a remuneration.' Why, it carries it. Remuneration! Why, it is a fairer name than French crown. I will never buy and sell out of this word.

Enter BEROWNE

BEROWNE. My good knave Costard, exceedingly well met!

COSTARD. Pray you, sir, how much carnation ribbon may a man buy for a remuneration?

BEROWNE. What is a remuneration?

COSTARD. Marry, sir, halfpenny farthing.

BEROWNE. Why, then, three-farthing worth of silk.

COSTARD. I thank your worship. God be wi' you!

BEROWNE. Stay, slave; I must employ thee.

As thou wilt win my favour, good my knave,

Do one thing for me that I shall entreat.

COSTARD. When would you have it done, sir?

BEROWNE. This afternoon.

COSTARD. Well, I will do it, sir; fare you well.

BEROWNE. Thou knowest not what it is.

COSTARD. I shall know, sir, when I have done it.

BEROWNE. Why, villain, thou must know first.

COSTARD. I will come to your worship to-morrow morning.

BEROWNE. It must be done this afternoon.

Hark, slave, it is but this:

The Princess comes to hunt here in the park,

And in her train there is a gentle lady;

When tongues speak sweetly, then they name her name,

And Rosaline they call her. Ask for her,

And to her white hand see thou do commend

This seal'd-up counsel. There's thy guerdon; go.

[Giving him a shilling]

COSTARD. Gardon, O sweet gardon! better than remuneration; a

'leven-pence farthing better; most sweet gardon! I will do it, sir, in print. Gardon- remuneration!

Exit

BEROWNE. And I, forsooth, in love; I, that have been love's whip;

A very beadle to a humorous sigh;

A critic, nay, a night-watch constable;

A domineering pedant o'er the boy,

Than whom no mortal so magnificent!

This wimpled, whining, purblind, wayward boy,

This senior-junior, giant-dwarf, Dan Cupid;

Regent of love-rhymes, lord of folded arms,

Th' anointed sovereign of sighs and groans,

Liege of all loiterers and malcontents,

Dread prince of plackets, king of codpieces,

Sole imperator, and great general

Of trotting paritors. O my little heart!
And I to be a corporal of his field,
And wear his colours like a tumbler's hoop!
What! I love, I sue, I seek a wife-
A woman, that is like a German clock,
Still a-repairing, ever out of frame,
And never going aright, being a watch,
But being watch'd that it may still go right!
Nay, to be perjur'd, which is worst of all;
And, among three, to love the worst of all,
A whitely wanton with a velvet brow,
With two pitch balls stuck in her face for eyes;
Ay, and, by heaven, one that will do the deed,
Though Argus were her eunuch and her guard.
And I to sigh for her! to watch for her!
To pray for her! Go to; it is a plague
That Cupid will impose for my neglect
Of his almighty dreadful little might.
Well, I will love, write, sigh, pray, sue, and groan:
Some men must love my lady, and some Joan.
Exit

ACT IV. SCENE I.: THE PARK

Enter the PRINCESS, ROSALINE, MARIA, KATHARINE, BOYET, LORDS, ATTENDANTS, and a FORESTER

PRINCESS OF FRANCE. Was that the King that spurr'd his horse so hard

Against the steep uprising of the hill?

BOYET. I know not; but I think it was not he.

PRINCESS OF FRANCE. Whoe'er 'a was, 'a show'd a mounting mind.

Well, lords, to-day we shall have our dispatch;

On Saturday we will return to France.

Then, forester, my friend, where is the bush

That we must stand and play the murderer in?

FORESTER. Hereby, upon the edge of yonder coppice;

A stand where you may make the fairest shoot.

PRINCESS OF FRANCE. I thank my beauty I am fair that shoot,

And thereupon thou speak'st the fairest shoot.

FORESTER. Pardon me, madam, for I meant not so.

PRINCESS OF FRANCE. What, what? First praise me, and again say no?

O short-liv'd pride! Not fair? Alack for woe!

FORESTER. Yes, madam, fair.

PRINCESS OF FRANCE. Nay, never paint me now;

Where fair is not, praise cannot mend the brow.

Here, good my glass, take this for telling true:

[Giving him money]

Fair payment for foul words is more than due.

FORESTER. Nothing but fair is that which you inherit.

PRINCESS OF FRANCE. See, see, my beauty will be sav'd by merit.

O heresy in fair, fit for these days!

A giving hand, though foul, shall have fair praise.

But come, the bow. Now mercy goes to kill,

And shooting well is then accounted ill;

Thus will I save my credit in the shoot:

Not wounding, pity would not let me do't;

If wounding, then it was to show my skill,

That more for praise than purpose meant to kill.

And, out of question, so it is sometimes:

Glory grows guilty of detested crimes,
When, for fame's sake, for praise, an outward part,
We bend to that the working of the heart;
As I for praise alone now seek to spill
The poor deer's blood that my heart means no ill.

BOYET. Do not curst wives hold that self-sovereignty
Only for praise sake, when they strive to be
Lords o'er their lords?

PRINCESS OF FRANCE. Only for praise; and praise we may afford
To any lady that subdues a lord.

Enter COSTARD

BOYET. Here comes a member of the commonwealth.

COSTARD. God dig-you-den all! Pray you, which is the head lady?

PRINCESS OF FRANCE. Thou shalt know her, fellow, by the rest that have no heads.

COSTARD. Which is the greatest lady, the highest?

PRINCESS OF FRANCE. The thickest and the tallest.

COSTARD. The thickest and the tallest! It is so; truth is truth.
An your waist, mistress, were as slender as my wit,
One o' these maids' girdles for your waist should be fit.
Are not you the chief woman? You are the thickest here.

PRINCESS OF FRANCE. What's your will, sir? What's your will?

COSTARD. I have a letter from Monsieur Berowne to one
Lady Rosaline.

PRINCESS OF FRANCE. O, thy letter, thy letter! He's a good friend of mine.
Stand aside, good bearer. Boyet, you can carve.
Break up this capon.

BOYET. I am bound to serve.

This letter is mistook; it importeth none here.

It is writ to Jaquenetta.

PRINCESS OF FRANCE. We will read it, I swear.

Break the neck of the wax, and every one give ear.

BOYET. [Reads] 'By heaven, that thou art fair is most infallible; true that thou art beauteous; truth itself that thou art lovely.

More fairer than fair, beautiful than beauteous, truer than truth itself, have commiseration on thy heroical vassal. The magnanimous and most illustrate king Cophetua set eye upon the pernicious and indubitate beggar Zenelophon; and he it was that might rightly say, 'Veni, vidi, vici'; which to annothanize in the vulgar,- O base and obscure vulgar!- videlicet, He came, saw, and overcame. He came, one; saw, two; overcame, three. Who came?- the king. Why did he come?- to see. Why did he see?-to overcome.

To whom came he?- to the beggar. What saw he?- the beggar. Who overcame he?- the beggar. The conclusion is victory; on whose side?- the king's. The captive is enrich'd; on whose side?- the beggar's. The catastrophe is a nuptial; on whose side?- the king's. No, on both in one, or one in both. I am the king, for so stands the comparison; thou the beggar, for so witnesseth thy lowliness. Shall I command thy love? I may. Shall I enforce thy love? I could. Shall I entreat thy love? I will. What shalt thou exchange for rags?- robes, for tittles?- titles, for thyself? -me. Thus expecting thy reply, I profane my lips on thy foot, my eyes on thy picture, and my heart on thy every part.

Thine in the dearest design of industry,

DON ADRIANO DE ARMADO.

'Thus dost thou hear the Nemean lion roar
'Gainst thee, thou lamb, that standest as his prey;
Submissive fall his princely feet before,
And he from forage will incline to play.
But if thou strive, poor soul, what are thou then?
Food for his rage, repasture for his den.'

PRINCESS OF FRANCE. What plume of feathers is he that indited this letter?

What vane? What weathercock? Did you ever hear better?

BOYET. I am much deceived but I remember the style.

PRINCESS OF FRANCE. Else your memory is bad, going o'er it erewhile.

BOYET. This Armado is a Spaniard, that keeps here in court;

A phantasime, a Monarcho, and one that makes sport

To the Prince and his book-mates.

PRINCESS OF FRANCE. Thou fellow, a word.

Who gave thee this letter?

COSTARD. I told you: my lord.

PRINCESS OF FRANCE. To whom shouldst thou give it?

COSTARD. From my lord to my lady.

PRINCESS OF FRANCE. From which lord to which lady?

COSTARD. From my Lord Berowne, a good master of mine,

To a lady of France that he call'd Rosaline.

PRINCESS OF FRANCE. Thou hast mistaken his letter. Come, lords, away.

[To ROSALINE] Here, sweet, put up this; 'twill be thine another day. Exeunt PRINCESS and TRAIN

BOYET. Who is the shooter? who is the shooter?

ROSALINE. Shall I teach you to know?

BOYET. Ay, my continent of beauty.

ROSALINE. Why, she that bears the bow.

Finely put off!

BOYET. My lady goes to kill horns; but, if thou marry,

Hang me by the neck, if horns that year miscarry.

Finely put on!

ROSALINE. Well then, I am the shooter.

BOYET. And who is your deer?

ROSALINE. If we choose by the horns, yourself come not near.

Finely put on indeed!

MARIA. You Still wrangle with her, Boyet, and she strikes at the brow.

BOYET. But she herself is hit lower. Have I hit her now?

ROSALINE. Shall I come upon thee with an old saying, that was a man

when King Pepin of France was a little boy, as touching the hit it?

BOYET. So I may answer thee with one as old, that was a woman when

Queen Guinever of Britain was a little wench, as touching the hit it.

ROSALINE. [Singing]

Thou canst not hit it, hit it, hit it,

Thou canst not hit it, my good man.

BOYET. An I cannot, cannot, cannot,

An I cannot, another can.

Exeunt ROSALINE and KATHARINE

COSTARD. By my troth, most pleasant! How both did fit it!

MARIA. A mark marvellous well shot; for they both did hit it.

BOYET. A mark! O, mark but that mark! A mark, says my lady!

Let the mark have a prick in't, to mete at, if it may be.

MARIA. Wide o' the bow-hand! I' faith, your hand is out.

COSTARD. Indeed, 'a must shoot nearer, or he'll ne'er hit the clout.

BOYET. An if my hand be out, then belike your hand is in.

COSTARD. Then will she get the upshoot by cleaving the pin.

MARIA. Come, come, you talk greasily; your lips grow foul.

COSTARD. She's too hard for you at pricks, sir; challenge her to bowl.

BOYET. I fear too much rubbing; good-night, my good owl.

Exeunt BOYET and MARIA

COSTARD. By my soul, a swain, a most simple clown!

Lord, Lord! how the ladies and I have put him down!

O' my troth, most sweet jests, most incony vulgar wit!

When it comes so smoothly off, so obscenely, as it were, so fit.

Armado a th' t'one side- O, a most dainty man!

To see him walk before a lady and to bear her fan!

To see him kiss his hand, and how most sweetly 'a will swear!

And his page a t' other side, that handful of wit!

Ah, heavens, it is a most pathetical nit!

Sola, sola!

Exit COSTARD

SCENE II.: THE PARK

From the shooting within, enter HOLOFERNES, SIR NATHANIEL, and DULL

NATHANIEL. Very reverent sport, truly; and done in the testimony of a good conscience.

HOLOFERNES. The deer was, as you know, sanguis, in blood; ripe as the pomewater, who now hangeth like a jewel in the ear of caelo, the sky, the welkin, the heaven; and anon falleth like a crab on the face of terra, the soil, the land, the earth.

NATHANIEL. Truly, Master Holofernes, the epithets are sweetly varied, like a scholar at the least; but, sir, I assure ye it was a buck of the first head.

HOLOFERNES. Sir Nathaniel, haud credo.

DULL. 'Twas not a haud credo; 'twas a pricket.

HOLOFERNES. Most barbarous intimation! yet a kind of insinuation, as it were, in via, in way, of explication; facere, as it were, replication, or rather, ostentare, to show, as it were, his inclination, after his undressed, unpolished, uneducated, unpruned, untrained, or rather unlettered, or ratherest unconfirmed fashion, to insert again my haud credo for a deer.

DULL. I Said the deer was not a haud credo; 'twas a pricket.

HOLOFERNES. Twice-sod simplicity, bis coctus!

O thou monster Ignorance, how deformed dost thou look!

NATHANIEL. Sir, he hath never fed of the dainties that are bred in a book;

He hath not eat paper, as it were; he hath not drunk ink; his intellect is not replenished; he is only an animal, only sensible in the duller parts;

And such barren plants are set before us that we thankful should be-

Which we of taste and feeling are- for those parts that do fructify in us more than he.

For as it would ill become me to be vain, indiscreet, or a fool,

So, were there a patch set on learning, to see him in a school.

But, omne bene, say I, being of an old father's mind:

Many can brook the weather that love not the wind.

DULL. You two are book-men: can you tell me by your wit

What was a month old at Cain's birth that's not five weeks old as yet?

HOLOFERNES. Dictynna, goodman Dull; Dictynna, goodman Dull.

DULL. What is Dictynna?

NATHANIEL. A title to Phoebe, to Luna, to the moon.

HOLOFERNES. The moon was a month old when Adam was no more,

And raught not to five weeks when he came to five-score.

Th' allusion holds in the exchange.

DULL. 'Tis true, indeed; the collusion holds in the exchange.

HOLOFERNES. God comfort thy capacity! I say th' allusion holds in the exchange.

DULL. And I say the polusion holds in the exchange; for the moon is never but a month old; and I say, beside, that 'twas a pricket that the Princess kill'd.

HOLOFERNES. Sir Nathaniel, will you hear an extemporal epitaph on the death of the deer? And, to humour the ignorant, call the deer the Princess kill'd a pricket.

NATHANIEL. Perge, good Master Holofernes, perge, so it shall please you to abrogate scurrility.

HOLOFERNES. I Will something affect the letter, for it argues facility.

The preyful Princess pierc'd and prick'd a pretty pleasing pricket.
Some say a sore; but not a sore till now made sore with shooting.
The dogs did yell; put el to sore, then sorel jumps from thicket-
Or pricket sore, or else sorel; the people fall a-hooting.
If sore be sore, then L to sore makes fifty sores o' sorel.
Of one sore I an hundred make by adding but one more L.

NATHANIEL. A rare talent!

DULL. [Aside] If a talent be a claw, look how he claws him with a talent.

HOLOFERNES. This is a gift that I have, simple, simple; a foolish extravagant spirit, full of forms, figures, shapes, objects, ideas, apprehensions, motions, revolutions. These are begot in the ventricle of memory, nourish'd in the womb of pia mater, and delivered upon the mellowing of occasion. But the gift is good in those in whom it is acute, and I am thankful for it.

NATHANIEL. Sir, I praise the Lord for you, and so may my parishioners; for their sons are well tutor'd by you, and their daughters profit very greatly under you. You are a good member of the commonwealth.

HOLOFERNES. Mehercle, if their sons be ingenious, they shall want no instruction; if their daughters be capable, I will put it to them; but, vir sapit qui pauca loquitur. A soul feminine saluteth us.

Enter JAQUENETTA and COSTARD

JAQUENETTA. God give you good morrow, Master Person.

HOLOFERNES. Master Person, quasi pers-one. And if one should be pierc'd which is the one?

COSTARD. Marry, Master Schoolmaster, he that is likest to a hogshead.

HOLOFERNES. Piercing a hogshead! A good lustre of conceit in a turf of earth; fire enough for a flint, pearl enough for a swine; 'tis pretty; it is well.

JAQUENETTA. Good Master Parson, be so good as read me this letter; it was given me by Costard, and sent me from Don Armado. I beseech you read it.

HOLOFERNES. Fauste, precor gelida quando pecus omne sub umbra Ruminat- and so forth. Ah, good old Mantuan! I may speak of thee as the traveller doth of Venice:

Venetia, Venetia,

Chi non ti vede, non ti pretia.

Old Mantuan, old Mantuan! Who understandeth thee not, loves thee not-

Ut, re, sol, la, mi, fa.

Under pardon, sir, what are the contents? or rather as

Horace says in his- What, my soul, verses?

NATHANIEL. Ay, sir, and very learned.

HOLOFERNES. Let me hear a staff, a stanze, a verse; lege, domine.

NATHANIEL. [Reads] 'If love make me forsworn, how shall I swear to love?

Ah, never faith could hold, if not to beauty vowed!

Though to myself forsworn, to thee I'll faithful prove;

Those thoughts to me were oaks, to thee like osiers bowed.

Study his bias leaves, and makes his book thine eyes,

Where all those pleasures live that art would comprehend.

If knowledge be the mark, to know thee shall suffice;
Well learned is that tongue that well can thee commend;
All ignorant that soul that sees thee without wonder;
Which is to me some praise that I thy parts admire.
Thy eye Jove's lightning bears, thy voice his dreadful thunder,
Which, not to anger bent, is music and sweet fire.
Celestial as thou art, O, pardon love this wrong,
That singes heaven's praise with such an earthly tongue.'

HOLOFERNES. You find not the apostrophas, and so miss the accent: let me supervise the canzonet. Here are only numbers ratified; but, for the elegancy, facility, and golden cadence of poesy, caret. Ovidius Naso was the man. And why, indeed, 'Naso' but for smelling out the odoriferous flowers of fancy, the jerks of invention? Imitari is nothing: so doth the hound his master, the ape his keeper, the tired horse his rider. But, damosella virgin, was this directed to you?

JAQUENETTA. Ay, sir, from one Monsieur Berowne, one of the strange queen's lords.

HOLOFERNES. I will overglance the superscript: 'To the snow-white hand of the most beauteous Lady Rosaline.' I will look again on the intellect of the letter, for the nomination of the party writing to the person written unto: 'Your Ladyship's in all desired employment, Berowne.' Sir Nathaniel, this Berowne is one of the votaries with the King; and here he hath framed a letter to a sequent of the stranger queen's which accidentally, or by the way of progression, hath miscarried. Trip and go, my sweet; deliver this paper into the royal hand of the King; it may concern much. Stay not thy compliment; I forgive thy duty. Adieu.

JAQUENETTA. Good Costard, go with me. Sir, God save your life!

COSTARD. Have with thee, my girl.

Exeunt COSTARD and JAQUENETTA

NATHANIEL. Sir, you have done this in the fear of God, very religiously; and, as a certain father saith-

HOLOFERNES. Sir, tell not me of the father; I do fear colourable colours. But to return to the verses: did they please you, Sir Nathaniel?

NATHANIEL. Marvellous well for the pen.

HOLOFERNES. I do dine to-day at the father's of a certain pupil of mine; where, if, before repast, it shall please you to gratify the table with a grace, I will, on my privilege I have with the parents of the foresaid child or pupil, undertake your ben venuto; where I will prove those verses to be very unlearned, neither savouring of poetry, wit, nor invention. I beseech your society.

NATHANIEL. And thank you too; for society, saith the text, is the happiness of life.

HOLOFERNES. And certes, the text most infallibly concludes it.

[To DULL] Sir, I do invite you too; you shall not say me nay: pauca verba. Away; the gentles are at their game, and we will to our recreation.

Exeunt

SCENE III.: THE PARK

Enter BEROWNE, with a paper his band, alone

BEROWNE. The King he is hunting the deer: I am coursing myself. They have pitch'd a toil: I am tolling in a pitch- pitch that defiles. Defile! a foul word. Well, 'set thee down, sorrow!' for so they say the fool said, and so say I, and I am the fool. Well proved, wit. By the Lord, this love is as mad as Ajax: it kills sheep; it kills me- I a sheep. Well proved again o' my side. I will not love; if I do, hang me. I' faith, I will not. O, but her eye! By this light, but for her eye, I would not love her- yes, for her two eyes. Well, I do nothing in the world but lie, and lie in my throat. By heaven, I do love; and it hath taught me to rhyme, and to be melancholy; and here is part of my rhyme, and here my melancholy. Well, she hath one o' my sonnets already; the clown bore it, the fool sent it, and the lady hath it: sweet clown, sweeter fool, sweetest lady! By the world, I would not care a pin if the other three were in. Here comes one with a paper; God give him grace to groan!

[Climbs into a tree]

Enter the KING, with a paper

KING. Ay me!

BEROWNE. Shot, by heaven! Proceed, sweet Cupid; thou hast thump'd him with thy bird-bolt under the left pap. In faith, secrets!

KING. [Reads]

'So sweet a kiss the golden sun gives not
To those fresh morning drops upon the rose,
As thy eye-beams, when their fresh rays have smote
The night of dew that on my cheeks down flows;
Nor shines the silver moon one half so bright
Through the transparent bosom of the deep,
As doth thy face through tears of mine give light.
Thou shin'st in every tear that I do weep;
No drop but as a coach doth carry thee;
So ridest thou triumphing in my woe.
Do but behold the tears that swell in me,
And they thy glory through my grief will show.
But do not love thyself; then thou wilt keep
My tears for glasses, and still make me weep.
O queen of queens! how far dost thou excel
No thought can think nor tongue of mortal tell.'
How shall she know my griefs? I'll drop the paper-
Sweet leaves, shade folly. Who is he comes here?
[Steps aside]

Enter LONGAVILLE, with a paper

What, Longaville, and reading! Listen, car.

BEROWNE. Now, in thy likeness, one more fool appear!
LONGAVILLE. Ay me, I am forsworn!
BEROWNE. Why, he comes in like a perjure, wearing papers.
KING. In love, I hope; sweet fellowship in shame!
BEROWNE. One drunkard loves another of the name.
LONGAVILLE. Am I the first that have been perjur'd so?
BEROWNE. I could put thee in comfort: not by two that I know;
Thou makest the triumviry, the corner-cap of society,
The shape of Love's Tyburn that hangs up simplicity.
LONGAVILLE. I fear these stubborn lines lack power to move.
O sweet Maria, empress of my love!
These numbers will I tear, and write in prose.
BEROWNE. O, rhymes are guards on wanton Cupid's hose:
Disfigure not his slop.
LONGAVILLE. This same shall go. [He reads the sonnet]
'Did not the heavenly rhetoric of thine eye,
'Gainst whom the world cannot hold argument,
Persuade my heart to this false perjury?
Vows for thee broke deserve not punishment.
A woman I forswore; but I will prove,
Thou being a goddess, I forswore not thee:
My vow was earthly, thou a heavenly love;
Thy grace being gain'd cures all disgrace in me.
Vows are but breath, and breath a vapour is;
Then thou, fair sun, which on my earth dost shine,
Exhal'st this vapour-vow; in thee it is.
If broken, then it is no fault of mine;
If by me broke, what fool is not so wise
To lose an oath to win a paradise?'

BEROWNE. This is the liver-vein, which makes flesh a deity,
A green goose a goddess- pure, pure idolatry.
God amend us, God amend! We are much out o' th' way.

Enter DUMAIN, with a paper

LONGAVILLE. By whom shall I send this?- Company! Stay.
[Steps aside]
BEROWNE. 'All hid, all hid'- an old infant play.
Like a demigod here sit I in the sky,
And wretched fools' secrets heedfully o'er-eye.
More sacks to the mill! O heavens, I have my wish!
Dumain transformed! Four woodcocks in a dish!
DUMAIN. O most divine Kate!
BEROWNE. O most profane coxcomb!
DUMAIN. By heaven, the wonder in a mortal eye!
BEROWNE. By earth, she is not, corporal: there you lie.
DUMAIN. Her amber hairs for foul hath amber quoted.
BEROWNE. An amber-colour'd raven was well noted.
DUMAIN. As upright as the cedar.
BEROWNE. Stoop, I say;
Her shoulder is with child.
DUMAIN. As fair as day.
BEROWNE. Ay, as some days; but then no sun must shine.
DUMAIN. O that I had my wish!
LONGAVILLE. And I had mine!
KING. And I mine too,.good Lord!
BEROWNE. Amen, so I had mine! Is not that a good word?
DUMAIN. I would forget her; but a fever she
Reigns in my blood, and will rememb'red be.
BEROWNE. A fever in your blood? Why, then incision
Would let her out in saucers. Sweet misprision!

DUMAIN. Once more I'll read the ode that I have writ.
BEROWNE. Once more I'll mark how love can vary wit.
DUMAIN. [Reads]
'On a day-alack the day!-
Love, whose month is ever May,
Spied a blossom passing fair
Playing in the wanton air.
Through the velvet leaves the wind,
All unseen, can passage find;
That the lover, sick to death,
Wish'd himself the heaven's breath.
"Air," quoth he "thy cheeks may blow;
Air, would I might triumph so!
But, alack, my hand is sworn
Ne'er to pluck thee from thy thorn;
Vow, alack, for youth unmeet,
Youth so apt to pluck a sweet.
Do not call it sin in me
That I am forsworn for thee;
Thou for whom Jove would swear
Juno but an Ethiope were;
And deny himself for Jove,
Turning mortal for thy love."'
This will I send; and something else more plain
That shall express my true love's fasting pain.
O, would the King, Berowne and Longaville,
Were lovers too! Ill, to example ill,
Would from my forehead wipe a perjur'd note;
For none offend where all alike do dote.

LONGAVILLE. [Advancing] Dumain, thy love is far from charity,

That in love's grief desir'st society;
You may look pale, but I should blush, I know,
To be o'erheard and taken napping so.
KING. [Advancing] Come, sir, you blush; as his, your case is such.
You chide at him, offending twice as much:
You do not love Maria! Longaville
Did never sonnet for her sake compile;
Nor never lay his wreathed arms athwart
His loving bosom, to keep down his heart.
I have been closely shrouded in this bush,
And mark'd you both, and for you both did blush.
I heard your guilty rhymes, observ'd your fashion,
Saw sighs reek from you, noted well your passion.
'Ay me!' says one. 'O Jove!' the other cries.
One, her hairs were gold; crystal the other's eyes.
[To LONGAVILLE] You would for paradise break faith and troth;
[To Dumain] And Jove for your love would infringe an oath.
What will Berowne say when that he shall hear
Faith infringed which such zeal did swear?
How will he scorn, how will he spend his wit!
How will he triumph, leap, and laugh at it!
For all the wealth that ever I did see,
I would not have him know so much by me.
BEROWNE. [Descending] Now step I forth to whip hypocrisy,
Ah, good my liege, I pray thee pardon me.
Good heart, what grace hast thou thus to reprove
These worms for loving, that art most in love?
Your eyes do make no coaches; in your tears
There is no certain princess that appears;

You'll not be perjur'd; 'tis a hateful thing;
Tush, none but minstrels like of sonneting.
But are you not ashamed? Nay, are you not,
All three of you, to be thus much o'ershot?
You found his mote; the King your mote did see;
But I a beam do find in each of three.
O, what a scene of fool'ry have I seen,
Of sighs, of groans, of sorrow, and of teen!
O, me, with what strict patience have I sat,
To see a king transformed to a gnat!
To see great Hercules whipping a gig,
And profound Solomon to tune a jig,
And Nestor play at push-pin with the boys,
And critic Timon laugh at idle toys!
Where lies thy grief, O, tell me, good Dumain?
And, gentle Longaville, where lies thy pain?
And where my liege's? All about the breast.
A caudle, ho!
KING. Too bitter is thy jest.
Are we betrayed thus to thy over-view?
BEROWNE. Not you by me, but I betrayed to you.
I that am honest, I that hold it sin
To break the vow I am engaged in;
I am betrayed by keeping company
With men like you, men of inconstancy.
When shall you see me write a thing in rhyme?
Or groan for Joan? or spend a minute's time
In pruning me? When shall you hear that I
Will praise a hand, a foot, a face, an eye,
A gait, a state, a brow, a breast, a waist,

A leg, a limb-

KING. Soft! whither away so fast?

A true man or a thief that gallops so?

BEROWNE. I post from love; good lover, let me go.

Enter JAQUENETTA and COSTARD

JAQUENETTA. God bless the King!

KING. What present hast thou there?

COSTARD. Some certain treason.

KING. What makes treason here?

COSTARD. Nay, it makes nothing, sir.

KING. If it mar nothing neither,

The treason and you go in peace away together.

JAQUENETTA. I beseech your Grace, let this letter be read;

Our person misdoubts it: 'twas treason, he said.

KING. Berowne, read it over. [BEROWNE reads the letter]

Where hadst thou it?

JAQUENETTA. Of Costard.

KING. Where hadst thou it?

COSTARD. Of Dun Adramadio, Dun Adramadio.

[BEROWNE tears the letter]

KING. How now! What is in you? Why dost thou tear it?

BEROWNE. A toy, my liege, a toy! Your Grace needs not fear it.

LONGAVILLE. It did move him to passion, and therefore let's hear it.

DUMAIN. It is Berowne's writing, and here is his name.

[Gathering up the pieces]

BEROWNE. [To COSTARD] Ah, you whoreson loggerhead, you were born to do me shame.

Guilty, my lord, guilty! I confess, I confess.

KING. What?

BEROWNE. That you three fools lack'd me fool to make up the mess;

He, he, and you- and you, my liege!- and I
Are pick-purses in love, and we deserve to die.
O, dismiss this audience, and I shall tell you more.

DUMAIN. Now the number is even.

BEROWNE. True, true, we are four.
Will these turtles be gone?

KING. Hence, sirs, away.

COSTARD. Walk aside the true folk, and let the traitors stay.

Exeunt COSTARD and JAQUENETTA

BEROWNE. Sweet lords, sweet lovers, O, let us embrace!
As true we are as flesh and blood can be.
The sea will ebb and flow, heaven show his face;
Young blood doth not obey an old decree.
We cannot cross the cause why we were born,
Therefore of all hands must we be forsworn.

KING. What, did these rent lines show some love of thine?

BEROWNE. 'Did they?' quoth you. Who sees the heavenly Rosaline

That, like a rude and savage man of Inde
At the first op'ning of the gorgeous east,
Bows not his vassal head and, strucken blind,
Kisses the base ground with obedient breast?
What peremptory eagle-sighted eye
Dares look upon the heaven of her brow
That is not blinded by her majesty?

KING. What zeal, what fury hath inspir'd thee now?
My love, her mistress, is a gracious moon;
She, an attending star, scarce seen a light.

BEROWNE. My eyes are then no eyes, nor I Berowne.
O, but for my love, day would turn to night!
Of all complexions the cull'd sovereignty
Do meet, as at a fair, in her fair cheek,
Where several worthies make one dignity,
Where nothing wants that want itself doth seek.
Lend me the flourish of all gentle tongues-
Fie, painted rhetoric! O, she needs it not!
To things of sale a seller's praise belongs:
She passes praise; then praise too short doth blot.
A wither'd hermit, five-score winters worn,
Might shake off fifty, looking in her eye.
Beauty doth varnish age, as if new-born,
And gives the crutch the cradle's infancy.
O, 'tis the sun that maketh all things shine!
KING. By heaven, thy love is black as ebony.
BEROWNE. Is ebony like her? O wood divine!
A wife of such wood were felicity.
O, who can give an oath? Where is a book?
That I may swear beauty doth beauty lack,
If that she learn not of her eye to look.
No face is fair that is not full so black.
KING. O paradox! Black is the badge of hell,
The hue of dungeons, and the school of night;
And beauty's crest becomes the heavens well.
BEROWNE. Devils soonest tempt, resembling spirits of light.
O, if in black my lady's brows be deckt,
It mourns that painting and usurping hair
Should ravish doters with a false aspect;
And therefore is she born to make black fair.

Her favour turns the fashion of the days;
For native blood is counted painting now;
And therefore red that would avoid dispraise
Paints itself black, to imitate her brow.
DUMAIN. To look like her are chimney-sweepers black.
LONGAVILLE. And since her time are colliers counted bright.
KING. And Ethiopes of their sweet complexion crack.
DUMAIN. Dark needs no candles now, for dark is light.
BEROWNE. Your mistresses dare never come in rain
For fear their colours should be wash'd away.
KING. 'Twere good yours did; for, sir, to tell you plain,
I'll find a fairer face not wash'd to-day.
BEROWNE. I'll prove her fair, or talk till doomsday here.
KING. No devil will fright thee then so much as she.
DUMAIN. I never knew man hold vile stuff so dear.
LONGAVILLE. Look, here's thy love: my foot and her face see.
[Showing his shoe]
BEROWNE. O, if the streets were paved with thine eyes,
Her feet were much too dainty for such tread!
DUMAIN. O vile! Then, as she goes, what upward lies
The street should see as she walk'd overhead.
KING. But what of this? Are we not all in love?
BEROWNE. Nothing so sure; and thereby all forsworn.
KING. Then leave this chat; and, good Berowne, now prove
Our loving lawful, and our faith not torn.
DUMAIN. Ay, marry, there; some flattery for this evil.
LONGAVILLE. O, some authority how to proceed;
Some tricks, some quillets, how to cheat the devil!
DUMAIN. Some salve for perjury.
BEROWNE. 'Tis more than need.

Have at you, then, affection's men-at-arms.
Consider what you first did swear unto:
To fast, to study, and to see no woman-
Flat treason 'gainst the kingly state of youth.
Say, can you fast? Your stomachs are too young,
And abstinence engenders maladies.
And, where that you you have vow'd to study, lords,
In that each of you have forsworn his book,
Can you still dream, and pore, and thereon look?
For when would you, my lord, or you, or you,
Have found the ground of study's excellence
Without the beauty of a woman's face?
From women's eyes this doctrine I derive:
They are the ground, the books, the academes,
From whence doth spring the true Promethean fire.
Why, universal plodding poisons up
The nimble spirits in the arteries,
As motion and long-during action tires
The sinewy vigour of the traveller.
Now, for not looking on a woman's face,
You have in that forsworn the use of eyes,
And study too, the causer of your vow;
For where is author in the world
Teaches such beauty as a woman's eye?
Learning is but an adjunct to ourself,
And where we are our learning likewise is;
Then when ourselves we see in ladies' eyes,
With ourselves.
Do we not likewise see our learning there?
O, we have made a vow to study, lords,

And in that vow we have forsworn our books.
For when would you, my liege, or you, or you,
In leaden contemplation have found out
Such fiery numbers as the prompting eyes
Of beauty's tutors have enrich'd you with?
Other slow arts entirely keep the brain;
And therefore, finding barren practisers,
Scarce show a harvest of their heavy toil;
But love, first learned in a lady's eyes,
Lives not alone immured in the brain,
But with the motion of all elements
Courses as swift as thought in every power,
And gives to every power a double power,
Above their functions and their offices.
It adds a precious seeing to the eye:
A lover's eyes will gaze an eagle blind.
A lover's ear will hear the lowest sound,
When the suspicious head of theft is stopp'd.
Love's feeling is more soft and sensible
Than are the tender horns of cockled snails:
Love's tongue proves dainty Bacchus gross in taste.
For valour, is not Love a Hercules,
Still climbing trees in the Hesperides?
Subtle as Sphinx; as sweet and musical
As bright Apollo's lute, strung with his hair.
And when Love speaks, the voice of all the gods
Make heaven drowsy with the harmony.
Never durst poet touch a pen to write
Until his ink were temp'red with Love's sighs;
O, then his lines would ravish savage ears,

And plant in tyrants mild humility.
From women's eyes this doctrine I derive.
They sparkle still the right Promethean fire;
They are the books, the arts, the academes,
That show, contain, and nourish, all the world,
Else none at all in aught proves excellent.
Then fools you were these women to forswear;
Or, keeping what is sworn, you will prove fools.
For wisdom's sake, a word that all men love;
Or for Love's sake, a word that loves all men;
Or for men's sake, the authors of these women;
Or women's sake, by whom we men are men-
Let us once lose our oaths to find ourselves,
Or else we lose ourselves to keep our oaths.
It is religion to be thus forsworn;
For charity itself fulfils the law,
And who can sever love from charity?
KING. Saint Cupid, then! and, soldiers, to the field!
BEROWNE. Advance your standards, and upon them, lords;
Pell-mell, down with them! be first advis'd,
In conflict, that you get the sun of them.
LONGAVILLE. Now to plain-dealing; lay these glozes by.
Shall we resolve to woo these girls of France?
KING. And win them too; therefore let us devise
Some entertainment for them in their tents.
BEROWNE. First, from the park let us conduct them thither;
Then homeward every man attach the hand
Of his fair mistress. In the afternoon
We will with some strange pastime solace them,
Such as the shortness of the time can shape;

For revels, dances, masks, and merry hours,
Forerun fair Love, strewing her way with flowers.
KING. Away, away! No time shall be omitted
That will betime, and may by us be fitted.
BEROWNE. Allons! allons! Sow'd cockle reap'd no corn,
And justice always whirls in equal measure.
Light wenches may prove plagues to men forsworn;
If so, our copper buys no better treasure. Exeunt

ACT V. SCENE I.: THE PARK

Enter HOLOFERNES, SIR NATHANIEL, and DULL

HOLOFERNES. Satis quod sufficit.

NATHANIEL. I praise God for you, sir. Your reasons at dinner have been sharp and sententious; pleasant without scurrility, witty without affection, audacious without impudency, learned without opinion, and strange without heresy. I did converse this quondam day with a companion of the King's who is intituled, nominated, or called, Don Adriano de Armado.

HOLOFERNES. Novi hominem tanquam te. His humour is lofty, his discourse peremptory, his tongue filed, his eye ambitious, his gait majestical and his general behaviour vain, ridiculous, and thrasonical. He is too picked, too spruce, too affected, too odd, as it were, too peregrinate, as I may call it.

NATHANIEL. A most singular and choice epithet.

[Draws out his table-book]

HOLOFERNES. He draweth out the thread of his verbosity finer than the staple of his argument. I abhor such fanatical phantasimes, such insociable and point-devise companions; such rackers of orthography, as to speak 'dout' fine, when he should say 'doubt'; 'det' when he should pronounce 'debt'- d, e, b, t, not d, e, t. He clepeth a calf 'cauf,' half 'hauf'; neighbour vocatur 'nebour'; 'neigh' abbreviated 'ne.' This is abhominable- which he would call 'abbominable.' It insinuateth me of insanie: ne intelligis, domine? to make frantic, lunatic.

NATHANIEL. Laus Deo, bone intelligo.

HOLOFERNES. 'Bone'?- 'bone' for 'bene.' Priscian a little scratch'd; 'twill serve.

Enter ARMADO, MOTH, and COSTARD

NATHANIEL. Videsne quis venit?

HOLOFERNES. Video, et gaudeo.

ARMADO. [To MOTH] Chirrah!

HOLOFERNES. Quare 'chirrah,' not 'sirrah'?

ARMADO. Men of peace, well encount'red.

HOLOFERNES. Most military sir, salutation.

MOTH. [Aside to COSTARD] They have been at a great feast of languages and stol'n the scraps.

COSTARD. O, they have liv'd long on the alms-basket of words. I marvel thy master hath not eaten thee for a word, for thou are not so long by the head as honorificabilitudinitatibus; thou art easier swallowed than a flap-dragon.

MOTH. Peace! the peal begins.

ARMADO. [To HOLOFERNES] Monsieur, are you not lett'red?

MOTH. Yes, yes; he teaches boys the hornbook. What is a, b, spelt backward with the horn on his head?

HOLOFERNES. Ba, pueritia, with a horn added.

MOTH. Ba, most silly sheep with a horn. You hear his learning.

HOLOFERNES. Quis, quis, thou consonant?

MOTH. The third of the five vowels, if You repeat them; or the fifth, if I.

HOLOFERNES. I will repeat them: a, e, I-

MOTH. The sheep; the other two concludes it: o, U.

ARMADO. Now, by the salt wave of the Mediterraneum, a sweet touch, a quick venue of wit- snip, snap, quick and home. It rejoiceth my intellect. True wit!

MOTH. Offer'd by a child to an old man; which is wit-old.

HOLOFERNES. What is the figure? What is the figure?

MOTH. Horns.

HOLOFERNES. Thou disputes like an infant; go whip thy gig.

MOTH. Lend me your horn to make one, and I will whip about your infamy circum circa- a gig of a cuckold's horn.

COSTARD. An I had but one penny in the world, thou shouldst have it to buy ginger-bread. Hold, there is the very remuneration I had of thy master, thou halfpenny purse of wit, thou pigeon-egg of discretion. O, an the heavens were so pleased that thou wert but my bastard, what a joyful father wouldst thou make me! Go to; thou hast it ad dunghill, at the fingers' ends, as they say.

HOLOFERNES. O, I smell false Latin; 'dunghill' for unguem.

ARMADO. Arts-man, preambulate; we will be singuled from the barbarous. Do you not educate youth at the charge-house on the top of the mountain?

HOLOFERNES. Or mons, the hill.

ARMADO. At your sweet pleasure, for the mountain.

HOLOFERNES. I do, sans question.

ARMADO. Sir, it is the King's most sweet pleasure and affection to congratulate the Princess at her pavilion, in the posteriors of this day; which the rude multitude call the afternoon.

HOLOFERNES. The posterior of the day, most generous sir, is liable, congruent, and measurable, for the afternoon. The word is well cull'd, chose, sweet, and apt, I do assure you, sir, I do assure.

ARMADO. Sir, the King is a noble gentleman, and my familiar, I do assure ye, very good friend. For what is inward between us, let it pass. I do beseech thee, remember thy courtesy. I beseech thee, apparel thy head. And among other importunate and most serious designs, and of great import indeed, too- but let that pass; for I must tell thee it will please his Grace, by the world, sometime to lean upon my poor shoulder, and with his royal finger thus dally with my excrement, with my mustachio; but, sweet heart, let that pass. By the world, I recount no fable: some certain special honours it pleaseth his greatness to impart to Armado, a soldier, a man of travel, that hath seen the world; but let that pass. The very all of all is- but, sweet heart, I do implore secrecy- that the King would have me present the Princess, sweet chuck, with some delightful ostentation, or show, or pageant, or antic, or firework. Now, understanding that the curate and your sweet self are good at such eruptions and sudden breaking-out of mirth, as it were, I have acquainted you withal, to the end to crave your assistance.

HOLOFERNES. Sir, you shall present before her the Nine Worthies.

Sir Nathaniel, as concerning some entertainment of time, some show in the posterior of this day, to be rend'red by our assistance, the King's command, and this most gallant, illustrate, and learned gentleman, before the Princess- I say none so fit as to present the Nine Worthies.

NATHANIEL. Where will you find men worthy enough to present them?

HOLOFERNES. Joshua, yourself; myself, Alexander; this gallant gentleman, Judas Maccabaeus; this swain, because of his great limb or joint, shall pass Pompey the Great; the page, Hercules.

ARMADO. Pardon, sir; error: he is not quantity enough for that Worthy's thumb; he is not so big as the end of his club.

HOLOFERNES. Shall I have audience? He shall present Hercules in minority: his enter and exit shall be strangling a snake; and I will have an apology for that purpose.

MOTH. An excellent device! So, if any of the audience hiss, you may cry 'Well done, Hercules; now thou crushest the snake!' That is the way to make an offence gracious, though few have the grace to do it.

ARMADO. For the rest of the Worthies?

HOLOFERNES. I will play three myself.

MOTH. Thrice-worthy gentleman!

ARMADO. Shall I tell you a thing?

HOLOFERNES. We attend.

ARMADO. We will have, if this fadge not, an antic. I beseech you, follow.

HOLOFERNES. Via, goodman Dull! Thou has spoken no word all this while.

DULL. Nor understood none neither, sir.

HOLOFERNES. Allons! we will employ thee.

DULL. I'll make one in a dance, or so, or I will play

On the tabor to the Worthies, and let them dance the hay.

HOLOFERNES. Most dull, honest Dull! To our sport, away.

Exeunt

SCENE II.: THE PARK

Enter the PRINCESS, MARIA, KATHARINE, and ROSALINE

PRINCESS OF FRANCE. Sweet hearts, we shall be rich ere we depart,

If fairings come thus plentifully in.

A lady wall'd about with diamonds!

Look you what I have from the loving King.

ROSALINE. Madam, came nothing else along with that?

PRINCESS OF FRANCE. Nothing but this! Yes, as much love in rhyme

As would be cram.n'd up in a sheet of paper

Writ o' both sides the leaf, margent and all,

That he was fain to seal on Cupid's name.

ROSALINE. That was the way to make his godhead wax;

For he hath been five thousand year a boy.

KATHARINE. Ay, and a shrewd unhappy gallows too.

ROSALINE. You'll ne'er be friends with him: 'a kill'd your sister.

KATHARINE. He made her melancholy, sad, and heavy;
And so she died. Had she been light, like you,
Of such a merry, nimble, stirring spirit,
She might 'a been a grandam ere she died.
And so may you; for a light heart lives long.
ROSALINE. What's your dark meaning, mouse, of this light word?
KATHARINE. A light condition in a beauty dark.
ROSALINE. We need more light to find your meaning out.
KATHARINE. You'll mar the light by taking it in snuff;
Therefore I'll darkly end the argument.
ROSALINE. Look what you do, you do it still i' th' dark.
KATHARINE. So do not you; for you are a light wench.
ROSALINE. Indeed, I weigh not you; and therefore light.
KATHARINE. You weigh me not? O, that's you care not for me.
ROSALINE. Great reason; for 'past cure is still past care.'
PRINCESS OF FRANCE. Well bandied both; a set of wit well play'd.
But, Rosaline, you have a favour too?
Who sent it? and what is it?
ROSALINE. I would you knew.
An if my face were but as fair as yours,
My favour were as great: be witness this.
Nay, I have verses too, I thank Berowne;
The numbers true, and, were the numb'ring too,
I were the fairest goddess on the ground.
I am compar'd to twenty thousand fairs.
O, he hath drawn my picture in his letter!
PRINCESS OF FRANCE. Anything like?
ROSALINE. Much in the letters; nothing in the praise.

PRINCESS OF FRANCE. Beauteous as ink- a good conclusion.
KATHARINE. Fair as a text B in a copy-book.
ROSALINE. Ware pencils, ho! Let me not die your debtor,
My red dominical, my golden letter:
O that your face were not so full of O's!
KATHARINE. A pox of that jest! and I beshrew all shrows!
PRINCESS OF FRANCE. But, Katharine, what was sent to you from fair Dumain?
KATHARINE. Madam, this glove.
PRINCESS OF FRANCE. Did he not send you twain?
KATHARINE. Yes, madam; and, moreover,
Some thousand verses of a faithful lover;
A huge translation of hypocrisy,
Vilely compil'd, profound simplicity.
MARIA. This, and these pearl, to me sent Longaville;
The letter is too long by half a mile.
PRINCESS OF FRANCE. I think no less. Dost thou not wish in heart
The chain were longer and the letter short?
MARIA. Ay, or I would these hands might never part.
PRINCESS OF FRANCE. We are wise girls to mock our lovers so.
ROSALINE. They are worse fools to purchase mocking so.
That same Berowne I'll torture ere I go.
O that I knew he were but in by th' week!
How I would make him fawn, and beg, and seek,
And wait the season, and observe the times,
And spend his prodigal wits in bootless rhymes,
And shape his service wholly to my hests,
And make him proud to make me proud that jests!
So pertaunt-like would I o'ersway his state

That he should be my fool, and I his fate.

PRINCESS OF FRANCE. None are so surely caught, when they are catch'd,

As wit turn'd fool; folly, in wisdom hatch'd,

Hath wisdom's warrant and the help of school,

And wit's own grace to grace a learned fool.

ROSALINE. The blood of youth burns not with such excess

As gravity's revolt to wantonness.

MARIA. Folly in fools bears not so strong a note

As fool'ry in the wise when wit doth dote,

Since all the power thereof it doth apply

To prove, by wit, worth in simplicity.

Enter BOYET

PRINCESS OF FRANCE. Here comes Boyet, and mirth is in his face.

BOYET. O, I am stabb'd with laughter! Where's her Grace?

PRINCESS OF FRANCE. Thy news, Boyet?

BOYET. Prepare, madam, prepare!

Arm, wenches, arm! Encounters mounted are

Against your peace. Love doth approach disguis'd,

Armed in arguments; you'll be surpris'd.

Muster your wits; stand in your own defence;

Or hide your heads like cowards, and fly hence.

PRINCESS OF FRANCE. Saint Dennis to Saint Cupid! What are they

That charge their breath against us? Say, scout, say.

BOYET. Under the cool shade of a sycamore

I thought to close mine eyes some half an hour;

When, lo, to interrupt my purpos'd rest,

Toward that shade I might behold addrest

The King and his companions; warily
I stole into a neighbour thicket by,
And overheard what you shall overhear-
That, by and by, disguis'd they will be here.
Their herald is a pretty knavish page,
That well by heart hath conn'd his embassage.
Action and accent did they teach him there:
'Thus must thou speak' and 'thus thy body bear,'
And ever and anon they made a doubt
Presence majestical would put him out;
'For' quoth the King 'an angel shalt thou see;
Yet fear not thou, but speak audaciously.'
The boy replied 'An angel is not evil;
I should have fear'd her had she been a devil.'
With that all laugh'd, and clapp'd him on the shoulder,
Making the bold wag by their praises bolder.
One rubb'd his elbow, thus, and fleer'd, and swore
A better speech was never spoke before.
Another with his finger and his thumb
Cried 'Via! we will do't, come what will come.'
The third he caper'd, and cried 'All goes well.'
The fourth turn'd on the toe, and down he fell.
With that they all did tumble on the ground,
With such a zealous laughter, so profound,
That in this spleen ridiculous appears,
To check their folly, passion's solemn tears.

PRINCESS OF FRANCE. But what, but what, come they to visit us?

BOYET. They do, they do, and are apparell'd thus,
Like Muscovites or Russians, as I guess.

Their purpose is to parley, court, and dance;
And every one his love-feat will advance
Unto his several mistress; which they'll know
By favours several which they did bestow.

PRINCESS OF FRANCE. And will they so? The gallants shall be task'd,
For, ladies, we will every one be mask'd;
And not a man of them shall have the grace,
Despite of suit, to see a lady's face.
Hold, Rosaline, this favour thou shalt wear,
And then the King will court thee for his dear;
Hold, take thou this, my sweet, and give me thine,
So shall Berowne take me for Rosaline.
And change you favours too; so shall your loves
Woo contrary, deceiv'd by these removes.

ROSALINE. Come on, then, wear the favours most in sight.

KATHARINE. But, in this changing, what is your intent?

PRINCESS OF FRANCE. The effect of my intent is to cross theirs.
They do it but in mocking merriment,
And mock for mock is only my intent.
Their several counsels they unbosom shall
To loves mistook, and so be mock'd withal
Upon the next occasion that we meet
With visages display'd to talk and greet.

ROSALINE. But shall we dance, if they desire us to't?

PRINCESS OF FRANCE. No, to the death, we will not move a foot,
Nor to their penn'd speech render we no grace;
But while 'tis spoke each turn away her face.

BOYET. Why, that contempt will kill the speaker's heart,
And quite divorce his memory from his part.
PRINCESS OF FRANCE. Therefore I do it; and I make no doubt
The rest will ne'er come in, if he be out.
There's no such sport as sport by sport o'erthrown,
To make theirs ours, and ours none but our own;
So shall we stay, mocking intended game,
And they well mock'd depart away with shame.
[Trumpet sounds within]
BOYET. The trumpet sounds; be mask'd; the maskers come.
[The LADIES mask]

Enter BLACKAMOORS music, MOTH as Prologue, the KING and his LORDS as maskers, in the guise of Russians

MOTH. All hail, the richest heauties on the earth!
BOYET. Beauties no richer than rich taffeta.
MOTH. A holy parcel of the fairest dames
[The LADIES turn their backs to him]
That ever turn'd their- backs- to mortal views!
BEROWNE. Their eyes, villain, their eyes.
MOTH. That ever turn'd their eyes to mortal views!
Out-
BOYET. True; out indeed.
MOTH. Out of your favours, heavenly spirits, vouchsafe
Not to behold-
BEROWNE. Once to behold, rogue.
MOTH. Once to behold with your sun-beamed eyes- with your sun-beamed eyes-
BOYET. They will not answer to that epithet;
You were best call it 'daughter-beamed eyes.'

MOTH. They do not mark me, and that brings me out.

BEROWNE. Is this your perfectness? Be gone, you rogue.

Exit MOTH

ROSALINE. What would these strangers? Know their minds, Boyet.

If they do speak our language, 'tis our will
That some plain man recount their purposes.
Know what they would.

BOYET. What would you with the Princess?

BEROWNE. Nothing but peace and gentle visitation.

ROSALINE. What would they, say they?

BOYET. Nothing but peace and gentle visitation.

ROSALINE. Why, that they have; and bid them so be gone.

BOYET. She says you have it, and you may be gone.

KING. Say to her we have measur'd many miles
To tread a measure with her on this grass.

BOYET. They say that they have measur'd many a mile
To tread a measure with you on this grass.

ROSALINE. It is not so. Ask them how many inches
Is in one mile? If they have measured many,
The measure, then, of one is eas'ly told.

BOYET. If to come hither you have measur'd miles,
And many miles, the Princess bids you tell
How many inches doth fill up one mile.

BEROWNE. Tell her we measure them by weary steps.

BOYET. She hears herself.

ROSALINE. How many weary steps
Of many weary miles you have o'ergone
Are numb'red in the travel of one mile?

BEROWNE. We number nothing that we spend for you;
Our duty is so rich, so infinite,

That we may do it still without accompt.
Vouchsafe to show the sunshine of your face,
That we, like savages, may worship it.
ROSALINE. My face is but a moon, and clouded too.
KING. Blessed are clouds, to do as such clouds do.
Vouchsafe, bright moon, and these thy stars, to shine,
Those clouds removed, upon our watery eyne.
ROSALINE. O vain petitioner! beg a greater matter;
Thou now requests but moonshine in the water.
KING. Then in our measure do but vouchsafe one change.
Thou bid'st me beg; this begging is not strange.
ROSALINE. Play, music, then. Nay, you must do it soon.
Not yet? No dance! Thus change I like the moon.
KING. Will you not dance? How come you thus estranged?
ROSALINE. You took the moon at full; but now she's changed.
KING. Yet still she is the Moon, and I the Man.
The music plays; vouchsafe some motion to it.
ROSALINE. Our ears vouchsafe it.
KING. But your legs should do it.
ROSALINE. Since you are strangers, and come here by chance,
We'll not be nice; take hands. We will not dance.
KING. Why take we hands then?
ROSALINE. Only to part friends.
Curtsy, sweet hearts; and so the measure ends.
KING. More measure of this measure; be not nice.
ROSALINE. We can afford no more at such a price.
KING. Price you yourselves. What buys your company?
ROSALINE. Your absence only.
KING. That can never be.
ROSALINE. Then cannot we be bought; and so adieu-
Twice to your visor and half once to you.

KING. If you deny to dance, let's hold more chat.

ROSALINE. In private then.

KING. I am best pleas'd with that. [They converse apart]

BEROWNE. White-handed mistress, one sweet word with thee.

PRINCESS OF FRANCE. Honey, and milk, and sugar; there is three.

BEROWNE. Nay, then, two treys, an if you grow so nice,
Metheglin, wort, and malmsey; well run dice!
There's half a dozen sweets.

PRINCESS OF FRANCE. Seventh sweet, adieu!
Since you can cog, I'll play no more with you.

BEROWNE. One word in secret.

PRINCESS OF FRANCE. Let it not be sweet.

BEROWNE. Thou grievest my gall.

PRINCESS OF FRANCE. Gall! bitter.

BEROWNE. Therefore meet. [They converse apart]

DUMAIN. Will you vouchsafe with me to change a word?

MARIA. Name it.

DUMAIN. Fair lady-

MARIA. Say you so? Fair lord-
Take that for your fair lady.

DUMAIN. Please it you,
As much in private, and I'll bid adieu.
[They converse apart]

KATHARINE. What, was your vizard made without a tongue?

LONGAVILLE. I know the reason, lady, why you ask.

KATHARINE. O for your reason! Quickly, sir; I long.

LONGAVILLE. You have a double tongue within your mask,
And would afford my speechless vizard half.

KATHARINE. 'Veal' quoth the Dutchman. Is not 'veal' a calf?

LONGAVILLE. A calf, fair lady!

KATHARINE. No, a fair lord calf.

LONGAVILLE. Let's part the word.

KATHARINE. No, I'll not be your half.

Take all and wean it; it may prove an ox.

LONGAVILLE. Look how you butt yourself in these sharp mocks!

Will you give horns, chaste lady? Do not so.

KATHARINE. Then die a calf, before your horns do grow.

LONGAVILLE. One word in private with you ere I die.

KATHARINE. Bleat softly, then; the butcher hears you cry.

[They converse apart]

BOYET. The tongues of mocking wenches are as keen

As is the razor's edge invisible,

Cutting a smaller hair than may be seen,

Above the sense of sense; so sensible

Seemeth their conference; their conceits have wings,

Fleeter than arrows, bullets, wind, thought, swifter things.

ROSALINE. Not one word more, my maids; break off, break off.

BEROWNE. By heaven, all dry-beaten with pure scoff!

KING. Farewell, mad wenches; you have simple wits.

Exeunt KING, LORDS, and BLACKAMOORS

PRINCESS OF FRANCE. Twenty adieus, my frozen Muscovits.

Are these the breed of wits so wondered at?

BOYET. Tapers they are, with your sweet breaths puff'd out.

ROSALINE. Well-liking wits they have; gross, gross; fat, fat.

PRINCESS OF FRANCE. O poverty in wit, kingly-poor flout!

Will they not, think you, hang themselves to-night?

Or ever but in vizards show their faces?

This pert Berowne was out of count'nance quite.

ROSALINE. They were all in lamentable cases!

The King was weeping-ripe for a good word.

PRINCESS OF FRANCE. Berowne did swear himself out of all suit.

MARIA. Dumain was at my service, and his sword.

'No point' quoth I; my servant straight was mute.

KATHARINE. Lord Longaville said I came o'er his heart;

And trow you what he call'd me?

PRINCESS OF FRANCE. Qualm, perhaps.

KATHARINE. Yes, in good faith.

PRINCESS OF FRANCE. Go, sickness as thou art!

ROSALINE. Well, better wits have worn plain statute-caps.

But will you hear? The King is my love sworn.

PRINCESS OF FRANCE. And quick Berowne hath plighted faith to me.

KATHARINE. And Longaville was for my service born.

MARIA. Dumain is mine, as sure as bark on tree.

BOYET. Madam, and pretty mistresses, give ear:

Immediately they will again be here

In their own shapes; for it can never be

They will digest this harsh indignity.

PRINCESS OF FRANCE. Will they return?

BOYET. They will, they will, God knows,

And leap for joy, though they are lame with blows;

Therefore, change favours; and, when they repair,

Blow like sweet roses in this summer air.

PRINCESS OF FRANCE. How blow? how blow? Speak to be understood.

BOYET. Fair ladies mask'd are roses in their bud:

Dismask'd, their damask sweet commixture shown,

Are angels vailing clouds, or roses blown.

PRINCESS OF FRANCE. Avaunt, perplexity! What shall we do

If they return in their own shapes to woo?

ROSALINE. Good madam, if by me you'll be advis'd,

Let's mock them still, as well known as disguis'd.

Let us complain to them what fools were here,

Disguis'd like Muscovites, in shapeless gear;

And wonder what they were, and to what end

Their shallow shows and prologue vilely penn'd,

And their rough carriage so ridiculous,

Should be presented at our tent to us.

BOYET. Ladies, withdraw; the gallants are at hand.

PRINCESS OF FRANCE. Whip to our tents, as roes run o'er land.

Exeunt PRINCESS, ROSALINE, KATHARINE, and MARIA

Re-enter the KING, BEROWNE, LONGAVILLE, and DUMAIN, in their proper habits

KING. Fair sir, God save you! Where's the Princess?

BOYET. Gone to her tent. Please it your Majesty

Command me any service to her thither?

KING. That she vouchsafe me audience for one word.

BOYET. I will; and so will she, I know, my lord.

Exit

BEROWNE. This fellow pecks up wit as pigeons pease,

And utters it again when God doth please.

He is wit's pedlar, and retails his wares

At wakes, and wassails, meetings, markets, fairs;

And we that sell by gross, the Lord doth know,

Have not the grace to grace it with such show.

This gallant pins the wenches on his sleeve;

Had he been Adam, he had tempted Eve.
'A can carve too, and lisp; why this is he
That kiss'd his hand away in courtesy;
This is the ape of form, Monsieur the Nice,
That, when he plays at tables, chides the dice
In honourable terms; nay, he can sing
A mean most meanly; and in ushering,
Mend him who can. The ladies call him sweet;
The stairs, as he treads on them, kiss his feet.
This is the flow'r that smiles on every one,
To show his teeth as white as whales-bone;
And consciences that will not die in debt
Pay him the due of 'honey-tongued Boyet.'
KING. A blister on his sweet tongue, with my heart,
That put Armado's page out of his part!

Re-enter the PRINCESS, ushered by BOYET; ROSALINE, MARIA, and KATHARINE

BEROWNE. See where it comes! Behaviour, what wert thou
Till this man show'd thee? And what art thou now?
KING. All hail, sweet madam, and fair time of day!
PRINCESS OF FRANCE. 'Fair' in 'all hail' is foul, as I conceive.
KING. Construe my speeches better, if you may.
PRINCESS OF FRANCE. Then wish me better; I will give you leave.
KING. We came to visit you, and purpose now
To lead you to our court; vouchsafe it then.
PRINCESS OF FRANCE. This field shall hold me, and so hold your vow:
Nor God, nor I, delights in perjur'd men.
KING. Rebuke me not for that which you provoke.

The virtue of your eye must break my oath.
PRINCESS OF FRANCE. You nickname virtue: vice you should have spoke;
For virtue's office never breaks men's troth.
Now by my maiden honour, yet as pure
As the unsullied lily, I protest,
A world of torments though I should endure,
I would not yield to be your house's guest;
So much I hate a breaking cause to be
Of heavenly oaths, vowed with integrity.
KING. O, you have liv'd in desolation here,
Unseen, unvisited, much to our shame.
PRINCESS OF FRANCE. Not so, my lord; it is not so, I swear;
We have had pastimes here, and pleasant game;
A mess of Russians left us but of late.
KING. How, madam! Russians!
PRINCESS OF FRANCE. Ay, in truth, my lord;
Trim gallants, full of courtship and of state.
ROSALINE. Madam, speak true. It is not so, my lord.
My lady, to the manner of the days,
In courtesy gives undeserving praise.
We four indeed confronted were with four
In Russian habit; here they stayed an hour
And talk'd apace; and in that hour, my lord,
They did not bless us with one happy word.
I dare not call them fools; but this I think,
When they are thirsty, fools would fain have drink.
BEROWNE. This jest is dry to me. Fair gentle sweet,
Your wit makes wise things foolish; when we greet,
With eyes best seeing, heaven's fiery eye,

By light we lose light; your capacity
Is of that nature that to your huge store
Wise things seem foolish and rich things but poor.
ROSALINE. This proves you wise and rich, for in my eye-
BEROWNE. I am a fool, and full of poverty.
ROSALINE. But that you take what doth to you belong,
It were a fault to snatch words from my tongue.
BEROWNE. O, I am yours, and all that I possess.
ROSALINE. All the fool mine?
BEROWNE. I cannot give you less.
ROSALINE. Which of the vizards was it that you wore?
BEROWNE. Where? when? what vizard? Why demand you this?
ROSALINE. There, then, that vizard; that superfluous case
That hid the worse and show'd the better face.
KING. We were descried; they'll mock us now downright.
DUMAIN. Let us confess, and turn it to a jest.
PRINCESS OF FRANCE. Amaz'd, my lord? Why looks your Highness sad?
ROSALINE. Help, hold his brows! he'll swoon! Why look you pale?
Sea-sick, I think, coming from Muscovy.
BEROWNE. Thus pour the stars down plagues for perjury.
Can any face of brass hold longer out?
Here stand I, lady- dart thy skill at me,
Bruise me with scorn, confound me with a flout,
Thrust thy sharp wit quite through my ignorance,
Cut me to pieces with thy keen conceit;
And I will wish thee never more to dance,
Nor never more in Russian habit wait.
O, never will I trust to speeches penn'd,

Nor to the motion of a school-boy's tongue,
Nor never come in vizard to my friend,
Nor woo in rhyme, like a blind harper's song.
Taffeta phrases, silken terms precise,
Three-pil'd hyperboles, spruce affectation,
Figures pedantical- these summer-flies
Have blown me full of maggot ostentation.
I do forswear them; and I here protest,
By this white glove- how white the hand, God knows!-
Henceforth my wooing mind shall be express'd
In russet yeas, and honest kersey noes.
And, to begin, wench- so God help me, law!-
My love to thee is sound, sans crack or flaw.
ROSALINE. Sans 'sans,' I pray you.
BEROWNE. Yet I have a trick
Of the old rage; bear with me, I am sick;
I'll leave it by degrees. Soft, let us see-
Write 'Lord have mercy on us' on those three;
They are infected; in their hearts it lies;
They have the plague, and caught it of your eyes.
These lords are visited; you are not free,
For the Lord's tokens on you do I see.

PRINCESS OF FRANCE. No, they are free that gave these tokens to us.

BEROWNE. Our states are forfeit; seek not to undo us.
ROSALINE. It is not so; for how can this be true,
That you stand forfeit, being those that sue?
BEROWNE. Peace; for I will not have to do with you.
ROSALINE. Nor shall not, if I do as I intend.
BEROWNE. Speak for yourselves; my wit is at an end.

KING. Teach us, sweet madam, for our rude transgression
Some fair excuse.
PRINCESS OF FRANCE. The fairest is confession.
Were not you here but even now, disguis'd?
KING. Madam, I was.
PRINCESS OF FRANCE. And were you well advis'd?
KING. I was, fair madam.
PRINCESS OF FRANCE. When you then were here,
What did you whisper in your lady's ear?
KING. That more than all the world I did respect her.
PRINCESS OF FRANCE. When she shall challenge this, you will reject her.
KING. Upon mine honour, no.
PRINCESS OF FRANCE. Peace, peace, forbear;
Your oath once broke, you force not to forswear.
KING. Despise me when I break this oath of mine.
PRINCESS OF FRANCE. I will; and therefore keep it. Rosaline,
What did the Russian whisper in your ear?
ROSALINE. Madam, he swore that he did hold me dear
As precious eyesight, and did value me
Above this world; adding thereto, moreover,
That he would wed me, or else die my lover.
PRINCESS OF FRANCE. God give thee joy of him! The noble lord
Most honourably doth uphold his word.
KING. What mean you, madam? By my life, my troth,
I never swore this lady such an oath.
ROSALINE. By heaven, you did; and, to confirm it plain,
You gave me this; but take it, sir, again.
KING. My faith and this the Princess I did give;
I knew her by this jewel on her sleeve.

PRINCESS OF FRANCE. Pardon me, sir, this jewel did she wear;
And Lord Berowne, I thank him, is my dear.
What, will you have me, or your pearl again?
BEROWNE. Neither of either; I remit both twain.
I see the trick on't: here was a consent,
Knowing aforehand of our merriment,
To dash it like a Christmas comedy.
Some carry-tale, some please-man, some slight zany,
Some mumble-news, some trencher-knight, some Dick
That smiles his cheek in years and knows the trick
To make my lady laugh when she's dispos'd,
Told our intents before; which once disclos'd,
The ladies did change favours; and then we,
Following the signs, woo'd but the sign of she.
Now, to our perjury to add more terror,
We are again forsworn in will and error.
Much upon this it is; [To BOYET] and might not you
Forestall our sport, to make us thus untrue?
Do not you know my lady's foot by th' squier,
And laugh upon the apple of her eye?
And stand between her back, sir, and the fire,
Holding a trencher, jesting merrily?
You put our page out. Go, you are allow'd;
Die when you will, a smock shall be your shroud.
You leer upon me, do you? There's an eye
Wounds like a leaden sword.
BOYET. Full merrily
Hath this brave manage, this career, been run.
BEROWNE. Lo, he is tilting straight! Peace; I have done.

Enter COSTARD

Welcome, pure wit! Thou part'st a fair fray.

COSTARD. O Lord, sir, they would know

Whether the three Worthies shall come in or no?

BEROWNE. What, are there but three?

COSTARD. No, sir; but it is vara fine,

For every one pursents three.

BEROWNE. And three times thrice is nine.

COSTARD. Not so, sir; under correction, sir,

I hope it is not so.

You cannot beg us, sir, I can assure you, sir; we know what we know;

I hope, sir, three times thrice, sir-

BEROWNE. Is not nine.

COSTARD. Under correction, sir, we know whereuntil it doth amount.

BEROWNE. By Jove, I always took three threes for nine.

COSTARD. O Lord, sir, it were pity you should get your living by reck'ning, sir.

BEROWNE. How much is it?

COSTARD. O Lord, sir, the parties themselves, the actors, sir, will show whereuntil it doth amount. For mine own part, I am, as they say, but to parfect one man in one poor man, Pompion the Great, sir.

BEROWNE. Art thou one of the Worthies?

COSTARD. It pleased them to think me worthy of Pompey the Great; for mine own part, I know not the degree of the Worthy; but I am to stand for him.

BEROWNE. Go, bid them prepare.

COSTARD. We will turn it finely off, sir; we will take some care.

Exit COSTARD

KING. Berowne, they will shame us; let them not approach.

BEROWNE. We are shame-proof, my lord, and 'tis some policy

To have one show worse than the King's and his company.

KING. I say they shall not come.

PRINCESS OF FRANCE. Nay, my good lord, let me o'errule you now.

That sport best pleases that doth least know how;

Where zeal strives to content, and the contents

Dies in the zeal of that which it presents.

Their form confounded makes most form in mirth,

When great things labouring perish in their birth.

BEROWNE. A right description of our sport, my lord.

Enter ARMADO

ARMADO. Anointed, I implore so much expense of thy royal sweet breath as will utter a brace of words.

[Converses apart with the KING, and delivers a paper]

PRINCESS OF FRANCE. Doth this man serve God?

BEROWNE. Why ask you?

PRINCESS OF FRANCE. 'A speaks not like a man of God his making.

ARMADO. That is all one, my fair, sweet, honey monarch; for, I protest, the schoolmaster is exceeding fantastical; too too vain, too too vain; but we will put it, as they say, to fortuna de la guerra. I wish you the peace of mind, most royal couplement!

Exit ARMADO

KING. Here is like to be a good presence of Worthies. He presents

Hector of Troy; the swain, Pompey the Great; the parish curate,

Alexander; Arinado's page, Hercules; the pedant, Judas Maccabaeus.

And if these four Worthies in their first show thrive,

These four will change habits and present the other five.

BEROWNE. There is five in the first show.

KING. You are deceived, 'tis not so.

BEROWNE. The pedant, the braggart, the hedge-priest, the fool, and the boy:

Abate throw at novum, and the whole world again

Cannot pick out five such, take each one in his vein.

KING. The ship is under sail, and here she comes amain.

Enter COSTARD, armed for POMPEY

COSTARD. I Pompey am-

BEROWNE. You lie, you are not he.

COSTARD. I Pompey am-

BOYET. With libbard's head on knee.

BEROWNE. Well said, old mocker; I must needs be friends with thee.

COSTARD. I Pompey am, Pompey surnam'd the Big-

DUMAIN. The Great.

COSTARD. It is Great, sir.

Pompey surnam'd the Great,

That oft in field, with targe and shield, did make my foe to sweat;

And travelling along this coast, I bere am come by chance,

And lay my arms before the legs of this sweet lass of France.

If your ladyship would say 'Thanks, Pompey,' I had done.

PRINCESS OF FRANCE. Great thanks, great Pompey.

COSTARD. 'Tis not so much worth; but I hope I was perfect. I made a little fault in Great.

BEROWNE. My hat to a halfpenny, Pompey proves the best Worthy.

Enter SIR NATHANIEL, for ALEXANDER

NATHANIEL. When in the world I liv'd, I was the world's commander;

By east, west, north, and south, I spread my conquering might.

My scutcheon plain declares that I am Alisander-

BOYET. Your nose says, no, you are not; for it stands to right.

BEROWNE. Your nose smells 'no' in this, most tender-smelling knight.

PRINCESS OF FRANCE. The conqueror is dismay'd. Proceed, good Alexander.

NATHANIEL. When in the world I liv'd, I was the world's commander-

BOYET. Most true, 'tis right, you were so, Alisander.

BEROWNE. Pompey the Great!

COSTARD. Your servant, and Costard.

BEROWNE. Take away the conqueror, take away Alisander.

COSTARD. [To Sir Nathaniel] O, Sir, you have overthrown Alisander the conqueror! You will be scrap'd out of the painted cloth for this. Your lion, that holds his poleaxe sitting on a close-stool, will be given to Ajax. He will be the ninth Worthy. A conqueror and afeard to speak! Run away for shame, Alisander.

[Sir Nathaniel retires] There, an't shall please you, a foolish mild man; an honest man, look you, and soon dash'd. He is a marvellous good neighbour, faith, and a very good bowler; but for Alisander-alas! you see how 'tis- a little o'erparted. But there are Worthies a-coming will speak their mind in some other sort.

PRINCESS OF FRANCE. Stand aside, good Pompey.

Enter HOLOFERNES, for JUDAS; and MOTH, for HERCULES

HOLOFERNES. Great Hercules is presented by this imp,

Whose club kill'd Cerberus, that three-headed canus;

And when be was a babe, a child, a shrimp,

Thus did he strangle serpents in his manus.

Quoniam he seemeth in minority,

Ergo I come with this apology.

Keep some state in thy exit, and vanish. [MOTH retires]

Judas I am-

DUMAIN. A Judas!

HOLOFERNES. Not Iscariot, sir.

Judas I am, ycliped Maccabaeus.

DUMAIN. Judas Maccabaeus clipt is plain Judas.

BEROWNE. A kissing traitor. How art thou prov'd Judas?

HOLOFERNES. Judas I am-

DUMAIN. The more shame for you, Judas!

HOLOFERNES. What mean you, sir?

BOYET. To make Judas hang himself.

HOLOFERNES. Begin, sir; you are my elder.

BEROWNE. Well followed: Judas was hanged on an elder.

HOLOFERNES. I will not be put out of countenance.

BEROWNE. Because thou hast no face.

HOLOFERNES. What is this?

BOYET. A cittern-head.

DUMAIN. The head of a bodkin.

BEROWNE. A death's face in a ring.

LONGAVILLE. The face of an old Roman coin, scarce seen.

BOYET. The pommel of Coesar's falchion.

DUMAIN. The carv'd-bone face on a flask.

BEROWNE. Saint George's half-cheek in a brooch.

DUMAIN. Ay, and in a brooch of lead.

BEROWNE. Ay, and worn in the cap of a tooth-drawer. And now, forward; for we have put thee in countenance.

HOLOFERNES. You have put me out of countenance.

BEROWNE. False: we have given thee faces.

HOLOFERNES. But you have outfac'd them all.

BEROWNE. An thou wert a lion we would do so.

BOYET. Therefore, as he is an ass, let him go.

And so adieu, sweet Jude! Nay, why dost thou stay?

DUMAIN. For the latter end of his name.

BEROWNE. For the ass to the Jude; give it him- Jud-as, away.

HOLOFERNES. This is not generous, not gentle, not humble.

BOYET. A light for Monsieur Judas! It grows dark, he may stumble.

[HOLOFERNES retires]

PRINCESS OF FRANCE. Alas, poor Maccabaeus, how hath he been baited!

Enter ARMADO, for HECTOR

BEROWNE. Hide thy head, Achilles; here comes Hector in arms.

DUMAIN. Though my mocks come home by me, I will now be merry.

KING. Hector was but a Troyan in respect of this.

BOYET. But is this Hector?

DUMAIN. I think Hector was not so clean-timber'd.

LONGAVILLE. His leg is too big for Hector's.

DUMAIN. More calf, certain.

BOYET. No; he is best indued in the small.

BEROWNE. This cannot be Hector.

DUMAIN. He's a god or a painter, for he makes faces.

ARMADO. The armipotent Mars, of lances the almighty,

Gave Hector a gift-

DUMAIN. A gilt nutmeg.

BEROWNE. A lemon.

LONGAVILLE. Stuck with cloves.

DUMAIN. No, cloven.

ARMADO. Peace!

The armipotent Mars, of lances the almighty,
Gave Hector a gift, the heir of Ilion;
A man so breathed that certain he would fight ye,
From morn till night out of his pavilion.
I am that flower-

DUMAIN. That mint.

LONGAVILLE. That columbine.

ARMADO. Sweet Lord Longaville, rein thy tongue.

LONGAVILLE. I must rather give it the rein, for it runs against Hector.

DUMAIN. Ay, and Hector's a greyhound.

ARMADO. The sweet war-man is dead and rotten; sweet chucks, beat not the bones of the buried; when he breathed, he was a man. But I will forward with my device. [To the PRINCESS] Sweet royalty, bestow on me the sense of hearing.

[BEROWNE steps forth, and speaks to COSTARD]

PRINCESS OF FRANCE. Speak, brave Hector; we are much delighted.

ARMADO. I do adore thy sweet Grace's slipper.

BOYET. [Aside to DUMAIN] Loves her by the foot.

DUMAIN. [Aside to BOYET] He may not by the yard.

ARMADO. This Hector far surmounted Hannibal-

COSTARD. The party is gone, fellow Hector, she is gone; she is two months on her way.

ARMADO. What meanest thou?

COSTARD. Faith, unless you play the honest Troyan, the poor wench is cast away. She's quick; the child brags in her belly already; 'tis yours.

ARMADO. Dost thou infamonize me among potentates? Thou shalt die.

COSTARD. Then shall Hector be whipt for Jaquenetta that is quick by him, and hang'd for Pompey that is dead by him.

DUMAIN. Most rare Pompey!

BOYET. Renowned Pompey!

BEROWNE. Greater than Great! Great, great, great Pompey! Pompey the Huge!

DUMAIN. Hector trembles.

BEROWNE. Pompey is moved. More Ates, more Ates! Stir them on! stir them on!

DUMAIN. Hector will challenge him.

BEROWNE. Ay, if 'a have no more man's blood in his belly than will sup a flea.

ARMADO. By the North Pole, I do challenge thee.

COSTARD. I will not fight with a pole, like a Northern man; I'll slash; I'll do it by the sword. I bepray you, let me borrow my arms again.

DUMAIN. Room for the incensed Worthies!

COSTARD. I'll do it in my shirt.

DUMAIN. Most resolute Pompey!

MOTH. Master, let me take you a buttonhole lower. Do you not see Pompey is uncasing for the combat? What mean you? You will lose your reputation.

ARMADO. Gentlemen and soldiers, pardon me; I will not combat in my shirt.

DUMAIN. You may not deny it: Pompey hath made the challenge.

ARMADO. Sweet bloods, I both may and will.

BEROWNE. What reason have you for 't?

ARMADO. The naked truth of it is: I have no shirt; I go woolward for penance.

BOYET. True, and it was enjoined him in Rome for want of linen; since when, I'll be sworn, he wore none but a dishclout of Jaquenetta's, and that 'a wears next his heart for a favour.

Enter as messenger, MONSIEUR MARCADE

MARCADE. God save you, madam!

PRINCESS OF FRANCE. Welcome, Marcade;

But that thou interruptest our merriment.

MARCADE. I am sorry, madam; for the news I bring

Is heavy in my tongue. The King your father-

PRINCESS OF FRANCE. Dead, for my life!

MARCADE. Even so; my tale is told.

BEROWNE. WOrthies away; the scene begins to cloud.

ARMADO. For mine own part, I breathe free breath. I have seen the day of wrong through the little hole of discretion, and I will right myself like a soldier. Exeunt WORTHIES

KING. How fares your Majesty?

PRINCESS OF FRANCE. Boyet, prepare; I will away to-night.

KING. Madam, not so; I do beseech you stay.

PRINCESS OF FRANCE. Prepare, I say. I thank you, gracious lords,

For all your fair endeavours, and entreat,
Out of a new-sad soul, that you vouchsafe
In your rich wisdom to excuse or hide
The liberal opposition of our spirits,
If over-boldly we have borne ourselves
In the converse of breath- your gentleness
Was guilty of it. Farewell, worthy lord.
A heavy heart bears not a nimble tongue.
Excuse me so, coming too short of thanks
For my great suit so easily obtain'd.

KING. The extreme parts of time extremely forms
All causes to the purpose of his speed;
And often at his very loose decides

That which long process could not arbitrate.
And though the mourning brow of progeny
Forbid the smiling courtesy of love
The holy suit which fain it would convince,
Yet, since love's argument was first on foot,
Let not the cloud of sorrow justle it
From what it purpos'd; since to wail friends lost
Is not by much so wholesome-profitable
As to rejoice at friends but newly found.

PRINCESS OF FRANCE. I understand you not; my griefs are double.

BEROWNE. Honest plain words best pierce the ear of grief;
And by these badges understand the King.
For your fair sakes have we neglected time,
Play'd foul play with our oaths; your beauty, ladies,
Hath much deformed us, fashioning our humours
Even to the opposed end of our intents;
And what in us hath seem'd ridiculous,
As love is full of unbefitting strains,
All wanton as a child, skipping and vain;
Form'd by the eye and therefore, like the eye,
Full of strange shapes, of habits, and of forms,
Varying in subjects as the eye doth roll
To every varied object in his glance;
Which parti-coated presence of loose love
Put on by us, if in your heavenly eyes
Have misbecom'd our oaths and gravities,
Those heavenly eyes that look into these faults
Suggested us to make. Therefore, ladies,
Our love being yours, the error that love makes

Is likewise yours. We to ourselves prove false,
By being once false for ever to be true
To those that make us both- fair ladies, you;
And even that falsehood, in itself a sin,
Thus purifies itself and turns to grace.
PRINCESS OF FRANCE. We have receiv'd your letters, full of love;
Your favours, the ambassadors of love;
And, in our maiden council, rated them
At courtship, pleasant jest, and courtesy,
As bombast and as lining to the time;
But more devout than this in our respects
Have we not been; and therefore met your loves
In their own fashion, like a merriment.
DUMAIN. Our letters, madam, show'd much more than jest.
LONGAVILLE. So did our looks.
ROSALINE. We did not quote them so.
KING. Now, at the latest minute of the hour,
Grant us your loves.
PRINCESS OF FRANCE. A time, methinks, too short
To make a world-without-end bargain in.
No, no, my lord, your Grace is perjur'd much,
Full of dear guiltiness; and therefore this,
If for my love, as there is no such cause,
You will do aught- this shall you do for me:
Your oath I will not trust; but go with speed
To some forlorn and naked hermitage,
Remote from all the pleasures of the world;
There stay until the twelve celestial signs
Have brought about the annual reckoning.

If this austere insociable life
Change not your offer made in heat of blood,
If frosts and fasts, hard lodging and thin weeds,
Nip not the gaudy blossoms of your love,
But that it bear this trial, and last love,
Then, at the expiration of the year,
Come, challenge me, challenge me by these deserts;
And, by this virgin palm now kissing thine,
I will be thine; and, till that instant, shut
My woeful self up in a mournful house,
Raining the tears of lamentation
For the remembrance of my father's death.
If this thou do deny, let our hands part,
Neither intitled in the other's heart.
KING. If this, or more than this, I would deny,
To flatter up these powers of mine with rest,
The sudden hand of death close up mine eye!
Hence hermit then, my heart is in thy breast.
BEROWNE. And what to me, my love? and what to me?
ROSALINE. You must he purged too, your sins are rack'd;
You are attaint with faults and perjury;
Therefore, if you my favour mean to get,
A twelvemonth shall you spend, and never rest,
But seek the weary beds of people sick.
DUMAIN. But what to me, my love? but what to me?
A wife?
KATHARINE. A beard, fair health, and honesty;
With threefold love I wish you all these three.
DUMAIN. O, shall I say I thank you, gentle wife?
KATHARINE. No so, my lord; a twelvemonth and a day

I'll mark no words that smooth-fac'd wooers say.
Come when the King doth to my lady come;
Then, if I have much love, I'll give you some.
DUMAIN. I'll serve thee true and faithfully till then.
KATHARINE. Yet swear not, lest ye be forsworn again.
LONGAVILLE. What says Maria?
MARIA. At the twelvemonth's end
I'll change my black gown for a faithful friend.
LONGAVILLE. I'll stay with patience; but the time is long.
MARIA. The liker you; few taller are so young.
BEROWNE. Studies my lady? Mistress, look on me;
Behold the window of my heart, mine eye,
What humble suit attends thy answer there.
Impose some service on me for thy love.
ROSALINE. Oft have I heard of you, my Lord Berowne,
Before I saw you; and the world's large tongue
Proclaims you for a man replete with mocks,
Full of comparisons and wounding flouts,
Which you on all estates will execute
That lie within the mercy of your wit.
To weed this wormwood from your fruitful brain,
And therewithal to win me, if you please,
Without the which I am not to be won,
You shall this twelvemonth term from day to day
Visit the speechless sick, and still converse
With groaning wretches; and your task shall be,
With all the fierce endeavour of your wit,
To enforce the pained impotent to smile.
BEROWNE. To move wild laughter in the throat of death?
It cannot be; it is impossible;

Mirth cannot move a soul in agony.
ROSALINE. Why, that's the way to choke a gibing spirit,
Whose influence is begot of that loose grace
Which shallow laughing hearers give to fools.
A jest's prosperity lies in the ear
Of him that hears it, never in the tongue
Of him that makes it; then, if sickly ears,
Deaf'd with the clamours of their own dear groans,
Will hear your idle scorns, continue then,
And I will have you and that fault withal.
But if they will not, throw away that spirit,
And I shall find you empty of that fault,
Right joyful of your reformation.

BEROWNE. A twelvemonth? Well, befall what will befall, I'll jest a twelvemonth in an hospital.

PRINCESS OF FRANCE. [To the King] Ay, sweet my lord, and so I take my leave.

KING. No, madam; we will bring you on your way.
BEROWNE. Our wooing doth not end like an old play:
Jack hath not Jill. These ladies' courtesy
Might well have made our sport a comedy.
KING. Come, sir, it wants a twelvemonth an' a day,
And then 'twill end.
BEROWNE. That's too long for a play.

BEROWNE, LONGAVILLE, and DUMAIN

KING. Let fame, that all hunt after in their lives,
Live regist'red upon our brazen tombs,
And then grace us in the disgrace of death;
When, spite of cormorant devouring Time,
Th' endeavour of this present breath may buy

That honour which shall bate his scythe's keen edge,
And make us heirs of all eternity.
Therefore, brave conquerors- for so you are
That war against your own affections
And the huge army of the world's desires-
Our late edict shall strongly stand in force:
Navarre shall be the wonder of the world;
Our court shall be a little Academe,
Still and contemplative in living art.
You three, Berowne, Dumain, and Longaville,
Have sworn for three years' term to live with me
My fellow-scholars, and to keep those statutes
That are recorded in this schedule here.
Your oaths are pass'd; and now subscribe your names,
That his own hand may strike his honour down
That violates the smallest branch herein.
If you are arm'd to do as sworn to do,
Subscribe to your deep oaths, and keep it too.
LONGAVILLE. I am resolv'd; 'tis but a three years' fast.
The mind shall banquet, though the body pine.
Fat paunches have lean pates; and dainty bits
Make rich the ribs, but bankrupt quite the wits.
DUMAIN. My loving lord, Dumain is mortified.
The grosser manner of these world's delights
He throws upon the gross world's baser slaves;
To love, to wealth, to pomp, I pine and die,
With all these living in philosophy.
BEROWNE. I can but say their protestation over;
So much, dear liege, I have already sworn,
That is, to live and study here three years.

But there are other strict observances,
As: not to see a woman in that term,
Which I hope well is not enrolled there;
And one day in a week to touch no food,
And but one meal on every day beside,
The which I hope is not enrolled there;
And then to sleep but three hours in the night
And not be seen to wink of all the day-
When I was wont to think no harm all night,
And make a dark night too of half the day-
Which I hope well is not enrolled there.
O, these are barren tasks, too hard to keep,
Not to see ladies, study, fast, not sleep!
KING. Your oath is pass'd to pass away from these.
BEROWNE. Let me say no, my liege, an if you please:
I only swore to study with your Grace,
And stay here in your court for three years' space.
LONGAVILLE. You swore to that, Berowne, and to the rest.
BEROWNE. By yea and nay, sir, then I swore in jest.
What is the end of study, let me know.
KING. Why, that to know which else we should not know.
BEROWNE. Things hid and barr'd, you mean, from common sense?
KING. Ay, that is study's god-like recompense.
BEROWNE. Come on, then; I will swear to study so,
To know the thing I am forbid to know,
As thus: to study where I well may dine,
When I to feast expressly am forbid;
Or study where to meet some mistress fine,
When mistresses from common sense are hid;

Or, having sworn too hard-a-keeping oath,
Study to break it, and not break my troth.
If study's gain be thus, and this be so,
Study knows that which yet it doth not know.
Swear me to this, and I will ne'er say no.
KING. These be the stops that hinder study quite,
And train our intellects to vain delight.
BEROWNE. Why, all delights are vain; but that most vain
Which, with pain purchas'd, doth inherit pain,
As painfully to pore upon a book
To seek the light of truth; while truth the while
Doth falsely blind the eyesight of his look.
Light, seeking light, doth light of light beguile;
So, ere you find where light in darkness lies,
Your light grows dark by losing of your eyes.
Study me how to please the eye indeed,
By fixing it upon a fairer eye;
Who dazzling so, that eye shall be his heed,
And give him light that it was blinded by.
Study is like the heaven's glorious sun,
That will not be deep-search'd with saucy looks;
Small have continual plodders ever won,
Save base authority from others' books.
These earthly godfathers of heaven's lights
That give a name to every fixed star
Have no more profit of their shining nights
Than those that walk and wot not what they are.
Too much to know is to know nought but fame;
And every godfather can give a name.
KING. How well he's read, to reason against reading!

DUMAIN. Proceeded well, to stop all good proceeding!

LONGAVILLE. He weeds the corn, and still lets grow the weeding.

BEROWNE. The spring is near, when green geese are a-breeding.

DUMAIN. How follows that?

BEROWNE. Fit in his place and time.

DUMAIN. In reason nothing.

BEROWNE. Something then in rhyme.

LONGAVILLE. Berowne is like an envious sneaping frost
That bites the first-born infants of the spring.

BEROWNE. Well, say I am; why should proud summer boast
Before the birds have any cause to sing?
Why should I joy in any abortive birth?
At Christmas I no more desire a rose
Than wish a snow in May's new-fangled shows;
But like of each thing that in season grows;
So you, to study now it is too late,
Climb o'er the house to unlock the little gate.

KING. Well, sit out; go home, Berowne; adieu.

BEROWNE. No, my good lord; I have sworn to stay with you;
And though I have for barbarism spoke more
Than for that angel knowledge you can say,
Yet confident I'll keep what I have swore,
And bide the penance of each three years' day.
Give me the paper; let me read the same;
And to the strictest decrees I'll write my name.

KING. How well this yielding rescues thee from shame!

BEROWNE. [Reads] 'Item. That no woman shall come within a mile of my court'- Hath this been proclaimed?

LONGAVILLE. Four days ago.

BEROWNE. Let's see the penalty. [Reads] '-on pain of losing her tongue.' Who devis'd this penalty?

LONGAVILLE. Marry, that did I.

BEROWNE. Sweet lord, and why?

LONGAVILLE. To fright them hence with that dread penalty.

BEROWNE. A dangerous law against gentility.

[Reads] 'Item. If any man be seen to talk with a woman within the term of three years, he shall endure such public shame as the rest of the court can possibly devise.'

This article, my liege, yourself must break;
For well you know here comes in embassy
The French king's daughter, with yourself to speak-
A mild of grace and complete majesty-
About surrender up of Aquitaine
To her decrepit, sick, and bedrid father;
Therefore this article is made in vain,
Or vainly comes th' admired princess hither.

KING. What say you, lords? Why, this was quite forgot.

BEROWNE. So study evermore is over-shot.
While it doth study to have what it would,
It doth forget to do the thing it should;
And when it hath the thing it hunteth most,
'Tis won as towns with fire- so won, so lost.

KING. We must of force dispense with this decree;
She must lie here on mere necessity.

BEROWNE. Necessity will make us all forsworn
Three thousand times within this three years' space;
For every man with his affects is born,
Not by might mast'red, but by special grace.
If I break faith, this word shall speak for me:
I am forsworn on mere necessity.

So to the laws at large I write my name; [Subscribes]
And he that breaks them in the least degree
Stands in attainder of eternal shame.
Suggestions are to other as to me;
But I believe, although I seem so loath,
I am the last that will last keep his oath.
But is there no quick recreation granted?
KING. Ay, that there is. Our court, you know, is haunted
With a refined traveller of Spain,
A man in all the world's new fashion planted,
That hath a mint of phrases in his brain;
One who the music of his own vain tongue
Doth ravish like enchanting harmony;
A man of complements, whom right and wrong
Have chose as umpire of their mutiny.
This child of fancy, that Armado hight,
For interim to our studies shall relate,
In high-born words, the worth of many a knight
From tawny Spain lost in the world's debate.
How you delight, my lords, I know not, I;
But I protest I love to hear him lie,
And I will use him for my minstrelsy.
BEROWNE. Armado is a most illustrious wight,
A man of fire-new words, fashion's own knight.
LONGAVILLE. Costard the swain and he shall be our sport;
And so to study three years is but short.

Enter DULL, a constable, with a letter, and COSTARD

DULL. Which is the Duke's own person?
BEROWNE. This, fellow. What wouldst?

DULL. I myself reprehend his own person, for I am his Grace's farborough; but I would see his own person in flesh and blood.

BEROWNE. This is he.

DULL. Signior Arme- Arme- commends you. There's villainy abroad; this letter will tell you more.

COSTARD. Sir, the contempts thereof are as touching me.

KING. A letter from the magnificent Armado.

BEROWNE. How low soever the matter, I hope in God for high words.

LONGAVILLE. A high hope for a low heaven. God grant us patience!

BEROWNE. To hear, or forbear hearing?

LONGAVILLE. To hear meekly, sir, and to laugh moderately; or, to forbear both.

BEROWNE. Well, sir, be it as the style shall give us cause to climb in the merriness.

COSTARD. The matter is to me, sir, as concerning Jaquenetta. The manner of it is, I was taken with the manner.

BEROWNE. In what manner?

COSTARD. In manner and form following, sir; all those three: I was seen with her in the manor-house, sitting with her upon the form, and taken following her into the park; which, put together, is in manner and form following. Now, sir, for the manner- it is the manner of a man to speak to a woman. For the form- in some form.

BEROWNE. For the following, sir?

COSTARD. As it shall follow in my correction; and God defend the right!

KING. Will you hear this letter with attention?

BEROWNE. As we would hear an oracle.

COSTARD. Such is the simplicity of man to hearken after the flesh.

KING. [Reads] 'Great deputy, the welkin's vicegerent and sole dominator of Navarre, my soul's earth's god and body's fost'ring patron'-

COSTARD. Not a word of Costard yet.

KING. [Reads] 'So it is'-

COSTARD. It may be so; but if he say it is so, he is, in telling true, but so.

KING. Peace!

COSTARD. Be to me, and every man that dares not fight!

KING. No words!

COSTARD. Of other men's secrets, I beseech you.

KING. [Reads] 'So it is, besieged with sable-coloured melancholy, I did commend the black oppressing humour to the most wholesome physic of thy health-giving air; and, as I am a gentleman, betook myself to walk. The time When? About the sixth hour; when beasts most graze, birds best peck, and men sit down to that nourishment which is called supper.

So much for the time When. Now for the ground Which? which, I mean, I upon; it is ycleped thy park. Then for the place Where? where, I mean, I did encounter that obscene and most prepost'rous event that draweth from my snow-white pen the ebon-coloured ink which here thou viewest, beholdest, surveyest, or seest. But to the place Where? It standeth north-north-east and by east from the west corner of thy curious-knotted garden. There did I see that low-spirited swain, that base minnow of thy mirth,'

COSTARD. Me?

KING. 'that unlettered small-knowing soul,'

COSTARD. Me?

KING. 'that shallow vassal,'

COSTARD. Still me?

KING. 'which, as I remember, hight Costard,'

COSTARD. O, me!

KING. 'sorted and consorted, contrary to thy established proclaimed edict and continent canon; which, with, O, with- but with this I passion to say wherewith-'

COSTARD. With a wench.

King. 'with a child of our grandmother Eve, a female; or, for thy more sweet understanding, a woman. Him I, as my ever-esteemed duty pricks me on, have sent to thee, to receive the meed of punishment, by thy sweet Grace's officer, Antony Dull, a man of good repute, carriage, bearing, and estimation.'

DULL. Me, an't shall please you; I am Antony Dull.

KING. 'For Jaquenetta- so is the weaker vessel called, which I apprehended with the aforesaid swain- I keep her as a vessel of thy law's fury; and shall, at the least of thy sweet notice, bring her to trial. Thine, in all compliments of devoted and heart-burning heat of duty,

DON ADRIANO DE ARMADO.'

BEROWNE. This is not so well as I look'd for, but the best that ever I heard.

KING. Ay, the best for the worst. But, sirrah, what say you to this?

COSTARD. Sir, I confess the wench.

KING. Did you hear the proclamation?

COSTARD. I do confess much of the hearing it, but little of the marking of it.

KING. It was proclaimed a year's imprisonment to be taken with a wench.

COSTARD. I was taken with none, sir; I was taken with a damsel.

KING. Well, it was proclaimed damsel.

COSTARD. This was no damsel neither, sir; she was a virgin.

KING. It is so varied too, for it was proclaimed virgin.

COSTARD. If it were, I deny her virginity; I was taken with a maid.

KING. This 'maid' not serve your turn, sir.

COSTARD. This maid will serve my turn, sir.

KING. Sir, I will pronounce your sentence: you shall fast a week with bran and water.

COSTARD. I had rather pray a month with mutton and porridge.

KING. And Don Armado shall be your keeper.

My Lord Berowne, see him delivered o'er;

And go we, lords, to put in practice that

Which each to other hath so strongly sworn.

Exeunt KING, LONGAVILLE, and DUMAIN

BEROWNE. I'll lay my head to any good man's hat

These oaths and laws will prove an idle scorn.

Sirrah, come on.

COSTARD. I suffer for the truth, sir; for true it is I was taken with Jaquenetta, and Jaquenetta is a true girl; and therefore welcome the sour cup of prosperity! Affliction may one day smile again; and till then, sit thee down, sorrow.

Exeunt

SCENE II.: THE PARK

Enter ARMADO and MOTH, his page

ARMADO. Boy, what sign is it when a man of great spirit grows melancholy?

MOTH. A great sign, sir, that he will look sad.

ARMADO. Why, sadness is one and the self-same thing, dear imp.

MOTH. No, no; O Lord, sir, no!

ARMADO. How canst thou part sadness and melancholy, my tender juvenal?

MOTH. By a familiar demonstration of the working, my tough signior.

ARMADO. Why tough signior? Why tough signior?

MOTH. Why tender juvenal? Why tender juvenal?

ARMADO. I spoke it, tender juvenal, as a congruent epitheton appertaining to thy young days, which we may nominate tender.

MOTH. And I, tough signior, as an appertinent title to your old time, which we may name tough.

ARMADO. Pretty and apt.

MOTH. How mean you, sir? I pretty, and my saying apt? or I apt, and my saying pretty?

ARMADO. Thou pretty, because little.

MOTH. Little pretty, because little. Wherefore apt?

ARMADO. And therefore apt, because quick.

MOTH. Speak you this in my praise, master?

ARMADO. In thy condign praise.

MOTH. I will praise an eel with the same praise.

ARMADO. that an eel is ingenious?

MOTH. That an eel is quick.

ARMADO. I do say thou art quick in answers; thou heat'st my blood.

MOTH. I am answer'd, sir.

ARMADO. I love not to be cross'd.

MOTH. [Aside] He speaks the mere contrary: crosses love not him.

ARMADO. I have promised to study three years with the Duke.

MOTH. You may do it in an hour, sir.

ARMADO. Impossible.

MOTH. How many is one thrice told?

ARMADO. I am ill at reck'ning; it fitteth the spirit of a tapster.

MOTH. You are a gentleman and a gamester, sir.

ARMADO. I confess both; they are both the varnish of a complete man.

MOTH. Then I am sure you know how much the gross sum of deuce-ace amounts to.

ARMADO. It doth amount to one more than two.

MOTH. Which the base vulgar do call three.

ARMADO. True.

MOTH. Why, sir, is this such a piece of study? Now here is three studied ere ye'll thrice wink; and how easy it is to put 'years' to the word 'three,' and study three years in two words, the dancing horse will tell you.

ARMADO. A most fine figure!

MOTH. [Aside] To prove you a cipher.

ARMADO. I will hereupon confess I am in love. And as it is base for a soldier to love, so am I in love with a base wench. If drawing my sword against the humour of affection would deliver me from the reprobate thought of it, I would take Desire prisoner, and ransom him to any French courtier for a new-devis'd curtsy. I think scorn to sigh; methinks I should out-swear Cupid. Comfort me, boy; what great men have been in love?

MOTH. Hercules, master.

ARMADO. Most sweet Hercules! More authority, dear boy, name more; and, sweet my child, let them be men of good repute and carriage.

MOTH. Samson, master; he was a man of good carriage, great carriage, for he carried the town gates on his back like a porter; and he was in love.

ARMADO. O well-knit Samson! strong-jointed Samson! I do excel thee in my rapier as much as thou didst me in carrying gates. I am in love too. Who was Samson's love, my dear Moth?

MOTH. A woman, master.

ARMADO. Of what complexion?

MOTH. Of all the four, or the three, or the two, or one of the four.

ARMADO. Tell me precisely of what complexion.

MOTH. Of the sea-water green, sir.

ARMADO. Is that one of the four complexions?

MOTH. As I have read, sir; and the best of them toc.

ARMADO. Green, indeed, is the colour of lovers; but to have a love of that colour, methinks Samson had small reason for it. He surely affected her for her wit.

MOTH. It was so, sir; for she had a green wit.

ARMADO. My love is most immaculate white and red.

MOTH. Most maculate thoughts, master, are mask'd under such colours.

ARMADO. Define, define, well-educated infant.

MOTH. My father's wit my mother's tongue assist me!

ARMADO. Sweet invocation of a child; most pretty, and pathetical!

MOTH. If shé be made of white and red,
Her faults will ne'er be known;
For blushing cheeks by faults are bred,
And fears by pale white shown.
Then if she fear, or be to blame,
By this you shall not know;
For still her cheeks possess the same
Which native she doth owe.

A dangerous rhyme, master, against the reason of white and red.

ARMADO. Is there not a ballad, boy, of the King and the Beggar?

MOTH. The world was very guilty of such a ballad some three ages since; but I think now 'tis not to be found; or if it were, it would neither serve for the writing nor the tune.

ARMADO. I will have that subject newly writ o'er, that I may example my digression by some mighty precedent. Boy, I do love that country girl that I took in the park with the rational hind Costard; she deserves well.

MOTH. [Aside] To be whipt; and yet a better love than my master.

ARMADO. Sing, boy; my spirit grows heavy in love.

MOTH. And that's great marvel, loving a light wench.

ARMADO. I say, sing.

MOTH. Forbear till this company be past.

Enter DULL, COSTARD, and JAQUENETTA

DULL. Sir, the Duke's pleasure is that you keep Costard safe; and you must suffer him to take no delight nor no penance; but 'a must fast three days a week. For this damsel, I must keep her at the park; she is allow'd for the day-woman. Fare you well.

ARMADO. I do betray myself with blushing. Maid!

JAQUENETTA. Man!

ARMADO. I will visit thee at the lodge.

JAQUENETTA. That's hereby.

ARMADO. I know where it is situate.

JAQUENETTA. Lord, how wise you are!

ARMADO. I will tell thee wonders.

JAQUENETTA. With that face?

ARMADO. I love thee.

JAQUENETTA. So I heard you say.

ARMADO. And so, farewell.

JAQUENETTA. Fair weather after you!

DULL. Come, Jaquenetta, away. Exit with JAQUENETTA

ARMADO. Villain, thou shalt fast for thy offences ere thou be pardoned.

COSTARD. Well, sir, I hope when I do it I shall do it on a full stomach.

ARMADO. Thou shalt be heavily punished.

COSTARD. I am more bound to you than your fellows, for they are but lightly rewarded.

ARMADO. Take away this villain; shut him up.

MOTH. Come, you transgressing slave, away.

COSTARD. Let me not be pent up, sir; I will fast, being loose.

MOTH. No, sir; that were fast, and loose. Thou shalt to prison.

COSTARD. Well, if ever I do see the merry days of desolation that I have seen, some shall see.

MOTH. What shall some see?

COSTARD. Nay, nothing, Master Moth, but what they look upon. It is not for prisoners to be too silent in their words, and therefore

I will say nothing. I thank God I have as little patience as another man, and therefore I can be quiet.

Exeunt MOTH and COSTARD

ARMADO. I do affect the very ground, which is base, where her shoe, which is baser, guided by her foot, which is basest, doth tread.

I shall be forsworn- which is a great argument of falsehood- if I love. And how can that be true love which is falsely attempted?

Love is a familiar; Love is a devil. There is no evil angel but

Love. Yet was Samson so tempted, and he had an excellent strength; yet was Solomon so seduced, and he had a very good wit.

Cupid's butt-shaft is too hard for Hercules' club, and therefore too much odds for a Spaniard's rapier. The first and second cause will not serve my turn; the passado he respects not, the duello he regards not; his disgrace is to be called boy, but his glory is to subdue men. Adieu, valour; rust, rapier; be still, drum; for your manager is in love; yea, he loveth. Assist me, some extemporal god of rhyme, for I am sure I shall turn sonnet. Devise, wit; write, pen; for I am for whole volumes in folio.

Exit

SCENE I.: THE PARK

Enter the PRINCESS OF FRANCE, with three attending ladies,

ROSALINE, MARIA, KATHARINE, BOYET, and two other LORDS

BOYET. Now, madam, summon up your dearest spirits.
Consider who the King your father sends,
To whom he sends, and what's his embassy:
Yourself, held precious in the world's esteem,
To parley with the sole inheritor
Of all perfections that a man may owe,
Matchless Navarre; the plea of no less weight
Than Aquitaine, a dowry for a queen.
Be now as prodigal of all dear grace
As Nature was in making graces dear,
When she did starve the general world beside
And prodigally gave them all to you.

PRINCESS OF FRANCE. Good Lord Boyet, my beauty, though but mean,
Needs not the painted flourish of your praise.
Beauty is bought by judgment of the eye,
Not utt'red by base sale of chapmen's tongues;
I am less proud to hear you tell my worth
Than you much willing to be counted wise
In spending your wit in the praise of mine.
But now to task the tasker: good Boyet,
You are not ignorant all-telling fame
Doth noise abroad Navarre hath made a vow,
Till painful study shall outwear three years,
No woman may approach his silent court.
Therefore to's seemeth it a needful course,
Before we enter his forbidden gates,
To know his pleasure; and in that behalf,
Bold of your worthiness, we single you

As our best-moving fair solicitor.

Tell him the daughter of the King of France,

On serious business, craving quick dispatch,

Importunes personal conference with his Grace.

Haste, signify so much; while we attend,

Like humble-visag'd suitors, his high will.

BOYET. Proud of employment, willingly I go.

PRINCESS OF FRANCE. All pride is willing pride, and yours is so.

Exit BOYET

Who are the votaries, my loving lords,

That are vow-fellows with this virtuous duke?

FIRST LORD. Lord Longaville is one.

PRINCESS OF FRANCE. Know you the man?

MARIA. I know him, madam; at a marriage feast,

Between Lord Perigort and the beauteous heir

Of Jaques Falconbridge, solemnized

In Normandy, saw I this Longaville.

A man of sovereign parts, peerless esteem'd,

Well fitted in arts, glorious in arms;

Nothing becomes him ill that he would well.

The only soil of his fair virtue's gloss,

If virtue's gloss will stain with any soil,

Is a sharp wit match'd with too blunt a will,

Whose edge hath power to cut, whose will still wills

It should none spare that come within his power.

PRINCESS OF FRANCE. Some merry mocking lord, belike; is't so?

MARIA. They say so most that most his humours know.

PRINCESS OF FRANCE. Such short-liv'd wits do wither as they grow.

Who are the rest?
KATHARINE. The young Dumain, a well-accomplish'd youth,
Of all that virtue love for virtue loved;
Most power to do most harm, least knowing ill,
For he hath wit to make an ill shape good,
And shape to win grace though he had no wit.
I saw him at the Duke Alencon's once;
And much too little of that good I saw
Is my report to his great worthiness.
ROSALINE. Another of these students at that time
Was there with him, if I have heard a truth.
Berowne they call him; but a merrier man,
Within the limit of becoming mirth,
I never spent an hour's talk withal.
His eye begets occasion for his wit,
For every object that the one doth catch
The other turns to a mirth-moving jest,
Which his fair tongue, conceit's expositor,
Delivers in such apt and gracious words
That aged ears play truant at his tales,
And younger hearings are quite ravished;
So sweet and voluble is his discourse.
PRINCESS OF FRANCE. God bless my ladies! Are they all in love,
That every one her own hath garnished
With such bedecking ornaments of praise?
FIRST LORD. Here comes Boyet.

Re-enter BOYET

PRINCESS OF FRANCE. Now, what admittance, lord?
BOYET. Navarre had notice of your fair approach,

And he and his competitors in oath

Were all address'd to meet you, gentle lady,

Before I came. Marry, thus much I have learnt:

He rather means to lodge you in the field,

Like one that comes here to besiege his court,

Than seek a dispensation for his oath,

To let you enter his unpeopled house.

[The LADIES-IN-WAITING mask]

Enter KING, LONGAVILLE, DUMAIN, BEROWNE, and ATTENDANTS

Here comes Navarre.

KING. Fair Princess, welcome to the court of Navarre.

PRINCESS OF FRANCE. 'Fair' I give you back again; and 'welcome' I have not yet. The roof of this court is too high to be yours, and welcome to the wide fields too base to be mine.

KING. You shall be welcome, madam, to my court.

PRINCESS OF FRANCE. I will be welcome then; conduct me thither.

KING. Hear me, dear lady: I have sworn an oath-

PRINCESS OF FRANCE. Our Lady help my lord! He'll be forsworn.

KING. Not for the world, fair madam, by my will.

PRINCESS OF FRANCE. Why, will shall break it; will, and nothing else.

KING. Your ladyship is ignorant what it is.

PRINCESS OF FRANCE. Were my lord so, his ignorance were wise,

Where now his knowledge must prove ignorance.

I hear your Grace hath sworn out house-keeping.

'Tis deadly sin to keep that oath, my lord,

And sin to break it.

But pardon me, I am too sudden bold;
To teach a teacher ill beseemeth me.
Vouchsafe to read the purpose of my coming,
And suddenly resolve me in my suit. [Giving a paper]
KING. Madam, I will, if suddenly I may.
PRINCESS OF FRANCE. YOU Will the sooner that I were away,
For you'll prove perjur'd if you make me stay.
BEROWNE. Did not I dance with you in Brabant once?
KATHARINE. Did not I dance with you in Brabant once?
BEROWNE. I know you did.
KATHARINE. How needless was it then to ask the question!
BEROWNE. You must not be so quick.
KATHARINE. 'Tis long of you, that spur me with such questions.
BEROWNE. Your wit 's too hot, it speeds too fast, 'twill tire.
KATHARINE. Not till it leave the rider in the mire.
BEROWNE. What time o' day?
KATHARINE. The hour that fools should ask.
BEROWNE. Now fair befall your mask!
KATHARINE. Fair fall the face it covers!
BEROWNE. And send you many lovers!
KATHARINE. Amen, so you be none.
BEROWNE. Nay, then will I be gone.
KING. Madam, your father here doth intimate
The payment of a hundred thousand crowns;
Being but the one half of an entire sum
Disbursed by my father in his wars.
But say that he or we, as neither have,
Receiv'd that sum, yet there remains unpaid

A hundred thousand more, in surety of the which,
One part of Aquitaine is bound to us,
Although not valued to the money's worth.
If then the King your father will restore
But that one half which is unsatisfied,
We will give up our right in Aquitaine,
And hold fair friendship with his Majesty.
But that, it seems, he little purposeth,
For here he doth demand to have repaid
A hundred thousand crowns; and not demands,
On payment of a hundred thousand crowns,
To have his title live in Aquitaine;
Which we much rather had depart withal,
And have the money by our father lent,
Than Aquitaine so gelded as it is.
Dear Princess, were not his requests so far
From reason's yielding, your fair self should make
A yielding 'gainst some reason in my breast,
And go well satisfied to France again.

PRINCESS OF FRANCE. You do the King my father too much wrong,
And wrong the reputation of your name,
In so unseeming to confess receipt
Of that which hath so faithfully been paid.

KING. I do protest I never heard of it;
And, if you prove it, I'll repay it back
Or yield up Aquitaine.

PRINCESS OF FRANCE. We arrest your word.
Boyet, you can produce acquittances
For such a sum from special officers

Of Charles his father.

KING. Satisfy me so.

BOYET. So please your Grace, the packet is not come,
Where that and other specialties are bound;
To-morrow you shall have a sight of them.

KING. It shall suffice me; at which interview
All liberal reason I will yield unto.
Meantime receive such welcome at my hand
As honour, without breach of honour, may
Make tender of to thy true worthiness.
You may not come, fair Princess, within my gates;
But here without you shall be so receiv'd
As you shall deem yourself lodg'd in my heart,
Though so denied fair harbour in my house.
Your own good thoughts excuse me, and farewell.
To-morrow shall we visit you again.

PRINCESS OF FRANCE. Sweet health and fair desires consort your Grace!

KING. Thy own wish wish I thee in every place.

Exit with attendants

BEROWNE. Lady, I will commend you to mine own heart.

ROSALINE. Pray you, do my commendations;
I would be glad to see it.

BEROWNE. I would you heard it groan.

ROSALINE. Is the fool sick?

BEROWNE. Sick at the heart.

ROSALINE. Alack, let it blood.

BEROWNE. Would that do it good?

ROSALINE. My physic says 'ay.'

BEROWNE. Will YOU prick't with your eye?

ROSALINE. No point, with my knife.

BEROWNE. Now, God save thy life!

ROSALINE. And yours from long living!

BEROWNE. I cannot stay thanksgiving. [Retiring]

DUMAIN. Sir, I pray you, a word: what lady is that same?

BOYET. The heir of Alencon, Katharine her name.

DUMAIN. A gallant lady! Monsieur, fare you well.

Exit

LONGAVILLE. I beseech you a word: what is she in the white?

BOYET. A woman sometimes, an you saw her in the light.

LONGAVILLE. Perchance light in the light. I desire her name.

BOYET. She hath but one for herself; to desire that were a shame.

LONGAVILLE. Pray you, sir, whose daughter?

BOYET. Her mother's, I have heard.

LONGAVILLE. God's blessing on your beard!

BOYET. Good sir, be not offended;

She is an heir of Falconbridge.

LONGAVILLE. Nay, my choler is ended.

She is a most sweet lady.

BOYET. Not unlike, sir; that may be. Exit LONGAVILLE

BEROWNE. What's her name in the cap?

BOYET. Rosaline, by good hap.

BEROWNE. Is she wedded or no?

BOYET. To her will, sir, or so.

BEROWNE. You are welcome, sir; adieu!

BOYET. Farewell to me, sir, and welcome to you.

Exit BEROWNE. LADIES Unmask

MARIA. That last is Berowne, the merry mad-cap lord;

Not a word with him but a jest.

BOYET. And every jest but a word.

PRINCESS OF FRANCE. It was well done of you to take him at his word.

BOYET. I was as willing to grapple as he was to board.

KATHARINE. Two hot sheeps, marry!

BOYET. And wherefore not ships?
No sheep, sweet lamb, unless we feed on your lips.

KATHARINE. You sheep and I pasture- shall that finish the jest?

BOYET. So you grant pasture for me. [Offering to kiss her]

KATHARINE. Not so, gentle beast;
My lips are no common, though several they be.

BOYET. Belonging to whom?

KATHARINE. To my fortunes and me.

PRINCESS OF FRANCE. Good wits will be jangling; but, gentles, agree;
This civil war of wits were much better used
On Navarre and his book-men, for here 'tis abused.

BOYET. If my observation, which very seldom lies,
By the heart's still rhetoric disclosed with eyes,
Deceive me not now, Navarre is infected.

PRINCESS OF FRANCE. With what?

BOYET. With that which we lovers entitle 'affected.'

PRINCESS OF FRANCE. Your reason?

BOYET. Why, all his behaviours did make their retire
To the court of his eye, peeping thorough desire.
His heart, like an agate, with your print impressed,
Proud with his form, in his eye pride expressed;
His tongue, all impatient to speak and not see,
Did stumble with haste in his eyesight to be;
All senses to that sense did make their repair,
To feel only looking on fairest of fair.

Methought all his senses were lock'd in his eye,
As jewels in crystal for some prince to buy;
Who, tend'ring their own worth from where they were glass'd,
Did point you to buy them, along as you pass'd.
His face's own margent did quote such amazes
That all eyes saw his eyes enchanted with gazes.
I'll give you Aquitaine and all that is his,
An you give him for my sake but one loving kiss.

PRINCESS OF FRANCE. Come, to our pavilion. Boyet is dispos'd.

BOYET. But to speak that in words which his eye hath disclos'd;
I only have made a mouth of his eye,
By adding a tongue which I know will not lie.

MARIA. Thou art an old love-monger, and speakest skilfully.

KATHARINE. He is Cupid's grandfather, and learns news of him.

ROSALINE. Then was Venus like her mother; for her father is but grim.

BOYET. Do you hear, my mad wenches?

MARIA. No.

BOYET. What, then; do you see?

MARIA. Ay, our way to be gone.

BOYET. You are too hard for me. Exeunt

THE END.

3

Romance of the Shakespeare's

INTRODUCTION

The romance form is difficult to define, particularly because it has appeared and reappeared repeatedly in the history of literature. I do not wish to suggest that romance - or any of the modes I have discussed - is a transhistorical category that works the same across all cultures and all periods. But there is something familiar about romance, as Howard Felperin points out: "To the extent that all literary experience involves a journey into another world inherently removed from present time and place, all literature is fundamentally romantic". Romance seems to exhibit many of the same properties in its various manifestations, whether in the mode of Greek romance, from which much Renaissance literature derives; or in medieval quest romance, such as Sir Thomas Malory's Morte d'Arthur; in Edmund Spenser's epic poem The Faerie Queene; in its later appearance among the nineteenth-century poets we know as the Romantics; and in modern cinematic versions, such as the Western or the space epic.

A touchstone for the formal and tonal properties we are concerned with is George Lucas's Star Wars, with its otherworldly locations, youthful hero, displaced princess, battles between the agents of good and evil, and supernatural Force. The most productive approach to Shakespearean romance is to offer a series of descriptions, none comprehensive but each contributing a partial explanation of the effect or shape of the form. As a distinctive kind of comedy, romance arrives at a happy ending by an unusually perilous route. As our sense of the term implies, the action usually involves amorous desire and fulfillment, but the essential characteristic of fictional romance is an adventure story. Etymologically the word derives from the same root that gives us both the French and German words for "novel," roman. The main characters must endure a series of hazards and trials that lead ultimately to success and reward. The form is given to extremes, for the ending is not only happy but joyous, even revelatory, and the progression to that ending is much more arduous than in traditional comedy. In other words, the fundamentally comic shape of the action is darkly colored by tragic concerns and perceptions: the marriage or reunion that ends the play is preceded in the middle by some form of catastrophe, either death or some similarly grave loss.

These tonal oppositions of inexpressible despair and joy are matched by other extremes. Pericles, for example, opens with a riddle that the hero must solve for King Antiochus; the answer reveals the king's incest with his daughter. A wide geographical range is employed as well. Pericles travels throughout the Mediterranean; Cymbeline takes place in ancient Britain, ancient Rome, and the wilds of Wales; and The Tempest is set on a magical island. Often temporal limits are ignored: The Winter's Tale covers a period of sixteen years. At the conclusion of the hero's trials, magic or the supernatural contributes to the ending, often creating a sense of miracle. The vaguely providential force that, in the earlier comedies, seems to safeguard the characters and bring about a happy resolution is here specifically identified with divine protection, and in several of the plays this immortal force is theatrically incarnated, as in Jupiter's appearance in a dream at the end of Cymbeline or Diana's in Pericles. Such instances of theophany, or the appearance of a god or goddess, attest to the religious affinities of Shakespearean romance.

The cardinal feature of the form, the key to its emotional power, is the gap between the desperate middle and the joyful ending.

Characters in these plays are able to recover what seemed irretrievably lost, what they themselves have foolishly attempted to destroy: penitent husbands find themselves reunited with wives they wished dead; lost children are restored to their parents; impossible wishes are granted. It has often been pointed out that the Odyssey is the first romance, an adventure story that is also a love story, and one that delays the pleasure of Ulysses' homecoming for twenty years by taking him all over the known world (not to mention a visit to the underworld). And it is this wandering

that makes the poem; that's what it's about. So with Shakespeare's romances.

Although we look forward to the endings, the playwright spends most of his time not ending the play and then, when he finally does so, surprising us. So crucial is this incongruity that we might say that Shakespeare makes his romances about endings, playing self-consciously on the audience's desire for a happy outcome. These are fantasy plays that stimulate, frustrate, and fulfill our fantasies of resolution, but above all they force us to examine and evaluate our need for satisfactory closure. At the end of Cymbeline, the sleeping hero dreams that Jupiter descends from above and explains to his family why their son has had to endure such misery: "Whom best I love, I cross; to make my gift/the more delay'd, delighted". The god insists that waiting for fulfillment intensifies the emotion, that the more difficult the trial, the more satisfying the victory.

But Jupiter appears in a character's dream, distanced from the audience and even from the reality of the play-world. In other words, the deity's appearance is a form of illusion occurring within a play that is itself an illusion. This dramatic tactic confirms the principle that the choice of a mode implies particular meanings about the world and the human experience of it. By turning at the end of his career to stories of fantasy and magic, Shakespeare has committed himself not only to the power of the imaginary, but also to the value of fiction in general. This turn to romance is especially revealing because the tragedies seem obsessed with the perils and deceits of illusion. The apparitions of the deceptive witches in Macbetb, the fatal trickery of Iago's performance in Othello, or the lies of the elder daughters in King Lear - all these betray Shakespeare's mistrust of theatricality and perhaps even doubt about his own profession. As Anne Righter puts it in discussing the "Tomorrow and tomorrow and tomorrow" speech, "The final attitude of Macbeth, the passionate reduction of all human endeavour to the meaningless posturing of a player on a darkening stage, is scarcely flattering to the theatre. Such an image expresses not only the hollowness of life, but also the degradation and stupidity of the actor's profession" (169). Shakespeare's late interest in romance suggests a reversal in his thinking; his professional doubts, if not dismissed, appear to have been at least allayed.

Thus in the last plays the instances of spectacle tend to be affirmative rather than threatening, a point best demonstrated in the powerful last scene of The Winter's Tale. Hermione, dead, or apparently dead, for sixteen years, has been memorialized in a statue, and as her penitent husband, the one responsible for her death, stands before it, the statue comes to life. This spectacular moment could be terrifying: as Paulina puts it, ". . . you'll think / (Which I protest against) I am assisted / By wicked powers" (5.3.89-91). But instead of a demonic show, Paulina presents her audiences, both onstage and in the theater, with what amounts to a miracle. The appropriate response is spiritual wonder at an act of grace. As Paulina also says, "It is requir'd / You do awake your faith" (5.3.94-95). A statue, a work of art, an imitation of life, suddenly becomes "real," a miracle that occurs in a play that is itself an imitation of life, a fiction in which imaginary persons come to life for the pleasure of a credulous audience. Shakespeare prizes the indistin-guishability of the illusory and the actual. The artificiality of all experience, with Providence as the artist, the devine playwright, is the great theme of Shakespeare's last phase. Here it would be fitting to cite Prospero's famous "Revels" speech from the fourth act of The Tempest about the unreality of the whole world; instead, I shall quote a much more contemporary instance of the same perception, from Cormac McCarthy's novel The Crossing (1994): "For this world also which seems to us to sing of stone and flower and blood is not a thing at all but is a tale. And all in it is a tale and each tale the sum of all lesser tales and yet these also are the selfsame tale and contain as well all else within them".

LECTURE ONE—CYMBELINE

Shakespeare's career spans some 20 or 25 years, from the early 1590s to around 1611 or so, beginning under Elizabeth I in an expanding commercial theater and ending under James I in a theater more in tune with the aesthetic of the court. Cymbeline is among Shakespeare's last plays. But Shakespeare's career consists of a constant, and increasingly self-conscious, process of writing and rewriting. The same themes emerge and retreat at various stages in his career, and the same situations are dealt with in different ways and with different thematic implication. Perhaps because there is such a strong and well-established tradition of presenting, observing, and studying Shakespeare plays, it is hard, and perhaps not particularly productive, to see the plays entirely in isolation from one another. Cymbeline seems to have more echoes of other plays and other stories than any of the others, even more than Pericles. Such superabundance of what modern critics would call narremes is close to overwhelming. "This play," writes the great Samuel Johnson, never a mincer of words, "has many just sentiments, some natural dialogues, and some pleasing scenes, but they are obtained at the expense of much incongruity. To remark the folly of the fiction, the absurdity of the conduct, the confusion of the names, and manners of different times, and the impossibility of the events in any system of life, were to waste criticism upon unresisting imbecility, upon faults too evident for detection, and too gross for aggravation" (quoted by Nosworthy, p. xl).

The Augustan Johnson was writing in a very different time from our own, in the eighteenth century, and was more concerned with externalities than we in our post- Freudian day are apt to be. We also need to understand the circumstances of the initial production, since this play was in certain respects a new departure for Shakespeare. In the winter of 1608-09, Shakespeare's company of players, the King's Men, moved into the Blackfriars Theatre, previously occupied by the Children of the Chapel, the "little eyases" alluded to in Hamlet. Unlike the Globe, the Blackfriars had a roof, and the audience it attracted was a considerably more up-market crowd than the one at the Globe.

It was an audience that expected more of a technical kind from the acting companies it went to see. James I, who came to the throne in 1603, was particularly fond of the masque, courtly entertainment involving elaborate scenery and highly stylized action and stage effects, and each of the plays Shakespeare wrote for the Blackfriars Theatre, probably beginning with Cymbeline (1609), contained masque material. We know more or less nothing about the nature of the special effects in these plays, but we are reasonably certain that they went beyond anything that had been seen in Shakespeare's earlier efforts.

So spectacle was probably an important element in the original production. Hence the inclusion of a masque in the fifth act, for example. Furthermore, we make a big mistake if we allow our attention to stay only at the surface level of this play and the other romances: underneath the particularities of plot are much larger thematic concerns. Mark Lamos, when he directed Cymbeline for Hartford Stage a few years ago, saw the plot as essentially something that had to be accommodated, the mere vehicle of such larger thematic concerns (he called them "experience of the plays themselves in performance") – concerns having to do with the reversals of fortune and the triumph of a benign universe over the evils that it inevitably contains.

The elements that make up the plot, apart from the main historical thread derived from Holinshed, are generic and folkloric, or common elements in the literature of the period:

- the cruel stepmother (cf. Dionyza in Pericles),
- the sleeping potion (cf. Romeo and Juliet),
- changeling princes (cf. Perdita in The Winter's Tale),
- the wife wrongly accused (cf. Hero in Much Ado),
- the wager (the test of truth of a man's wife: cf. the story of Lucretia and Tarquin, which begins with such a wager, here derived, though, mostly from Boccaccio),
- the oracle (cf. Macbeth, The Winter's Tale),
- the wandering and unprotected maiden (cf. Julia in Two Gentlemen or Viola in Twelfth Night),
- the intruder who eats the family's food (the story of Goldilocks, here presented by Imogen's eating of the food of Belarius and his sons),
- nobility that reveals itself in spite of the surroundings (cf. Marina in Pericles, or Perdita), and of course
- girls disguised as boys.

Here, we also have a wife separated from her husband, and sons separated from their father, plus a king who successfully defends his country against an invasion. Like Pericles, this is a play of scrapes and adventures. As a piece of drama, it is full of set scenes and sudden reversals, accidents and coincidences, unwieldy, but good theater.

The key to its success on the stage (and Johnson's problem may have been that he read it rather than seeing it) is getting the tension between absurdity and sublimity just right. Notice how the play actually emerges: a first scene is shared by two gentlemen – nameless gentlemen whose function is essentially to provide us with narrative background: the play emerges rather clearly from the printed page, from the realm of narrative. As is so often the case in Shakespeare, the play is clearly a dramatized narrative.

Indeed perhaps to stress the point I should emphasize that we should not see the play (as we are inclined to see modern drama) as a stage version of reality, but rather as an acted version of narrative: it is not fictionalized down but concretized up. If we can accept such absurdities when we read The Faerie Queene or Ovid's Metamorphoses, we should be able to do the same when we see them on stage. But in amongst the "impossibility of the events in any system of life," as Dr. Johnson puts it, is a collection of interesting and intriguing characters: the Queen, Machiavellian and scheming, yet standing up for British independence (a kind of Lady Macbeth who ultimately goes mad and dies); Cymbeline himself, a kind of disoriented and ineffectual Lear; Posthumus, a kind of shape-changer. Bringing this together into a coherent whole requires a focus on theme and broader purpose, yet also a sacrifice of the particular in ways that are barely acceptable. To put it another way, comedy may have to slip over into farce more frequently than we would like, and dramatic tension may have on occasion to give way to visual patterning.

The following scene introduces us to this Queen who is surely larger than life, a schemer, a manipulator, loud, absurd, coarse. Poor Posthumus and Imogen scuttle about the stage like so many sheep, and Cymbeline is massively outwitted by his triumphant spouse. She, in turn, is followed by a scene involving Cloten, her nitwit of a son, where two Lords (again, they have no particular names or faces) play the role of straight man and interpreter (the latter for the benefit of the audience), as Cloten himself makes a bigger and bigger ass of himself. There is really no way of taking such figures entirely seriously. Pisanio tells Imogen about the departure of Posthumus right after this scene, and the lyricism of the episode contrasts sharply with what has gone before and sets Imogen off from her surroundings. She imagines how Posthumus must have faded off into the distance as his ship set sail:

I would have broke mine eye-strings, crack'd them, but
To look upon him, till the diminution
Of space had pointed him sharp as my needle:
Nay, followed him, till he had melted from

The smallness of a gnat, to air: and then
Have turn'd mine eye, and wept. (1.4.17-22)

She tells us how she was cheated of the opportunity to say to him the things she had wanted to say:

I did not take my leave of him, but had
Most pretty things to say: ere I could tell him
How I would think on him at certain hours,
Such thoughts, and such: or I could make him swear
The shes of Italy should not betray
Mine interest, and his honour; or have charg'd him,
At the sixth hour of morn, at noon, at midnight,
T' encounter me with orisons, for then
I am in heaven for him; or ere I could
Give him that parting kiss, which I had set
Betwixt two charming words, comes in my father,
And like the tyrannous breathing of the north,
Shakes all our buds from growing. (1.4.25-37)

Of course, it is this "tyrannous breathing of the north" that wafts Posthumus steadily southwards, away from Imogen: Imogen is another of those daughters (like Desdemona, Hermia, Cordelia, Juliet) at odds with uncomprehending fathers. The fifth scene of the first act sets up the terms of the wager, so we move to Italy for the occasion. In a sixth scene, the Queen, like the Wicked Witch of the West, is practicing her chemistry with Cornelius – fortunately under circumstances in which her mentor is able to substitute a sleeping potion for the poison she is eager to acquire. No wonder that at the end of this succession of scenes, Imogen comes forward to address the audience directly:

A father cruel, and a step-dame false,
A foolish suitor to a wedded lady,
That hath her husband banish'd: -- O, that husband,
My supreme crown of grief! and those repeated

Vexations of it! (1.7.1-4)

Her little speech sums up her situation, and in effect completes the introductory cycle of the play: we move from here to the arrival of Iachimo and the further development of the test of chastity. Be it fictionalization or concretization, the quality of complex and intertwined narrative in Cymbeline – what Johnson calls absurdity and confusion – is none the less likely to throw us off and require a moment of explanation. As a general rule of thumb, it seems legitimate to suggest that tragedies are dependent upon the development of the character of a particular individual – humans enmeshed by circumstances, either internal to themselves or external (much of what happens to Romeo and Juliet happens through no fault of their own – indeed the play is arguably concerned with how adults make use of their offspring to perpetuate their vendettas; most of what happens to Macbeth is his own doing; either way, circumstances get the better of the heroes). Comedies, on the other hand, depend upon triumph over adverse circumstances, either through coincidence and good luck, as in The Comedy of Errors or through the healing power of love, as in As You Like It, or through magic (which may in turn be a metaphor for something else), as in A Midsummer Night's Dream. Fundamental to comedies is the simple fact that good triumphs under the most unlikely of circumstances. In other words, a measure of coincidence and happy surprise is necessary to the effect of the denouement.

Comedies are dependent less on probability than on a certain level of plausibility: the coming together of their elements at the end brings tears to our eyes precisely because the possibilities of tragedy in the course of the play are considerable, and because the chances of a happy ending may in certain respects seem slight (happy endings are made happy because we worry that they may not be happy; if you do not collapse in floods of tears at the end of The Comedy of Errors, you are either unwilling to accept the plot premises of the play, or you actually believe that things like this happen every day).

In fact, many of the comedies and some of the tragedies, situated as they are in an era of shifting economic values in England, when dynastic and mercantile concerns are being edged out by notions of individual liberty and the integrity of the individual, focus on two views of love, the one dynastic and the other romantic. In Romeo and Juliet these two sets of values collide head-on as they do again in Othello. They are the beginning point of A Midsummer Night's Dream, which ends by affirming romantic over dynastic.

They are also the beginning point of Cymbeline: Imogen marries Posthumus despite the fact that her family has other plans. Posthumus, an orphan of no importance but much virtue (after-death is his name because he is the posthumous, or surviving, Leonatus), is preferred over the odious Cloten, who, by marrying Imogen, might capture the throne. The "confusion of the names" that Johnson refers to points to a coming together of a number of generic elements in a truly unusual combination. Cymbeline, like Lear, is a play about ancient Britain.

Lear takes us back even before the coming of the Romans, but Cymbeline deals with Roman times. Its huge geographical canvas takes in Rome as well as Britain. Like Antony and Cleopatra before it, which oscillates between Rome and Alexandria (with Rome as the desiccated center and Alexandria as the exotic outer rim of empire, and with political empires and erotic empires in competition), and like Pericles, which moves across the map of the Mediterranean, the play is anchored in two worlds.

Such contrast, such separation of two dramatic locations, is everywhere in Shakespeare – Verona and Mantua in Romeo and Juliet, Verona and Milan in Two Gentlemen, Venice and Cyprus (center and periphery, like Antony and Cleopatra) in Othello, Orsino's palace and Olivia's house in Twelfth Night, Venice and Belmont inThe Merchant of Venice.

Sometimes, as in Othello or Pericles, the chaos of the ocean separates these locations, and the threat of shipwreck or the actuality of it is a factor. But the Rome of this play is really two worlds, or two aspects of this locus of values: imperial Rome, the Rome of Caius Lucius and the rest, and the conventional Italy of intrigue and love games such as we find in many of the comedies of the era and some of the tragedies (Othello for example): Roman honor and Italian trickery. Thus characters like Iachimo and Philario (with Italian names) inhabit a sophisticated, not to say decadent, Italy, while Caius Lucius (with his Roman name) represent a set of old values. The age was conflicted about Italy – home of Cicero and Julius Caesar and Vitruvius, but home also of Alexander VI and Caesar Borgia and of the Neapolitan bone-ache.

As for Britain, like Lear's world, it is pre-Christian: the Roman gods, Jupiter at their head, preside over it. The play oscillates not only between London (capital of the Britain that existed before England was founded) and Rome, on a north-south axis, as it were, but also between London and Milford Haven, an east-west axis. Southeastern London, close to the Continent and meeting point of lines of communication, was seen by Shakespeare's age as the center of sophistication in England (as indeed it was), but also as the center of citified corruption, with the hinterlands, extended northwards to Scotland and westwards to Wales, and of course beyond to Ireland, as areas either of natural virtue or of unmitigated barbarism.

The Tudors claimed to come from Wales, and they saw Arthur as their ancestor; the Stuarts, coming from the north, were at least perceived by those with an interest in perceiving them as such, as unsullied outsiders, with British virtue on their side. Milford Haven is in Pembrokeshire, due west of London, and out beyond Cardiff and Swansea in South Wales. It was an embarkation point for Ireland (Richard II went that way to his Irish wars) and for the Mediterranean. But reaching it meant passing through what was then wild and mountainous country in southern Wales – the kind of place in which unspoiled natural virtue, or the perils of savage nature, were equally likely to appear (see Boling 2000 on the role of Wales and the Welsh in this play). In effect, such territory allows for two views of nature: the chivalric (the castle contains virtue; the wilderness contains dragons), or the pastoral (the castle contains corruption; the countryside contains virtue).

A second, east-west movement, then, is overlaid on the north-south one. This second movement emerges in the second half of the play, but is hinted at from the beginning, for example in Imogen's "Would I were / A neat-herd's daughter, and my Leonatus / Our neighbor-shepherd's son" (1.2.79-81). But it is in Act III that it actually begins, at the point where this production, very logically, puts the intermission (at the end of Act III, sc. ii)

This second movement features exiles – an older man (Belarius) who is in fact a trusted courtier, who, like Kent in Lear, has assumed a disguise in order to survive, and two young princes, also disguised, whose virtue (a point under-stressed in this production) comes through in their behavior because aristocratic virtue is ultimately genetic, not learned, at least in this world-view. Exile, in fact, is the only way to deal with the corrupt court over which Cymbeline presides – either voluntary or involuntary exile: the goal is to bring these scattered elements back together again in harmony.

In other words, we have here, at least in this context, a pastoral retreat – a retreat into the forest, where true values can be found and brought back to restore order in the court and the kingdom. This forest is a place where personalities are put off and exchanged, and where things are not as they seem. In this regard it resembles A Midsummer Night's Dream. This pastoral dynamic itself occurs in numerous plays, among them Two Gentlemen, As You Like It, and Lear.

It is also, by the way, a story about Britain's refusal to be subject to Rome (cf. King John's defiance of Pandulph at the beginning of the third act of King John, the same location as Cymbeline's defiance of the Romans), but, interestingly, the final resolution is one of peaceful coexistence: the British and Roman worlds, in conflict during much of the play, are ultimately brought into harmony. In its largest sense, though, Cymbeline is about separation and realignment, loss and rediscovery.

In Mark Lamos's production of a few years ago, the extreme beauty of this production made these contrasting worlds very clear to us: the black clothes and red velvet of Roman love-games; the court of Cymbeline (a riot of costuming that perhaps overplayed the exotic somewhat); the hills of Wales (all brown clothing and sack-cloth); the Roman army (ensigns and standards and armor). However, one of the consequences of the sheer quantity and richness of spectacle was that it tended to flatten characterization. Just as the profusion of settings and scenery gives the play richness, so the interaction of character is of crucial importance. Take for example 1.7, the crucial scene of Iachimo's attempted seduction of Imogen, following her soliloquy that I have just quoted.

It is a reprise of the great scene of attempted seduction between Angelo and Isabella in Act 2 of Measure for Measure, where Isabella holds to her virtue even at the cost of her brother Claudio's death. On the great empty stage it is hard to give it the intensity, the claustrophobia, that it potentially can carry. It is a scene focused not so much on Iachimo, who is, after all, only an instrument of the plot, but on Imogen.

Iachimo, good psychologist, must first separate Imogen from Posthumus, which he does by painting Posthumus's behavior in a particular way, and then, having persuaded Imogen, must work on the notion of revenge. Imogen, desperate, cries out for Pisanio, but in fact Iachimo misreads Imogen: she is not Italian and does not see revenge as an appropriate goal. In a superb shift of tactics, Iachimo goes for the next best thing: if he cannot have Imogen, he can at least pretend to have had her by describing the details of her bedchamber and the intimacies of her body.

This scene establishes the centrality of Imogen: this is a play about a virtuous princess who is estranged from a false family and drawn to a true one, which, in turn, unites, aided by romantic love, to topple a corrupt establishment – or, more to the point, to stamp out the corruption and re-establish a new order based on the old. It is thus, for example, that we should read Cymbeline's final submission to Roman tribute: the good Rome pushes out the bad, and the old order returns, with its strong sinews and its honest relationships.

The seduction scene at the end of the first act is followed by another scene involving Cloten and his two sidekicks at the opening of the second. Again, this is a piece of absurd comedy, offering a diversion between the seduction scene and the Tarquin-like episode of Iachimo's emergence from the trunk in Imogen's bedchamber (put there, we remember, because of some creaky plot-device involving Iachimo's wish to protect his valuables). This is a powerful episode:

The crickets sing, and man's o'er-labour'd sense
Repairs itself by rest. Our Tarquin thus
Did softly press the rushes, ere he waken'd
The chastity he wounded. Cytherea,
How bravely thou becom'st thy bed! fresh lily!
And whiter than the sheets! That I might touch!
But kiss, one kiss! Rubies unparagon'd,
How dearly they do't: 'tis her breathing that
Perfumes the chamber thus: the flame o' th' taper
Bows toward her, and would under-peep her lids,
To see th' enclosed lights, now canopied
Under these windows, white and azure lac'd
With blue of heaven's own tinct. But my design.
To note the chamber... (2.2.11-24)

The chamber that he notes is richly and abundantly ornamented – like the chamber in Keats's "Eve of St. Agnes," for example (Walter Jackson Bate, in his biography of Keats, suggests that Cymbeline was in Keats's mind as he wrote). Imogen herself has been reading before sleep, and the story is the story of Tereus, who raped Philomela, cutting out her tongue so that she cannot tell her story. She was later transformed by Jove into a nightingale.

From here we go back to Cloten, but now with one of Shakespeare's greatest songs thrown in, "Hark, hark, the lark at heaven's gate sings," clearly offered here as a piece ofentertainment to tame the restless Blackfriars crowd (and with larks and lark's tongues and Philomela and nightingales as background images perhaps). Even as the arrival of ambassadors from Rome is announced, Cloten attempts to woo Imogen and is rebuffed contemptuously.

As for Posthumus, his stay in Rome is a disaster from the beginning. This is not the first time he has been drawn into a wager of this kind, as we are told. Last time, the\ Frenchman bailed him out; this time, no one is able to do so. Lamos dressed him in blue, and these blue garments among the black and the red of the other Italians displayed a quite different set of values. Iachimo's lies to Posthumus in Rome bring us to what might be described as the turning point in the story, Posthumus's long soliloquy at the end of Act 2, with its tirade against women. We have reached a low point. What do we make of the opening of the third act, in which the Queen and Cloten defy the Roman embassy? Was this played as a kind of comic reprise of King John,

Shakespeare's play of ten or fifteen years before? For a moment the Queen comes across as Queen Boadicea herself, defying the Roman army with the image of a moated island, secure from the confusions of (to quote Richard II, where the original speech of this kind is to be found) "the envy of less happier lands." Remember, sir, my liege,

The kings your ancestors, together with

The natural bravery of your isle, which stands

As Neptune's park, ribb'd and pal'd in

With rocks unscaleable and roaring waters,

With sands that will not bear your enemies' boats,

But suck them up to th' topmast. A kind of conquest

Shakespeare's most direct treatment of the myth is in Titus Andronicus.

Caesar made here, but made not here his brag
Of 'Came, and saw, and overcame:' with shame
(The first that ever touch'd him) he was carried
From off our coast, twice beaten: and his shipping
(Poor ignorant baubles!) on our terrible seas,
Like egg-shells mov'd upon their surges, crack'd
As easily 'gainst our rocks. (3.1.17-30)

Regardless of how we read the scene (and I am inclined to see it as a sudden access of patriotism that is at the same time a piece of humor), Cloten is destined for further discomfiture. Act 3 signals a new narrative movement as the test of chastity plays itself out with Posthumus's instructions to Pisanio to kill Imogen. Posthumus's seemingly conflicting messages have Imogen setting out for Milford Haven (into the hinterland of Britain, as it were) to meet Posthumus, and Pisanio setting out with the order to kill her. It is time indeed for us to find Cymbeline's two lost sons in the wilderness, virtuous both because they are cut off from the corruption of the court and because of their genetic nobility.

There is genuine tension in the scene (3.4) in which Pisanio reveals to Imogen the instructions from Posthumus, and his plan to have Imogen seek service with the Emperor Lucius (we seem to be at the beginning of Twelfth Night). Goldilocks Imogen transforms herself into a boy, and the confusion of brotherly and sexual love that ensues when she meets up with the two young princes is again cause for a measure of audience amusement (they think she's a boy, when actually she's a girl, who happens in reality to be their sister...). Cloten, also disguising himself and setting out into the woods, puts on the garments of Posthumus. He does so not because he is contemptuous at Imogen's suggestion that "his meanest garment / That ever hath but clipp'd his body, is dearer / In my respect, than all the hairs above thee" (2.3), but because he seeks, quite literally, to put on Posthumus's virtue and can't tell the difference between inward goodness and outward clothing. He does not understand the nature of metaphor, a poor fate for one inhabiting this particular play. True virtue, of course, does not depend on clothing, as Guiderius and Arviragus show. Indeed, while Cloten's borrowed garments survive, the "hairs" (and the head to which they are attached) do not, and are thrown "down the stream."

It would not be right to have Guiderius and Arviragus get clean away without a song, or rather a recitation (Guiderius says he is too sad to sing when they find Imogen, having taken her stepmother's potion, apparently dead). "Fear no more the heat o'th'sun" is another of the musical interludes inserted for the Blackfriars crowd, a sad and exquisite obsequy (4.2.257-281). But if it is one of the more improbable aspects of this duo that they can do stand-up songs, there are still bigger improbabilities to come.

How one deals with headless corpses on stage is one of the great directorial challenges of this play. Laughs may be the only way: such grand guignol is more than we can take seriously. But again much depends on the way in which Imogen is played. Arguably the challenge is to have Imogen's belief that she has lost Posthumus come through to us despite the macabre aspect of the scene (4.2). We, of course, know the truth, but Imogen is caught in the toils of our omniscience (in a way, the problem resembles what to do with the Nurse and Lady Capulet when they discover a sleeping Juliet whom they suppose dead). As she awakes from her dream and into her version of reality, she in effect underlines for us how uncertain that reality really is, and how truths may come through dreams as well as through the day-to-day meaninglessness of one-thing-after-another. As the deus ex machina and Posthumus's dream tells us in the final act of the play, providence is as important to the universe as incident.

I need not describe in detail the events that lead to the revealing of Guiderius and Arviragus (formerly Cadwal and Polydore), who, along with their Kent-like father, single-handedly beat back the Roman hordes. "This was a strange chance," says a Lord in 5.3., "A narrow lane, an old man, and two boys." Nor need I recount the details of the masque-like dream of Posthumus (5.4), or the agonizingly spun-out discovery scene with which the play ends. Free of his past, Cymbeline is able to find a new future, and in the reunion of Imogen and Posthumus and the return of her two brothers, memories of the Queen and her son and of the Roman wars are swept away and the old order returns. "Laud we the gods," he cries, "And let our crooked smokes climb to their nostrils / From our blest altars. Publish we this peace / To all our subjects."

Strikingly, Imogen's reunion with Posthumus and their receipt of Cymbeline's blessing seem overshadowed by what is in effect a political resolution at the end of the play. The play seems a kind of comic Lear in which the rehabilitation of Kent and Edgar takes precedence over the reunion with Cordelia. Though Shakespeare certainly kept worrying over the redemptive vision of the romances, the balance of this final scene seems oddly awry. There are ways of dealing with this imbalance, and modern directors do it quite successfully by some judicious rearrangement or cutting, but such is required to restore a certain coherence. One wonders what would happen if a director tried to turn the play into an authentic political statement – and one also wonders whether there was a political agenda behind the play in 1609. Be that as it may, Pericles and The Winter's Tale involve huge jumps from one generation to the next, and multiple locations for the action. They share with Cymbeline a focus on a virtuous woman and on uncomprehending fathers. They also share with the comedies an interest in disguise and in a kind of sexual equivocation that results from it: the assertion of gender and its role in generation is central to a comedic vision based on notions of a benign nature. In The Tempest, by putting his action on a magical island,

Shakespeare is able to make differences of place – Milan and Naples – become part of an off-stage geography, and differences of time – Prospero's banishment and Prospero's return – part on an off-stage history. But Prospero's narrative is barely sustainable before a sophisticated audience ("Your tale sir," says Miranda, "would cure deafness"), even if it leads, finally, to the proper and decorous transfer of authority from generation to generation, combined with due recognition of the power of romantic love. The Tempest solves the central problem of Shakespeare's plays – succession – through an assertion of the central power – that of nature benignly deployed. Cymbeline is an enchanting and entertaining stop on the way.

LECTURE TWO—THE WINTER'S TALE

The Winter's Tale is the third of the four plays generally categorized as Shakespeare's romances. The term is itself not that of Shakespeare and his contemporaries: the First Folio divides the plays into histories, tragedies and comedies. We have seen already that the keys to this mode of writing can be found, above all, in two places in Shakespeare: in the comedies of the 1590s and in King Lear. The early comedies, and particularly The Comedy of Errors, present a world that is full of adversities, but they describe adversities overcome, generally against impossible odds. The old man Egeon, wandering across the eastern Mediterranean like a lost Ulysses, miraculously finds his sons, and still more miraculously rediscovers his long-lost wife. The improbable ending of the play, when all the principals find themselves on the stage together, succeeds precisely because it is improbable. It presents for us a world of make-believe, or, rather, a world just this side of make-believe – a world in which divine providence takes precedence over probability. Shakespeare emphasizes the power of the family, guarantor of continuity in a world in which misfortune can strike at any time, and giver of life as well as sharer in the burden of death. Above all, The Comedy of Errors asserts that things do make sense, that life is not just one damn thing after another. In fact, the play turns on a paradox: to go right, we must first go wrong. The Comedy of Errors is a farce wrapped in a potential tragedy: the framing story is a story of imminent disaster – the execution of an old man whose only crime is to be in the wrong place at the wrong time. Of course, both because of its title and its mood, the play announces none the less that it is a comedy: we can only hope that the disorderly lives and misprisions of the early part of the play will be resolved in due course. But such tension between comedy and potential tragedy haunts more or less all of the comedies in one way or another. In the case of The Merchant of Venice it almost causes the play to overbalance.

Similar tensions rack Much Ado About Nothing. Both plays reconstitute their little communities along more stable lines, but only with the exclusion of Shylock in the first and the disappearance of Don John in the second. InTwelfth Night, Malvolio is shut out of the consensus at the end, and more than one modern production of that play has caused it (probably wrongly) to teeter on the edge of tragedy. For Shakespeare, what makes comedy happy is in part the fact that unhappiness is kept at bay only rather tenuously. When we move beyond Twelfth Night and into the comedies of the period of the great tragedies, increasingly the tension between comic conclusion and the actual course of events (the one-damn-thing-after-another sequence) is more difficult to reconcile.

In All's Well That Ends Well, Helena's cure of the King of France has the feeling and effect of a miracle, but such miraculous power does not make Bertram any less a reluctant husband. The bestower of miracles, Helena, has difficulty getting real life to fit the model. It is almost as though Shakespeare is operating in two realms – the realm of human feeling on the one hand, unpredictable, not given to miracles, intractable; and the realm of the miraculous on the other – offering solutions that are so incredible that they can solve nothing. How can we make the latter answer the former? How can we force our rather mundane human existence to be responsive to the grace contained in the miraculous? Elsewhere and in a different context – the poetry of Spenser rather than the plays of Shakespeare – I have alluded to something I describe as literary grace.

LECTURE THREE—PERICLES, PRINCE OF TYRE

Shakespeare's Antony and Cleopatra was probably first seen on the stage in about 1606, a couple of years before Pericles and about the same time as Macbeth was first performed. Antony and Cleopatra and Macbeth look in different directions. Macbeth, a tightly crafted and claustrophobic study of the ascent and decline of a man gripped by ambition, has much in common with the slightly earlier Othello, and with Hamlet. Antony and Cleopatra, though a dramatization of a piece of Roman history (its source is Plutarch's "Life of Mark Antony" as translated by Sir Thomas North in 1579) and therefore looking back to Julius Caesar and on to Coriolanus, covers a vast geographical area, seeming to embrace the Roman Empire from its center to its exotic periphery. It is a love story, a kind of Romeo and Juliet of the mature set: indeed, when seen through the prism of this early tragedy, from ten years before, the final scenes of Antony and Cleopatra take on a particular poignancy. In a way, the two plays form bookends to the tragedies, only Titus Andronicus and perhaps Richard III lying beyond their reach at the beginning, and Coriolanus at the end..

But the vast canvas on which the tragedy of Antony and Cleopatra is presented, along with the incident-packed nature of this presentation, gives the play something of the characteristics of romance. The kinship between this play and Pericles, a play also involving zigzags across the Mediterranean almost as bewildering as the Odyssey itself, is greater than it might at first sight appear. Pericles also looks back to a play at the very beginning of Shakespeare's career, The Comedy of Errors, likewise set in the Mediterranean and involving sea-voyages. Perhaps no other play in the canon (where it sits uneasily: more on this in a moment) has quite so many changes of geographical location, with quite such an array of characters, as

Pericles

In the course of the play we move around among the following:

- Antioch and King Antiochus (Act 1)
- Tyre, home of Pericles (1, 2)
- Tharsus, home of Cleon and Dionyza, where Marina grows up (1, 3, 4)

- Pentapolis, home of King Simonides and Thaisa (2)
- Ephesus, home of Cerimon, where Thaisa becomes a priestess (3, 5)
- Mytilene, home of Lysimachus, where Pericles finds Marina (4, 5)

These many locations, scattered across the eastern Mediterranean, are linked by perilous voyages, including:

- A shipwreck between Acts 1 and 2,
- Marina's birth and Thaisa's "burial" at sea at the beginning of Act 3.

The geographical breadth is matched by an equally vast chronology: fourteen years separate Acts 3 and 4, and in effect we witness the fortunes of two generations. More: the younger generation, born in the first half of the play, becomes the means of salvation of the older generation in the second half of the play. In this, the play particularly resembles The Winter's Tale.

So this is a play that is structured around disparate and widely scattered events strung out over a long period of time. If geography is attenuated and time is extended, we also move into the play through a series of fictional layers. This is, if I can use such a term, a highly fictionalized play. We move into the action through the figure of John Gower, contemporary of Chaucer, who, as it were, returns from the dead to present us with a dramatic rendering of one of his stories. The poet of Confessio Amantis, a narrative poem that was extremely popular in the fifteenth and sixteenth centuries as well as in its own day, comes back to us at various points in the action. The story of Pericles is in fact drawn from the Confessio, where it appears as a retelling of the ancient story known as "Apollonius of Tyre." Gower's appearance on the stage at the beginning of the play and at intervals thereafter serves to frame the play and stress its character as a dramatized fiction. The technique is reminiscent of Henry V or Romeo and Juliet. In a sense the dramatized action grows out of a non-dramatic narration. This creation of distance between ourselves and the play's fiction helps make the rather sketchy and disjointed nature of the play, and the improbability of much of its action, believable and acceptable. This is, in short, a highly formulaic play. The formulaic quality is reinforced by such devices as the dumb shows at intervals through the play, an old technique already passé in the 1590s, used, you will recall, by the players in Hamlet. The authors of Pericles (I use the plural advisedly) are at pains to give this story a kind of antique patina: it is an exemplary story from the distant English past.

Such distancing chimes with the work of such contemporaries as Spenser, whose stories in The Faerie Queene allegedly come from "antique rolls" – from the dim and distant past, much as Gower and his story do. In The Faerie Queene, Spenser is at pains to unite what might be called eclectic pan-European themes and motifs (stories from Ariosto, from the French chansons de geste, from classical authors) with native, home-grown elements (the world of the fairies, the rivers of Ireland, and so on), much as the architecture of the period unites classical and Renaissance motifs with echoes of English medieval forms, for example in Robert Smythson's grand houses Wollaton Hall or

Hardwick Hall

Shakespeare adopts this strategy in A Midsummer Night's Dream, where thoroughly native English craftsmen mingle with aristocratic Athenians, and echoes of Ovid and Apuleius combine with a rather English-looking fairyland. We pass through an English frame to an Italian story in The Taming of the Shrew. Pericles, too, is at once English (through Gower) and continental and classical (through setting and Gower's sources). The story of Pericles has as its hero a figure who is remarkably passive: things happen to

Pericles

He is not in control of the action, but the action drives him. One is reminded of a similar sense of powerlessness on the part of such near-contemporary creations as Macbeth and, most particularly, Timon. Pericles is also not a particularly clearly defined character: there is little sense of an inner life here, and certainly little sense of a continuity of characterization. He is, above all, an example of patience in adversity, or rather of patience in an adversity that ultimately deprives him of his wits (Lear comes to mind again), and he is a father – perhaps, in a sense, the father, just as Marina is the daughter, the two of them more representative than well-rounded as characters. But in reality this is a play driven by event, though event carefully iterated and reiterated. The mood of the play associates it with the formulaic prose romances that were so popular during this period, in which the hero suffers a series of reversals, often involving shipwrecks or attacks by wild creatures, young lovers and harsh fathers, oracles and prophecies, and particularly family members lost or given up for dead, only to live through a happy ending of rediscovery, rebirth, and the discovery of a new harmony (numerous scholars have written on this subject, Kermode particularly suggestively in his edition of The Tempest, now superseded, and in his anthology of pastoral poetry – and Scragg 1992). Lear has some of this same aura – a play from a time before time, a Cinderella story gone wrong. It is worth pointing out that these narratives were not only ancient and presented as ancient, but also extremely popular in Shakespeare's day. Such formulae of course underlie the dynamics of comedy: we recognize elements of romance in such plays as As You Like It, which really parodies these improbable stories, or in the shipwreck of Twelfth Night, or in the recognition scene of The Comedy of Errors. There is a strong deterministic element in romance: the actions of fortune determine events. But fortune in turn is tempered by an equally powerful force, that of providence, which in effect matches each unfortunate coincidence with a fortunate one. Indeed, one might say that romance presents for us a battle between fortune and providence in which providence ultimately wins.

The basic formulaic elements of romance can be traced back to the stories of late Greek literature. Six such "novels" of the Alexandrian period of Greek literature have survived, the most famous being Longus's Daphnis and Chloe (others are by Achilles Tatius, Heliodorus, Chariton, Xenophon, and Dio Chrysostom). The Latin writer Apuleius's Golden Ass, a story lying behind A Midsummer Night's Dream, is sometimes included in this category. They were translated and imitated in the Renaissance. Their spirit also underlay many of the stories told by Boccaccio and his successors. The story of Apollonius of Tyre is believed to have its origin in the late Greek romances, though the earliest surviving account is in Latin and dates from the fifth or sixth century A.D. Gower used a version by the 12th-century chronicler Godfrey of Viterbo. Shakespeare relied heavily on Gower, but also drew on the version in Laurence Twine's The Pattern of Painful Adventures (c. 1576), particularly for the Marina story (Hoeniger quotes relevant passages from Twine in his edition of the play). His decision to use Gower as a Chorus may have been inspired by Barnabe Barnes's The Devil's Charter, in which Barnes uses the Italian historian Guicciardini as a narrator.

Shakespeare's final plays bring the elements of romance to the fore. Pericles, Cymbeline, The Winter's Tale, and The Tempest all deal in their various ways with huge issues of life and death. One might argue that in this sense they hardly differ from the great tragedies, or from earlier plays as well. What is A Midsummer Night's Dream about if not the forward movement of youth and generation? The will to live and love overcomes the objections of a father at the beginning of the play, overcomes the constraints of society in the form of the rather constricted court of the Duke of Athens (and the perhaps somewhat unstable relationship between its two protagonists Theseus and Hippolyta), and ultimately is reintegrated and harmonized with those constraints in the final act of the play.

By the same token, Hamlet, in a very different way, confronts the problems of dealing with a tangled past in order to free young people up to live their lives. It is another version, from a very different perspective, of the Romeo and Juliet story: young people victimized by their elders' inability to lead their lives peacefully and harmoniously. If Hamlet fails to offer any alternative beyond the rather bloodless Fortinbras, Lear does go further. There are those who perceive in the final act (and I think I would count myself among them) a hint of redemption: Lear is at peace with himself, and his realization of Cordelia's sacrifice (once again a martyr to the older generation) opens him to the grace that comes with it.

An older Shakespeare writes a version of Romeo and Juliet: at the end of Romeo and Juliet the parents vow to erect a statue of Juliet. In Lear Shakespeare in effect rewrites the play from the point of view of Old Montague and Old Capulet, the perpetrators of the sacrifice of youth, much as Lear and Gloucester are unable to recognize virtue in the younger generation, and to shun its vicious elements. But behind the final acts of Lear, as Lear leaves the court behind and enters the storm and as the sun comes out and flowers bloom in its aftermath (flowers with which Lear is fantastically dressed in the fourth act), is a sense of the cyclical pattern of death and rebirth. It is this cyclical pattern that comes to dominate in the final plays. There are hints of it already in Timon, but in the four romances it becomes the dominant reading of the effects of time. Allied with it, and also apparent in Lear, is an interest in the relationship between art and nature, and in the enduring qualities of art.

A huge and thorny topic. A.C.Bradley 1905 suggests that Lear's discovery of the good transcends the world's evil, a view also held by G. Wilson Knight in his analysis in The Wheel of Fire 1949. Jan Kott 1964 famously takes the opposite view, arguing that the play is essentially nihilistic. For a helpful review of the argument of the play, see Mack 1965.

Indeed, one is tempted to conclude that Shakespeare's (voluntary or involuntary) publication of the Sonnets in 1609 was of a piece with the concern with time and generation, to say nothing of the interest in art, that is so important in the late plays. I think we are right to see most of the Sonnets as products of the mid-1590s, but the themes that they deal with are similar to those of the final plays. In a sense, in the final plays Shakespeare returns to the preoccupations of an earlier stage in his career, but now from a different and arresting viewpoint. Among the finest of the sonnets are poems of separation, of a longing for reunion – a variant of the theme of exile that goes back to Shakespeare's earliest plays (The Comedy of Errors, The Two Gentlemen of Verona, Romeo and Juliet), and that comes to the fore not only in Pericles but also in Cymbeline and The Tempest, and, in its way, in The Winter's Tale. How deep this theme runs in Shakespeare! There is hardly a play without it.

I spoke earlier of the "authors" of Pericles. There are huge problems with the text. The play was registered in 1608 and a pirated version was brought out by Henry Gosson in 1609 (the year, incidentally, of the first collected edition of Spenser's Faerie Queene). A second edition of Pericles appeared in that same year, 1609. The play was the only play generally regarded as canonical that was not included in the First Folio. In fact it does not appear until the second impression of the Third Folio in 1664.

This obviously raises the question of Shakespeare's authorship. We do not know precisely what criteria Shakespeare's colleagues John Heminge and Henry Condell (members, like Shakespeare, of the company called the King's Men) used for inclusion of plays in the First Folio. We do know that when Henry Gosson pirated the play in 1609 (it was a great success: a second quarto appeared in the same year), he attributed it to Shakespeare. and that this attribution continued with later quartos. Might the play have been excluded from the First Folio because of the overall condition of the text? There is considerable evidence that it is a reported version, perhaps simply too dirty and imprecise to meet Heminge and Condell's criteria.

The text of Pericles, unusually, is not divided into acts and scenes. The generally accepted attribution of acts and scenes to the play is a later addition. The play was originally presented with an intermission in the middle, at the point, now between Acts 3 and 4, where we pass over the gap of 14 years. Some critics have discerned in the play a kind of seven-movement structure, each set off by an intervention of Gower, in other words a series of dramatic sequences circling out from the narrative continuity that Gower provides. One theory even links them with the world's seven ages – a notion that works better in the earlier parts than it does in the later ones (see Marshall 1991). Of course Gosson's attribution of the play to Shakespeare would probably help sell copies. On the other hand, much of the text does have the feel and texture of Shakespeare's writing. It seems likely that we are dealing here with a collaboration.

Perhaps different parts of the play were done by different authors. Perhaps Shakespeare. patched up an earlier play by someone else. Acts 1 and 2, particularly, seem un-Shakespearian: the language lacks the textured feeling, the complexity of meanings and images, that we associate with Shakespeare. These acts have been attributed at various times to Thomas Heywood, George Wilkins and John Day. Putting on plays in Shakespeare's day was a collaborative activity, in which the author of the text was only one among many players. It is possible, indeed likely, that many hands had at least a minor part in many of Shakespeare's plays. In seeking to tease out such questions of authorship, there are of course a couple of assumptions that we must avoid making.

First, we must not assume that every word in every Shakespeare play is by Shakespeare. We know that the production and publication of the plays was an altogether messier process than that. There are several Shakespeare plays in which there are scenes that look un-Shakespearian and plays by other authors in which Shakespeare seems to have had a hand (such as Two Noble Kinsmen, which has a strong Shakespearian flavor).

Second, we should not suppose that all bad scenes are by someone else; all good ones are by Shakespeare. That argument is dangerously circular. However, when all is said and done, I favor the theory that the first two acts are largely, perhaps completely, someone else's work. F.D.Hoeniger and others make a strong case for John Day, who may also have had a hand in Timon and who was a frequent collaborator with other playwrights, among them Dekker,

Rowley, and possibly Marlowe. I will, however, in what follows, assume that we have here a single play, with the coherence of a single play, despite its episodic and sprawling structure.

In the first two acts we enter a chivalric world familiar to the readers of old romance. The two acts revolve around two motifs or themes – the so-called Custom of the Castle, and the tournament in which the hero wins lady.

The play begins with a story of incest, of love gone wrong. We come to it by way of Gower (who uses, by the way, the tetrameter couplets that he uses in the Confessio Amantis):

If you, born in these latter times,

When wit's more ripe, accept my rimes,

And that to hear an old man sing

May to your wishes pleasure bring,

I life would wish, and that I might

Waste it for you, like taper-light. (1.Chorus.11-16).

Thus Gower is given life by the light of a taper, which gradually burns down as the story progresses, much as the reader reads the story, perhaps last thing at night (like, I might add, some Winter's Tale).

The initial scene is an emblematic episode, only tangentially linked to what comes after it. The scene has a certain dance-like character, with music playing in the background, and with Pericles praising Antiochus's daughter (note she is never named) from a distance. Pericles is caught by King Antiochus: if he fails to interpret the riddle he is given, he dies; if he interprets it, he dies anyway. In the first case, he dies because if his ignorance, and in the second he dies because of his knowledge. We should not, by the way, spend too much time wondering why on earth Antiochus would risk so much with such a riddle, which does, after all, reveal his incest: this is a romance, and the normal principles of probability and of cause-and-effect, are only partially operative. Perhaps the collection of severed heads adorning Antiochus's castle is reminder enough of his symbolic nature: this waste-house is a house of love-as-death.

Incest of father and daughter forces the normal progress of generations back on itself. This emblematic episode at the beginning of the play starts a process in which Pericles tries to unlock or unblock (and so enable) the natural succession of generations, freeing daughter from father. Here, the normal order and succession is turned to poison and decay through incest:

... Where now you're both a father and a son,
By your uncomely claspings with your child, --
Which pleasures fits a husband, not a father;
And she an eater of her mother's flesh,
By the defiling of her parent's bed;
And both like serpents are, who though they feed
On sweetest flowers, yet they poison breed. (1.1.128-34).

"Lilies that fester smell far worse than weeds," says Shakespeare in the Sonnets. Like some prisoner in a knightly castle, where the custom of the castle (turning on a riddle) promises certain death, Pericles is able, providentially, to persuade Antiochus to relent just enough to give him a chance to flee. But what might feature in, say, a French romance as simply a chivalric episode, is here combined with politics: Antiochus is powerful enough to bring death and destruction to Tyre. Back in Tyre, Pericles is torn apart by the experience he has passed through, and concerned that the retribution he will bring on himself will also destroy his kingdom. The great Antiochus, 'Gainst whom I am too little to contend, Since he's so great can make his will his act, Will think me speaking, though I swear to silence;

Nor boots it me to say I honour him,
If he suspect I may dishonour him. (1.2.17-22)

Pursued by Antiochus's appointed assassin Thaliard, Pericles escapes by sea, a kind of Odysseus condemned to wandering, or a Prospero cast adrift, or perhaps like the Duke in Measure for Measure, separated from his kingdom out of his very concern for it. In a way this play is a Tempest, with uproar in the elements and miraculous gifts from the sea, along with a natural world that seems better than the humans who occupy it. It picks up on Lear and on Timon. I might add that it gives us a corrupt father/daughter relationship that is vaguely reminiscent of an incidental event at the beginning of Timon and very much reminiscent of the opening of Lear. Antiochus's court (like Lear's, or like Prospero's island) has no mother: in Pericles and in The Winter's Tale, particularly, the revival and rediscovery of the mother is of crucial importance. We end the act with an introduction to Tharsus, in the grips of a famine, presided over by Cleon and Dionyza. Pericles comes to them bearing grain, saving them from their famine.

We have heard your miseries as far as Tyre,
And seen the desolation of your streets;
Nor come we to add sorrow to your tears,
But to relieve them of their heavy load. (1.4.88-91)

The audience may be pardoned for wondering what this stop in Tharsus has to do with anything, but of course its significance will become apparent later on. Impelled by fear of Antiochus, Pericles takes again to the seas, only to be shipwrecked. The Pericles we meet at the beginning of Act 2 is a Pericles made poor, reduced to extremities", but in this sense mortified and purged of the contaminating sin to which he has been exposed by Antiochus ("Wind, rain and thunder, remember, earthly man / Is but a substance that must yield to you; / And I, as fits my nature, do obey you"). Baptized by the ocean, he is ready to be born again. Our three Fishermen, like peasants in a pastoral romance, comment on the action. Says Pericles, appearing to them (in lines, by the way, reminiscent of Egeon's long speech at the opening of The Comedy of Errors):

A man whom both the waters and the wind
In that vast tennis-court, hath made the ball
For them to play upon, entreats you pity him... (2.1.59-61)

Unlike Antiochus, these simple fishermen know goodness and happiness: they are unspoiled. Untutored in the ways of court and city, they give him back the breastplate miraculously caught in their nets: what the sea takes away it also gives back. Thus the natural world miraculously returns to its owner the badge of courtliness and chivalry, beginning thereby to rebuild his identity as a member of society, and Pericles uses a jewel that he still has on his arm (conveniently) to buy a horse. These are enough to allow him to enter the lists in Pentapolis and compete for Simonides' beautiful daughter Thaisa.

This episode is obviously intended to contrast with 1.1: the tournament takes the place of the riddle. Whereas Antiochus's palace is a Castle Perilous, the contest for the hand of Simonides' daughter is a knightly tournament -- though as each of the knights passes before Thaisa their devices in effect animate the static riddle of Antiochus and make of Pericles himself the biggest riddle of all. Stranger knights are common features in stories of such tournaments (note, by the way, that we have a Stranger Knight in Edgar in Lear).

This scene (one is reminded of the procession of Trojan warriors in Troilus and Cressida) bears some resemblance to actual tournaments conducted in the chivalric revival of Elizabeth's reign. This was an age that loved riddles and puzzles and devices. Pericles (no surprise) wins the tournament and wins Thaisa. Simonides' relationship with his daughter, as we learn in sc. 3 and later, is tight, but quite different in nature from that of Antiochus with his. In a brief return to Tyre we learn what has happened to Antiochus, burned to a crisp in his chariot, "even in the height and pride of all his glory" 2.4.6 (or, rather, not exactly a crisp, since father and daughter, incestuous to the last, "so stunk" after their death that their former admirers could hardly bring themselves to bury them. Angry nobles insist that Helicanus take control of the kingdom unless Pericles can be found, and Pericles is given a year to return. So we come back to Pentapolis. The other knights are sent away, and Pericles is singled out as Thaisa's intended.

Pericles, once bitten twice shy, reacts with considerable alarm to a letter shown him by Simonides in which Thaisa declares her love for him. Simonides feigns anger (in the way Prospero does with Miranda's intended Ferdinand in The Tempest), but this feint is only a modest rite of passage on the way to Thaisa's hand. It is not easy for a father to relinquish his daughter to a husband, as the case of Prospero makes abundantly clear, but ultimately she is freely given. This could be the end of the play: Antiochus is dead, Pericles has a wife, the bad example of Antiochus has been trumped by the good example of Simonides. But it is not to be. The third act deals with death and rebirth. A huge storm on their journey back to Tyre induces the pregnant Thaisa's labor. A daughter is born in the midst of the storm, but Thaisa is given up for dead, and must be cast overboard if the storm is to abate. Dead bodies on board cause storms to continue, according to the sailors' beliefs, and so Thaisa becomes a kind of sacrificial offering to the elements.

Pericles comments movingly on these events:

A terrible childbed hast thou had, my dear;
No light, no fire: th'unfriendly elements
Forgot thee utterly; nor have I time
To give thee hallow'd to thy grave, but straight
Must cast thee, scarcely coffin'd, in the ooze;
Where, for a monument upon thy bones,
And e'er remaining lamps, the belching whale
And humming water must o'erwhelm thy corpse.

"Thou met'st with things dying, I with things new-born," says the Shepherd to his son in The Winter's Tale. In the later play, we see very clearly that the deaths of Antigonus and, particularly, Mamillius, are a part of the sacrifice that must be made, the reversals that must be endured, for the world to be renewed. That same dynamic is at work here: the storm must claim its victims even as it renders up the new-born baby. We should note of this passage that the language and the movement of the verse seem suddenly

Shakespearean... as indeed we see from the beginning of the scene, both in the charming monologue of Gower (whose content and cadence take us back to A Midsummer Night's Dream) and in the crafted blank verse that follows. Thaisa's coffin floats ashore at Ephesus – a place, we remember from The Comedy of Errors, renowned for its magic and its witchcraft, as St. Paul and others tell us. Cerimon, the miraculous magus-physician who runs something that looks a little like ER, with a touch of Friar Lawrence's cell thrown in, and with more than a touch of Prospero, revives Thaisa, employing music and harmony to do so, in effect calling down to earth the music of the spheres:

'Tis known I ever
Have studied physic, through which secret art,
By turning o'er authorities, I have,
Together with my practice, made familiar
To me and to my aid the blest infusions
That dwells in vegetives, in metals, stones;
And can speak of the disturbances that
Nature works, and of her cures; which doth give me
A more content in course of true delight
Than to be thirsty after tottering honour,
Or tie my treasure up in silken bags,
To please the fool and death. (3.2.31-42)

As she revives, Thaisa calls on the goddess Diana. Indeed, she seems content to remain at Ephesus, where Cerimon locates her (The Comedy of Errors again) as a priestess at the temple of Diana (sc. 4). This revival, this return from death, makes of Thaisa a kind of spirit in waiting: there is no question at this stage of her reunion with Pericles, no indication of her eagerness to make contact with the larger world. The audience stores her away for use in future miracles....

As for the daughter born at sea, and called Marina, Pericles commits her to the keeping of Cleon and Dionyza in Tharsus and returns to Tyre. (Needless to say, there are a few improbabilities here too, particularly the 14-year abandonment of one's daughter, but we pass them by, as all part of the story.)

And so we jump over fourteen years. The theme of death and rebirth carries across the chronological gap between the third and fourth acts. Marina, Gower tells us, is "by Cleon train'd / In music's letters," causing her to gain by such education "all the grace, / Which makes her both the heart and place / Of general wonder." If Cleon is a good teacher, Dionyza, it turns out, is the next best thing to Lady Macbeth or Goneril -- and Cleon an Albany unable to stand up to her.

Leonine is given the task of killing Marina because she is too much competition for Dionyza's own daughter (envy seems a common thread in the final romances). Even as Leonine raises his arm to strike the blow on the seashore (that borderline between political stability and the formless chaos of the sea), a crowd of pirates emerges providentially from the sea and carries Marina away....

The sea seems to be rapidly achieving the status of character in the play. As for Leonine, he decides that Marina is not likely to reappear, and so he can save his skin by announcing to Dionyza that Marina is indeed dead. If this were a comedy of errors, by this time the sum of errors would threaten to overbalance the entire play: Cleon and Dionyza, misled by Leonine, think Marina dead; Leonine, seeing her carried off by parents, assumes her death; Pericles will also soon assume that she has died.

The setting changes yet again. Now we are in Mytilene with a new cast of characters. Business is bad at the local brothel: we are down to a couple of worn-out whores. Boult goes to the market to find women and returns with the supposedly dead Marina and the pirates. We move back, meanwhile, to Tharsus, where Dionyza tells Cleon that when and if Pericles comes back for Marina they will say she died and will erect a monument to her. And this is what happens in scene 4.

The brothel scenes are far and away the best written and most dramatically vivid scenes in the play, and they have been justly praised. Increasingly, the clientele is almost as down at heels as the disease-ridden merchandise, and Boult's repeated references to the need to take Marina's virginity in the interests of commercial profitability carry a deliciously absurd ring: "Faith, I must ravish her, or she'll disfurnish us of all our cavalleria, and make our swearers priests." The great spirit of virtue is splendidly reduced to a case of inconvenience. But quite apart from their comedic effectiveness, the scenes also play a symbolic role: Marina's sojourn in the brothel resembles Proserpine's in the underworld, or a kind of purgatory or hell: says Marina to Boult, "Thou hold'st a place, for which the pained'st fiend / Of hell would not in reputation change" (4.6.162-3). The beautiful maiden finds herself assailed on every side by the forces of corruption and hopelessness – but her education and her natural charm (aristocracy reveals itself in romance even when it is leveled with the peasantry) make her marvelously persuasive. She talks Lysimachus out of going to bed with her and he supplies her with money anyway. Like Isabella with Angelo in Measure for Measure, her rhetorical skills and her virtue go together. She uses the money she has received to buy off Boult and she proposes that she offer needlework lessons to the local population, a salutary diversification of the brothel business which should not be lost in those much-touted seminars on Shakespeare for executives. Thus she begins her return to life from her "death" on the beach at Tharsus. From prostitution to teaching, through rhetorical skill – this is the story of Marina's reemergence. But there is more, as the fifth act proceeds to tell us. Pericles, reduced to a kind of nervous breakdown through his various tribulations, comes to Mytilene (borne, we assume, by a friendly sea), where his daughter is. It is the time of "God Neptune's annual feast," celebrated in July – surely a propitious time for the fecund generosity of both sea and land, and a contrast to the time of winter tempests. There, Pericles is revived in 5.1. by the matchless Marina, brought on shipboard by Lysimachus with the express intention of doing so:

We have a maid in Mytilene, I durst wager,
Would win some words from him ...
She questionless, with her sweet harmony,
And other chosen attractions, would allure
And make a batt'ry through his deafened ports. (5.1.44ff)

And so it is. The very qualities of Marina -- her grace, her talk, her skills, her music–that caused Dionyza to seek to do away with her, here revive her father. Pericles himself has died and is revived, has lost his sense of self and is now induced back to it. This is Cordelia with Lear, or Helena with the King of France in All's Well. Thus, discovering one another's identity, they are reunited – both of them, in their ways, brought back to life:

O Helicanus, strike me, honour'd sir!
Give me a gash, put me to present pain,
Lest this great sea of joys rushing upon me
O'er bear the shores of my mortality,
And drown me with their sweetness. O, come hither,
Thou that beget'st him that did thee beget;
Thou that wast born at sea, buried at Tharsus,
And found at sea again. (1.1.191-98)

As Pericles, like Lear, falls into a contented sleep, hearing in the background what seems the music of the spheres, he dreams of Diana of Ephesus, who tells him to go to her temple. This time, the sea shows no anger: "In feather'd briefness sails are fill'd, / And wishes fall out as they're willed," remarks Gower. At Ephesus, preparing to do sacrifice to Diana (the virgin goddess par excellence, we might note, and therefore a suitable patroness most particularly for Marina), he tells his history in the hearing of Cerimon and Thaisa. Recognition follows and he is reunited with Thaisa ("That Thaisa am I, supposed dead / And drown'd"). "You gods," Pericles declares, "your present kindness / Makes my past miseries sports." In this grand recognition scene, it is Marina's turn next: "My heart / Leaps to be gone into my mother's bosom." Lysimachus, we are told, will marry Marina and reign in Tyre. And so the play ends. Recognition scenes are always good theatre, and the concluding act of Pericles is no exception. Its story of a family reunited takes us back to the beginning of Shakespeare's career, to The Comedy of Errors, with its grand finale in which twins are reunited, a father is reunited with his children, and their mother, lost for years, is found again. But there are two significant differences.

First, the family reunion at the end of The Comedy of Errors essentially restores the status quo ante: the play says nothing about questions of continuity, nothing about the succession of generations. Second, the story of Egeon and his sons which frames the farcical action of most of the play, draws much of its poignancy from the threat of execution that hangs over Egeon's head from the beginning: the providential ending averts a disaster of misfortune. Something different is going on in Pericles. Yes, there is abundance of action, as in the earlier play, and, yes, a family is brought together – but the reunion is, above all, an assertion of the triumphant powers of generation, of life. Furthermore, Pericles involves more than mere accident: the success is due to a certain miraculous collaboration between a provident nature and human affairs.

In The Comedy of Errors, the sea that separates the slips of land among which the family members navigate is an empty, lonely agglomeration of water-drops: in Pericles, the sea (and its representative collaborator Marina) is an actor in the affairs of human beings, a part of a demanding but ultimately benign universe. The last word goes to Gower, who reminds us that this is a fiction with a series of morals and a series of characters who offer lessons in morality: it is a story of "Virtue preserv'd from fell destruction's blast." The play itself becomes a kind of mine for the romances, its huge scope and scattered incidents not yet fully brought under control.

4

Beyond Tragedy of the Britain King Lear's

Enter Kent, Gloucester, and Edmund. (Kent and Glouceste converse. Edmund stands back.)

Kent. I thought the King had more affected the Duke of Albany than

Cornwall.

Glou. It did always seem so to us; but now, in the division of the kingdom, it appears not which of the Dukes he values most, for equalities are so weigh'd that curiosity in neither can make choice of either's moiety.

Kent. Is not this your son, my lord?

Glou. His breeding, sir, hath been at my charge. I have so often blush'd to acknowledge him that now I am braz'd to't.

Kent. I cannot conceive you.

Glou. Sir, this young fellow's mother could; whereupon she grew round-womb'd, and had indeed, sir, a son for her cradle ere she had a husband for her bed. Do you smell a fault?

Kent. I cannot wish the fault undone, the issue of it being so proper. Glou. But I have, sir, a son by order of law, some year elder than this, who yet is no dearer in my account. Though this knave came something saucily into the world before he was sent for, yet was his mother fair, there was good sport at his making, and the whoreson must be acknowledged.- Do you know this noble gentleman, Edmund?

Edm. [comes forward] No, my lord.

Glou. My Lord of Kent. Remember him hereafter as my honourable friend.

Edm. My services to your lordship.

Kent. I must love you, and sue to know you better.

Edm. Sir, I shall study deserving.

Glou. He hath been out nine years, and away he shall again.

Sound a sennet.

The King is coming.

Enter one bearing a coronet; then Lear; then the Dukes of

Albany and Cornwall; next, Goneril, Regan, Cordelia, with

Followers.

Lear. Attend the lords of France and Burgundy, Gloucester.

Glou. I shall, my liege.

Exeunt [Gloucester and Edmund].

Lear. Meantime we shall express our darker purpose.

Give me the map there. Know we have divided

In three our kingdom; and 'tis our fast intent

To shake all cares and business from our age,

Conferring them on younger strengths while we

Unburthen'd crawl toward death. Our son of Cornwall,

And you, our no less loving son of Albany,

We have this hour a constant will to publish

Our daughters' several dowers, that future strife

May be prevented now. The princes, France and Burgundy,

Great rivals in our youngest daughter's love,

Long in our court have made their amorous sojourn,

And here are to be answer'd. Tell me, my daughters (Since now we will divest us both of rule, Interest of territory, cares of state),

Which of you shall we say doth love us most?
That we our largest bounty may extend
Where nature doth with merit challenge. Goneril,
Our eldest-born, speak first.
Gon. Sir, I love you more than words can wield the matter;
Dearer than eyesight, space, and liberty;
Beyond what can be valued, rich or rare;
No less than life, with grace, health, beauty, honour;
As much as child e'er lov'd, or father found;
A love that makes breath poor, and speech unable.
Beyond all manner of so much I love you.
Cor. [aside] What shall Cordelia speak? Love, and be silent.
Lear. Of all these bounds, even from this line to this,
With shadowy forests and with champains rich'd,
With plenteous rivers and wide-skirted meads,
We make thee lady. To thine and Albany's issue
Be this perpetual.- What says our second daughter,
Our dearest Regan, wife to Cornwall? Speak.
Reg. Sir, I am made
Of the selfsame metal that my sister is,
And prize me at her worth. In my true heart
I find she names my very deed of love;
Only she comes too short, that I profess
Myself an enemy to all other joys
Which the most precious square of sense possesses,
And find I am alone felicitate
In your dear Highness' love.
Cor. [aside] Then poor Cordelia!
And yet not so; since I am sure my love's
More richer than my tongue.

Lear. To thee and thine hereditary ever
Remain this ample third of our fair kingdom,
No less in space, validity, and pleasure
Than that conferr'd on Goneril.- Now, our joy,
Although the last, not least; to whose young love
The vines of France and milk of Burgundy
Strive to be interest; what can you say to draw
A third more opulent than your sisters? Speak.
Cor. Nothing, my lord.
Lear. Nothing?
Cor. Nothing.
Lear. Nothing can come of nothing. Speak again.
Cor. Unhappy that I am, I cannot heave
My heart into my mouth. I love your Majesty
According to my bond; no more nor less.
Lear. How, how, Cordelia? Mend your speech a little,
Lest it may mar your fortunes.
Cor. Good my lord,
You have begot me, bred me, lov'd me; I
Return those duties back as are right fit,
Obey you, love you, and most honour you.
Why have my sisters husbands, if they say
They love you all? Haply, when I shall wed,
That lord whose hand must take my plight shall carry
Half my love with him, half my care and duty.
Sure I shall never marry like my sisters,
To love my father all.
Lear. But goes thy heart with this?
Cor. Ay, good my lord.
Lear. So young, and so untender?

Cor. So young, my lord, and true.
Lear. Let it be so! thy truth then be thy dower!
For, by the sacred radiance of the sun,
The mysteries of Hecate and the night;
By all the operation of the orbs
From whom we do exist and cease to be;
Here I disclaim all my paternal care,
Propinquity and property of blood,
And as a stranger to my heart and me
Hold thee from this for ever. The barbarous Scythian,
Or he that makes his generation messes
To gorge his appetite, shall to my bosom
Be as well neighbour'd, pitied, and reliev'd,
As thou my sometime daughter.
Kent. Good my liege-
Lear. Peace, Kent!
Come not between the dragon and his wrath.
I lov'd her most, and thought to set my rest
On her kind nursery.- Hence and avoid my sight!-
So be my grave my peace as here I give
Her father's heart from her! Call France! Who stirs?
Call Burgundy! Cornwall and Albany,
With my two daughters' dowers digest this third;
Let pride, which she calls plainness, marry her.
I do invest you jointly in my power,
Preeminence, and all the large effects
That troop with majesty. Ourself, by monthly course,
With reservation of an hundred knights,
By you to be sustain'd, shall our abode
Make with you by due turns. Only we still retain

The name, and all th' additions to a king. The sway,
Revenue, execution of the rest,
Beloved sons, be yours; which to confirm,
This coronet part betwixt you.
Kent. Royal Lear,
Whom I have ever honour'd as my king,
Lov'd as my father, as my master follow'd,
As my great patron thought on in my prayers-
Lear. The bow is bent and drawn; make from the shaft.
Kent. Let it fall rather, though the fork invade
The region of my heart! Be Kent unmannerly
When Lear is mad. What wouldst thou do, old man?
Think'st thou that duty shall have dread to speak
When power to flattery bows? To plainness honour's bound
When majesty falls to folly. Reverse thy doom;
And in thy best consideration check
This hideous rashness. Answer my life my judgment,
Thy youngest daughter does not love thee least,
Nor are those empty-hearted whose low sound
Reverbs no hollowness.
Lear. Kent, on thy life, no more!
Kent. My life I never held but as a pawn
To wage against thine enemies; nor fear to lose it,
Thy safety being the motive.
Lear. Out of my sight!
Kent. See better, Lear, and let me still remain
The true blank of thine eye.
Lear. Now by Apollo-
Kent. Now by Apollo, King,
Thou swear'st thy gods in vain.

Lear. O vassal! miscreant!
[Lays his hand on his sword.]
Alb., Corn. Dear sir, forbear!
Kent. Do!
Kill thy physician, and the fee bestow
Upon the foul disease. Revoke thy gift,
Or, whilst I can vent clamour from my throat,
I'll tell thee thou dost evil.
Lear. Hear me, recreant!
On thine allegiance, hear me!
Since thou hast sought to make us break our vow-
Which we durst never yet- and with strain'd pride
To come between our sentence and our power,-
Which nor our nature nor our place can bear,-
Our potency made good, take thy reward.
Five days we do allot thee for provision
To shield thee from diseases of the world,
And on the sixth to turn thy hated back
Upon our kingdom. If, on the tenth day following,
Thy banish'd trunk be found in our dominions,
The moment is thy death. Away! By Jupiter,
This shall not be revok'd.
Kent. Fare thee well, King. Since thus thou wilt appear,
Freedom lives hence, and banishment is here.
[To Cordelia] The gods to their dear shelter take thee, maid,
That justly think'st and hast most rightly said!
[To Regan and Goneril] And your large speeches may your deeds approve,
That good effects may spring from words of love.
Thus Kent, O princes, bids you all adieu;

He'll shape his old course in a country new.
Exit.

Flourish. Enter Gloucester, with France and Burgundy; Attendants.

Glou. Here's France and Burgundy, my noble lord.
Lear. My Lord of Burgundy,
We first address toward you, who with this king
Hath rivall'd for our daughter. What in the least
Will you require in present dower with her,
Or cease your quest of love?
Bur. Most royal Majesty,
I crave no more than hath your Highness offer'd,
Nor will you tender less.
Lear. Right noble Burgundy,
When she was dear to us, we did hold her so;
But now her price is fall'n. Sir, there she stands.
If aught within that little seeming substance,
Or all of it, with our displeasure piec'd,
And nothing more, may fitly like your Grace,
She's there, and she is yours.
Bur. I know no answer.
Lear. Will you, with those infirmities she owes,
Unfriended, new adopted to our hate,
Dow'r'd with our curse, and stranger'd with our oath,
Take her, or leave her?
Bur. Pardon me, royal sir.
Election makes not up on such conditions.
Lear. Then leave her, sir; for, by the pow'r that made me,
I tell you all her wealth. [To France] For you, great King,
I would not from your love make such a stray

To match you where I hate; therefore beseech you
T' avert your liking a more worthier way
Than on a wretch whom nature is asham'd
Almost t' acknowledge hers.
France. This is most strange,
That she that even but now was your best object,
The argument of your praise, balm of your age,
Most best, most dearest, should in this trice of time
Commit a thing so monstrous to dismantle
So many folds of favour. Sure her offence
Must be of such unnatural degree
That monsters it, or your fore-vouch'd affection
Fall'n into taint; which to believe of her
Must be a faith that reason without miracle
Should never plant in me.
Cor. I yet beseech your Majesty,
If for I want that glib and oily art
To speak and purpose not, since what I well intend,
I'll do't before I speak- that you make known
It is no vicious blot, murther, or foulness,
No unchaste action or dishonoured step,
That hath depriv'd me of your grace and favour;
But even for want of that for which I am richer-
A still-soliciting eye, and such a tongue
As I am glad I have not, though not to have it
Hath lost me in your liking.
Lear. Better thou
Hadst not been born than not t' have pleas'd me better.
France. Is it but this- a tardiness in nature
Which often leaves the history unspoke

That it intends to do? My Lord of Burgundy,
What say you to the lady? Love's not love
When it is mingled with regards that stands
Aloof from th' entire point. Will you have her?
She is herself a dowry.
Bur. Royal Lear,
Give but that portion which yourself propos'd,
And here I take Cordelia by the hand,
Duchess of Burgundy.
Lear. Nothing! I have sworn; I am firm.
Bur. I am sorry then you have so lost a father
That you must lose a husband.
Cor. Peace be with Burgundy!
Since that respects of fortune are his love,
I shall not be his wife.
France. Fairest Cordelia, that art most rich, being poor;
Most choice, forsaken; and most lov'd, despis'd!
Thee and thy virtues here I seize upon.
Be it lawful I take up what's cast away.
Gods, gods! 'tis strange that from their cold'st neglect
My love should kindle to inflam'd respect.
Thy dow'rless daughter, King, thrown to my chance,
Is queen of us, of ours, and our fair France.
Not all the dukes in wat'rish Burgundy
Can buy this unpriz'd precious maid of me.
Bid them farewell, Cordelia, though unkind.
Thou losest here, a better where to find.
Lear. Thou hast her, France; let her be thine; for we
Have no such daughter, nor shall ever see
That face of hers again. Therefore be gone

Without our grace, our love, our benison.

Come, noble Burgundy.

Flourish. Exeunt Lear, Burgundy, [Cornwall, Albany, Gloucester, and Attendants].

France. Bid farewell to your sisters.

Cor. The jewels of our father, with wash'd eyes Cordelia leaves you. I know you what you are;

And, like a sister, am most loath to call

Your faults as they are nam'd. Use well our father.

To your professed bosoms I commit him;

But yet, alas, stood I within his grace,

I would prefer him to a better place!

So farewell to you both.

Gon. Prescribe not us our duties.

Reg. Let your study

Be to content your lord, who hath receiv'd you

At fortune's alms. You have obedience scanted,

And well are worth the want that you have wanted.

Cor. Time shall unfold what plighted cunning hides.

Who cover faults, at last shame them derides.

Well may you prosper!

France. Come, my fair Cordelia.

Exeunt France and Cordelia.

Gon. Sister, it is not little I have to say of what most nearly appertains to us both. I think our father will hence to-night.

Reg. That's most certain, and with you; next month with us.

Gon. You see how full of changes his age is. The observation we have made of it hath not been little. He always lov'd our sister most, and with what poor judgment he hath now cast her off appears too grossly.

Reg. 'Tis the infirmity of his age; yet he hath ever but slenderly known himself.

Gon. The best and soundest of his time hath been but rash; then must we look to receive from his age, not alone the imperfections of long-ingraffed condition, but therewithal the unruly waywardness that infirm and choleric years bring with them.

Reg. Such unconstant starts are we like to have from him as this of Kent's banishment.

Gon. There is further compliment of leave-taking between France and him. Pray you let's hit together. If our father carry authority with such dispositions as he bears, this last surrender of his will but offend us.

Reg. We shall further think on't.

Gon. We must do something, and i' th' heat.

Exeunt.

SCENE I.: THE EARL OF GLOUCESTER'S CASTLE.

Enter [Edmund the] Bastard solus, [with a letter].

Edm. Thou, Nature, art my goddess; to thy law
My services are bound. Wherefore should I
Stand in the plague of custom, and permit
The curiosity of nations to deprive me,
For that I am some twelve or fourteen moonshines
Lag of a brother? Why bastard? wherefore base?
When my dimensions are as well compact,
My mind as generous, and my shape as true,
As honest madam's issue? Why brand they us
With base? with baseness? bastardy? base, base?
Who, in the lusty stealth of nature, take
More composition and fierce quality
Than doth, within a dull, stale, tired bed,
Go to th' creating a whole tribe of fops

Got 'tween asleep and wake? Well then,
Legitimate Edgar, I must have your land.
Our father's love is to the bastard Edmund
As to th' legitimate. Fine word- 'legitimate'!
Well, my legitimate, if this letter speed,
And my invention thrive, Edmund the base
Shall top th' legitimate. I grow; I prosper.
Now, gods, stand up for bastards!

Enter Gloucester.

Glou. Kent banish'd thus? and France in choler parted?
And the King gone to-night? subscrib'd his pow'r?
Confin'd to exhibition? All this done
Upon the gad? Edmund, how now? What news?
Edm. So please your lordship, none.
[Puts up the letter.]
Glou. Why so earnestly seek you to put up that letter?
Edm. I know no news, my lord.
Glou. What paper were you reading?
Edm. Nothing, my lord.

Glou. No? What needed then that terrible dispatch of it into your pocket? The quality of nothing hath not such need to hide itself. Let's see. Come, if it be nothing, I shall not need spectacles.

Edm. I beseech you, sir, pardon me. It is a letter from my brother that I have not all o'er-read; and for so much as I have perus'd, I find it not fit for your o'erlooking.

Glou. Give me the letter, sir.

Edm. I shall offend, either to detain or give it. The contents, as in part I understand them, are to blame.

Glou. Let's see, let's see!

Edm. I hope, for my brother's justification, he wrote this but as an essay or taste of my virtue.

Glou. (reads) 'This policy and reverence of age makes the world bitter to the best of our times; keeps our fortunes from us till our oldness cannot relish them. I begin to find an idle and fond bondage in the oppression of aged tyranny, who sways, not as it hath power, but as it is suffer'd. Come to me, that of this I may speak more. If our father would sleep till I wak'd him, you should enjoy half his revenue for ever, and live the beloved of your brother, 'EDGAR.'

Hum! Conspiracy? 'Sleep till I wak'd him, you should enjoy half his revenue.' My son Edgar! Had he a hand to write this? a heart and brain to breed it in? When came this to you? Who brought it?

Edm. It was not brought me, my lord: there's the cunning of it. I found it thrown in at the casement of my closet.

Glou. You know the character to be your brother's?

Edm. If the matter were good, my lord, I durst swear it were his; but in respect of that, I would fain think it were not.

Glou. It is his.

Edm. It is his hand, my lord; but I hope his heart is not in the contents.

Glou. Hath he never before sounded you in this business?

Edm. Never, my lord. But I have heard him oft maintain it to be fit that, sons at perfect age, and fathers declining, the father should be as ward to the son, and the son manage his revenue.

Glou. O villain, villain! His very opinion in the letter! Abhorred villain! Unnatural, detested, brutish villain! worse than brutish! Go, sirrah, seek him. I'll apprehend him. Abominable villain! Where is he? Edm. I do not well know, my lord. If it shall please you to suspend your indignation against my brother till you can derive from him better testimony of his intent, you should run a certain course; where, if you violently proceed against him, mistaking his purpose, it would make a great gap in your own honour and shake in pieces the heart of his obedience. I dare pawn down my life for him that he hath writ this to feel my affection to your honour, and to no other pretence of danger. Glou. Think you so?

Edm. If your honour judge it meet, I will place you where you shall hear us confer of this and by an auricular assurance have your satisfaction, and that without any further delay than this very evening. Glou. He cannot be such a monster.

Edm. Nor is not, sure.

Glou. To his father, that so tenderly and entirely loves him.

Heaven and earth! Edmund, seek him out; wind me into him, I pray you; frame the business after your own wisdom. I would unstate myself to be in a due resolution.

Edm. I will seek him, sir, presently; convey the business as I shall find means, and acquaint you withal.

Glou. These late eclipses in the sun and moon portend no good to us. Though the wisdom of nature can reason it thus and thus, yet nature finds itself scourg'd by the sequent effects. Love cools, friendship falls off, brothers divide. In cities, mutinies; in countries, discord; in palaces, treason; and the bond crack'd 'twixt son and father. This villain of mine comes under the prediction; there's son against father: the King falls from bias of nature; there's father against child. We have seen the best of our time. Machinations, hollowness, treachery, and all ruinous disorders follow us disquietly to our graves. Find out this villain, Edmund; it shall lose thee nothing; do it carefully. And the noble and true-hearted Kent banish'd! his offence, honesty! 'Tis strange.

Exit.

Edm. This is the excellent foppery of the world, that, when we are sick in fortune, often the surfeit of our own behaviour, we make guilty of our disasters the sun, the moon, and the stars; as if we were villains on necessity; fools by heavenly compulsion; knaves, thieves, and treachers by spherical pre-dominance; drunkards, liars, and adulterers by an enforc'd obedience of planetary influence; and all that we are evil in, by a divine thrusting on. An admirable evasion of whore-master man, to lay his goatish disposition to the charge of a star! My father compounded with my mother under the Dragon's

Tail, and my nativity was under Ursa Major, so that it follows I am rough and lecherous. Fut! I should have been that I am, had the maidenliest star in the firmament twinkled on my bastardizing. Edgar-

Enter Edgar.

And pat! he comes, like the catastrophe of the old comedy. My cue is villainous melancholy, with a sigh like Tom o' Bedlam.

O, these eclipses do portend these divisions! Fa, sol, la, mi.

Edg. How now, brother Edmund? What serious contemplation are you in?

Edm. I am thinking, brother, of a prediction I read this other day, what should follow these eclipses.

Edg. Do you busy yourself with that?

Edm. I promise you, the effects he writes of succeed unhappily: as of unnaturalness between the child and the parent; death, dearth, dissolutions of ancient amities; divisions in state, menaces and maledictions against king and nobles; needless diffidences, banishment of friends, dissipation of cohorts, nuptial breaches, and I know not what. Edg. How long have you been a sectary astronomical?

Edm. Come, come! When saw you my father last?

Edg. The night gone by.

Edm. Spake you with him?

Edg. Ay, two hours together.

Edm. Parted you in good terms? Found you no displeasure in him by word or countenance

Edg. None at all.

Edm. Bethink yourself wherein you may have offended him; and at my entreaty forbear his presence until some little time hath qualified the heat of his displeasure, which at this instant so rageth in him that with the mischief of your person it would scarcely allay.

Edg. Some villain hath done me wrong.

Edm. That's my fear. I pray you have a continent forbearance till the speed of his rage goes slower; and, as I say, retire with me to my lodging, from whence I will fitly bring you to hear my lord speak. Pray ye, go! There's my key. If you do stir abroad, go arm'd.

Edg. Arm'd, brother?

Edm. Brother, I advise you to the best. Go arm'd. I am no honest man if there be any good meaning toward you. I have told you what I have seen and heard; but faintly, nothing like the image and horror of it. Pray you, away!

Edg. Shall I hear from you anon?

Edm. I do serve you in this business.

Exit Edgar.

A credulous father! and a brother noble,

Whose nature is so far from doing harms

That he suspects none; on whose foolish honesty

My practices ride easy! I see the business.

Let me, if not by birth, have lands by wit;

All with me's meet that I can fashion fit.

Exit.

SCENE III.: THE DUKE OF ALBANY'S PALACE.

Enter Goneril and [her] Steward [Oswald].

Gon. Did my father strike my gentleman for chiding of his fool?

Osw. Ay, madam.

Gon. By day and night, he wrongs me! Every hour

He flashes into one gross crime or other

That sets us all at odds. I'll not endure it.

His knights grow riotous, and himself upbraids us

On every trifle. When he returns from hunting,

I will not speak with him. Say I am sick.
If you come slack of former services,
You shall do well; the fault of it I'll answer.
[Horns within.]
Osw. He's coming, madam; I hear him.
Gon. Put on what weary negligence you please,
You and your fellows. I'd have it come to question.
If he distaste it, let him to our sister,
Whose mind and mine I know in that are one,
Not to be overrul'd. Idle old man,
That still would manage those authorities
That he hath given away! Now, by my life,
Old fools are babes again, and must be us'd
With checks as flatteries, when they are seen abus'd.
Remember what I have said.
Osw. Very well, madam.
Gon. And let his knights have colder looks among you.
What grows of it, no matter. Advise your fellows so.
I would breed from hence occasions, and I shall,
That I may speak. I'll write straight to my sister
To hold my very course. Prepare for dinner.
Exeunt.

SCENE IV.: THE DUKE OF ALBANY'S PALACE.

Enter Kent, [disguised].
Kent. If but as well I other accents borrow,
That can my speech defuse, my good intent
May carry through itself to that full issue
For which I raz'd my likeness. Now, banish'd Kent,
If thou canst serve where thou dost stand condemn'd,
So may it come, thy master, whom thou lov'st,

Shall find thee full of labours.

Horns within. Enter Lear, [Knights,] and Attendants.

Lear. Let me not stay a jot for dinner; go get it ready. [Exit an Attendant.] How now? What art thou?

Kent. A man, sir.

Lear. What dost thou profess? What wouldst thou with us?

Kent. I do profess to be no less than I seem, to serve him truly that will put me in trust, to love him that is honest, to converse with him that is wise and says little, to fear judgment, to fight when I cannot choose, and to eat no fish. Lear. What art thou?

Kent. A very honest-hearted fellow, and as poor as the King.

Lear. If thou be'st as poor for a subject as he's for a king, thou art poor enough. What wouldst thou?

Kent. Service.

Lear. Who wouldst thou serve?

Kent. You.

Lear. Dost thou know me, fellow?

Kent. No, sir; but you have that in your countenance which I would fain call master.

Lear. What's that?

Kent. Authority.

Lear. What services canst thou do?

Kent. I can keep honest counsel, ride, run, mar a curious tale in telling it and deliver a plain message bluntly. That which ordinary men are fit for, I am qualified in, and the best of me is diligence.

Lear. How old art thou?

Kent. Not so young, sir, to love a woman for singing, nor so old to dote on her for anything. I have years on my back forty-eight.

Lear. Follow me; thou shalt serve me. If I like thee no worse after dinner, I will not part from thee yet. Dinner, ho, dinner!

Where's my knave? my fool? Go you and call my fool hither.

[Exit an attendant.]

Enter [Oswald the] Steward.

You, you, sirrah, where's my daughter?

Osw. So please you-

Exit.

Lear. What says the fellow there? Call the clotpoll back.

[Exit a Knight.] Where's my fool, ho? I think the world's asleep.

[Enter Knight]

How now? Where's that mongrel?

Knight. He says, my lord, your daughter is not well.

Lear. Why came not the slave back to me when I call'd him?

Knight. Sir, he answered me in the roundest manner, he would not.

Lear. He would not?

Knight. My lord, I know not what the matter is; but to my judgment your Highness is not entertain'd with that ceremonious affection as you were wont. There's a great abatement of kindness appears as well in the general dependants as in the Duke himself also and your daughter. Lear. Ha! say'st thou so?

Knight. I beseech you pardon me, my lord, if I be mistaken; for my duty cannot be silent when I think your Highness wrong'd.

Lear. Thou but rememb'rest me of mine own conception. I have perceived a most faint neglect of late, which I have rather blamed as mine own jealous curiosity than as a very pretence and purpose of unkindness. I will look further into't. But where's my fool? I have not seen him this two days.

Knight. Since my young lady's going into France, sir, the fool hath much pined away.

Lear. No more of that; I have noted it well. Go you and tell my daughter I would speak with her. [Exit Knight.] Go you, call hither my fool.

[Exit an Attendant.]

Enter [Oswald the] Steward.

O, you, sir, you! Come you hither, sir. Who am I, sir?

Osw. My lady's father.

Lear. 'My lady's father'? My lord's knave! You whoreson dog! you slave! you cur!

Osw. I am none of these, my lord; I beseech your pardon.

Lear. Do you bandy looks with me, you rascal?

[Strikes him.]

Osw. I'll not be strucken, my lord.

Kent. Nor tripp'd neither, you base football player?

[Trips up his heels.

Lear. I thank thee, fellow. Thou serv'st me, and I'll love thee.

Kent. Come, sir, arise, away! I'll teach you differences. Away, away! If you will measure your lubber's length again, tarry; but away! Go to! Have you wisdom? So.

[Pushes him out.]

Lear. Now, my friendly knave, I thank thee. There's earnest of thy service. [Gives money.]

Enter Fool.

Fool. Let me hire him too. Here's my coxcomb.

[Offers Kent his cap.]

Lear. How now, my pretty knave? How dost thou?

Fool. Sirrah, you were best take my coxcomb.

Kent. Why, fool?

Fool. Why? For taking one's part that's out of favour. Nay, an thou canst not smile as the wind sits, thou'lt catch cold shortly.

There, take my coxcomb! Why, this fellow hath banish'd two on's daughters, and did the third a blessing against his will. If thou follow him, thou must needs wear my coxcomb.- How now, nuncle? Would I had two coxcombs and two daughters!

Lear. Why, my boy?

Fool. If I gave them all my living, I'ld keep my coxcombs myself. There's mine! beg another of thy daughters.

Lear. Take heed, sirrah- the whip.

Fool. Truth's a dog must to kennel; he must be whipp'd out, when
Lady the brach may stand by th' fire and stink.

Lear. A pestilent gall to me!

Fool. Sirrah, I'll teach thee a speech.

Lear. Do.

Fool. Mark it, nuncle.

Have more than thou showest,
Speak less than thou knowest,
Lend less than thou owest,
Ride more than thou goest,
Learn more than thou trowest,
Set less than thou throwest;
Leave thy drink and thy whore,
And keep in-a-door,
And thou shalt have more
Than two tens to a score.

Kent. This is nothing, fool.

Fool. Then 'tis like the breath of an unfeed lawyer- you gave me nothing for't. Can you make no use of nothing, nuncle?

Lear. Why, no, boy. Nothing can be made out of nothing.

Fool. [to Kent] Prithee tell him, so much the rent of his land comes to. He will not believe a fool.

Lear. A bitter fool!

Fool. Dost thou know the difference, my boy, between a bitter fool and a sweet fool?

Lear. No, lad; teach me.

Fool. That lord that counsell'd thee

To give away thy land,

Come place him here by me-

Do thou for him stand.

The sweet and bitter fool

Will presently appear;

The one in motley here,

The other found out there.

Lear. Dost thou call me fool, boy?

Fool. All thy other titles thou hast given away; that thou wast born with.

Kent. This is not altogether fool, my lord.

Fool. No, faith; lords and great men will not let me. If I had a monopoly out, they would have part on't. And ladies too, they will not let me have all the fool to myself; they'll be snatching. Give me an egg, nuncle, and I'll give thee two crowns.

Lear. What two crowns shall they be?

Fool. Why, after I have cut the egg i' th' middle and eat up the meat, the two crowns of the egg. When thou clovest thy crown i' th' middle and gav'st away both parts, thou bor'st thine ass on thy back o'er the dirt. Thou hadst little wit in thy bald crown when thou gav'st thy golden one away. If I speak like myself in this, let him be whipp'd that first finds it so.

[Sings] Fools had ne'er less grace in a year,

For wise men are grown foppish;

They know not how their wits to wear,

Their manners are so apish.

Lear. When were you wont to be so full of songs, sirrah?

Fool. I have us'd it, nuncle, ever since thou mad'st thy daughters thy mother; for when thou gav'st them the rod, and put'st down thine own breeches,

[Sings] Then they for sudden joy did weep,
And I for sorrow sung,
That such a king should play bo-peep
And go the fools among.

Prithee, nuncle, keep a schoolmaster that can teach thy fool to lie. I would fain learn to lie.

Lear. An you lie, sirrah, we'll have you whipp'd.

Fool. I marvel what kin thou and thy daughters are. They'll have me whipp'd for speaking true; thou'lt have me whipp'd for lying; and sometimes I am whipp'd for holding my peace. I had rather be any kind o' thing than a fool! And yet I would not be thee, nuncle. Thou hast pared thy wit o' both sides and left nothing i' th' middle. Here comes one o' the parings. Enter Goneril.

Lear. How now, daughter? What makes that frontlet on? Methinks you are too much o' late i' th' frown.

Fool. Thou wast a pretty fellow when thou hadst no need to care for her frowning. Now thou art an O without a figure. I am better than thou art now: I am a fool, thou art nothing.

[To Goneril] Yes, forsooth, I will hold my tongue. So your face bids me, though you say nothing. Mum, mum!

He that keeps nor crust nor crum,
Weary of all, shall want some.-
[Points at Lear] That's a sheal'd peascod.

Gon. Not only, sir, this your all-licens'd fool,
But other of your insolent retinue
Do hourly carp and quarrel, breaking forth
In rank and not-to-be-endured riots. Sir,
I had thought, by making this well known unto you,
To have found a safe redress, but now grow fearful,

By what yourself, too, late have spoke and done,
That you protect this course, and put it on
By your allowance; which if you should, the fault
Would not scape censure, nor the redresses sleep,
Which, in the tender of a wholesome weal,
Might in their working do you that offence
Which else were shame, that then necessity
Must call discreet proceeding.
Fool. For you know, nuncle,
The hedge-sparrow fed the cuckoo so long
That it had it head bit off by it young.
So out went the candle, and we were left darkling.
Lear. Are you our daughter?
Gon. Come, sir,
I would you would make use of that good wisdom
Whereof I know you are fraught, and put away
These dispositions that of late transform you
From what you rightly are.
Fool. May not an ass know when the cart draws the horse?
Whoop, Jug, I love thee!
Lear. Doth any here know me? This is not Lear.
Doth Lear walk thus? speak thus? Where are his eyes?
Either his notion weakens, his discernings
Are lethargied- Ha! waking? 'Tis not so!
Who is it that can tell me who I am?
Fool. Lear's shadow.
Lear. I would learn that; for, by the marks of sovereignty,
Knowledge, and reason, I should be false persuaded
I had daughters.
Fool. Which they will make an obedient father.

Lear. Your name, fair gentlewoman?
Gon. This admiration, sir, is much o' th' savour
Of other your new pranks. I do beseech you
To understand my purposes aright.
As you are old and reverend, you should be wise.
Here do you keep a hundred knights and squires;
Men so disorder'd, so debosh'd, and bold
That this our court, infected with their manners,
Shows like a riotous inn. Epicurism and lust
Make it more like a tavern or a brothel
Than a grac'd palace. The shame itself doth speak
For instant remedy. Be then desir'd
By her that else will take the thing she begs
A little to disquantity your train,
And the remainder that shall still depend
To be such men as may besort your age,
Which know themselves, and you.
Lear. Darkness and devils!
Saddle my horses! Call my train together!
Degenerate bastard, I'll not trouble thee;
Yet have I left a daughter.
Gon. You strike my people, and your disorder'd rabble
Make servants of their betters.

Enter Albany.

Lear. Woe that too late repents!- O, sir, are you come?
Is it your will? Speak, sir!- Prepare my horses.
Ingratitude, thou marble-hearted fiend,
More hideous when thou show'st thee in a child
Than the sea-monster!

Alb. Pray, sir, be patient.
Lear. [to Goneril] Detested kite, thou liest!
My train are men of choice and rarest parts,
That all particulars of duty know
And in the most exact regard support
The worships of their name.- O most small fault,
How ugly didst thou in Cordelia show!
Which, like an engine, wrench'd my frame of nature
From the fix'd place; drew from my heart all love
And added to the gall. O Lear, Lear, Lear!
Beat at this gate that let thy folly in [Strikes his head.]
And thy dear judgment out! Go, go, my people.
Alb. My lord, I am guiltless, as I am ignorant
Of what hath mov'd you.
Lear. It may be so, my lord.
Hear, Nature, hear! dear goddess, hear!
Suspend thy purpose, if thou didst intend
To make this creature fruitful.
Into her womb convey sterility;
Dry up in her the organs of increase;
And from her derogate body never spring
A babe to honour her! If she must teem,
Create her child of spleen, that it may live
And be a thwart disnatur'd torment to her.
Let it stamp wrinkles in her brow of youth,
With cadent tears fret channels in her cheeks,
Turn all her mother's pains and benefits
To laughter and contempt, that she may feel
How sharper than a serpent's tooth it is
To have a thankless child! Away, away!

Exit.
Alb. Now, gods that we adore, whereof comes this?
Gon. Never afflict yourself to know the cause;
But let his disposition have that scope
That dotage gives it.

Enter Lear.

Lear. What, fifty of my followers at a clap?
Within a fortnight?
Alb. What's the matter, sir?
Lear. I'll tell thee. [To Goneril] Life and death! I am asham'd
That thou hast power to shake my manhood thus;
That these hot tears, which break from me perforce,
Should make thee worth them. Blasts and fogs upon thee!
Th' untented woundings of a father's curse
Pierce every sense about thee!- Old fond eyes,
Beweep this cause again, I'll pluck ye out,
And cast you, with the waters that you lose,
To temper clay. Yea, is it come to this?
Let it be so. Yet have I left a daughter,
Who I am sure is kind and comfortable.
When she shall hear this of thee, with her nails
She'll flay thy wolvish visage. Thou shalt find
That I'll resume the shape which thou dost think
I have cast off for ever; thou shalt, I warrant thee.
Exeunt [Lear, Kent, and Attendants].
Gon. Do you mark that, my lord?
Alb. I cannot be so partial, Goneril,
To the great love I bear you -
Gon. Pray you, content.- What, Oswald, ho!

[To the Fool] You, sir, more knave than fool, after your master!

Fool. Nuncle Lear, nuncle Lear, tarry! Take the fool with thee.

A fox when one has caught her,

And such a daughter,

Should sure to the slaughter,

If my cap would buy a halter.

So the fool follows after.

Exit.

Gon. This man hath had good counsel! A hundred knights?

'Tis politic and safe to let him keep

At point a hundred knights; yes, that on every dream,

Each buzz, each fancy, each complaint, dislike,

He may enguard his dotage with their pow'rs

And hold our lives in mercy.- Oswald, I say!

Alb. Well, you may fear too far.

Gon. Safer than trust too far.

Let me still take away the harms I fear,

Not fear still to be taken. I know his heart.

What he hath utter'd I have writ my sister.

If she sustain him and his hundred knights,

When I have show'd th' unfitness-

Enter [Oswald the] Steward.

How now, Oswald?

What, have you writ that letter to my sister?

Osw. Yes, madam.

Gon. Take you some company, and away to horse!

Inform her full of my particular fear,

And thereto add such reasons of your own

As may compact it more. Get you gone,

And hasten your return. [Exit Oswald.] No, no, my lord!
This milky gentleness and course of yours,
Though I condemn it not, yet, under pardon,
You are much more at task for want of wisdom
Than prais'd for harmful mildness.
Alb. How far your eyes may pierce I cannot tell.
Striving to better, oft we mar what's well.
Gon. Nay then-
Alb. Well, well; th' event. Exeunt.

SCENE V.: COURT BEFORE THE DUKE OF ALBANY'S PALACE.

Enter Lear, Kent, and Fool.

Lear. Go you before to Gloucester with these letters. Acquaint my daughter no further with anything you know than comes from her demand out of the letter. If your diligence be not speedy, I shall be there afore you.

Kent. I will not sleep, my lord, till I have delivered your letter. Exit.

Fool. If a man's brains were in's heels, were't not in danger of kibes?

Lear. Ay, boy.

Fool. Then I prithee be merry. Thy wit shall ne'er go slip-shod.

Lear. Ha, ha, ha!

Fool. Shalt see thy other daughter will use thee kindly; for though she's as like this as a crab's like an apple, yet I can tell what I can tell.

Lear. What canst tell, boy?

Fool. She'll taste as like this as a crab does to a crab. Thou canst tell why one's nose stands i' th' middle on's face?

Lear. No.

Fool. Why, to keep one's eyes of either side's nose, that what a man cannot smell out, 'a may spy into.

Lear. I did her wrong.

Fool. Canst tell how an oyster makes his shell?

Lear. No.

Fool. Nor I neither; but I can tell why a snail has a house.

Lear. Why?

Fool. Why, to put's head in; not to give it away to his daughters, and leave his horns without a case.

Lear. I will forget my nature. So kind a father!- Be my horses ready?

Fool. Thy asses are gone about 'em. The reason why the seven stars are no moe than seven is a pretty reason.

Lear. Because they are not eight?

Fool. Yes indeed. Thou wouldst make a good fool.

Lear. To tak't again perforce! Monster ingratitude!

Fool. If thou wert my fool, nuncle, I'ld have thee beaten for being old before thy time.

Lear. How's that?

Fool. Thou shouldst not have been old till thou hadst been wise.

Lear. O, let me not be mad, not mad, sweet heaven!

Keep me in temper; I would not be mad!

[Enter a Gentleman.]

How now? Are the horses ready?

Gent. Ready, my lord.

Lear. Come, boy.

Fool. She that's a maid now, and laughs at my departure,

Shall not be a maid long, unless things be cut shorter

Exeunt.

ACT II. SCENE I.

A court within the Castle of the Earl of Gloucester.

Enter [Edmund the] Bastard and Curan, meeting.

Edm. Save thee, Curan.

Cur. And you, sir. I have been with your father, and given him notice that the Duke of Cornwall and Regan his Duchess will be here with him this night.

Edm. How comes that?

Cur. Nay, I know not. You have heard of the news abroad- I mean the whisper'd ones, for they are yet but ear-kissing arguments?

Edm. Not I. Pray you, what are they?

Cur. Have you heard of no likely wars toward 'twixt the two Dukes of Cornwall and Albany?

Edm. Not a word.

Cur. You may do, then, in time. Fare you well, sir.

Exit.

Edm. The Duke be here to-night? The better! best!
This weaves itself perforce into my business.
My father hath set guard to take my brother;
And I have one thing, of a queasy question,
Which I must act. Briefness and fortune, work!
Brother, a word! Descend! Brother, I say!

Enter Edgar.

My father watches. O sir, fly this place!
Intelligence is given where you are hid.
You have now the good advantage of the night.
Have you not spoken 'gainst the Duke of Cornwall?
He's coming hither; now, i' th' night, i' th' haste,
And Regan with him. Have you nothing said
Upon his party 'gainst the Duke of Albany?

Advise yourself.

Edg. I am sure on't, not a word.

Edm. I hear my father coming. Pardon me!

In cunning I must draw my sword upon you.

Draw, seem to defend yourself; now quit you well.-

Yield! Come before my father. Light, ho, here!

Fly, brother.- Torches, torches!- So farewell.

Exit Edgar.

Some blood drawn on me would beget opinion

Of my more fierce endeavour. [Stabs his arm.] I have seen drunkards

Do more than this in sport.- Father, father!-

Stop, stop! No help?

Enter Gloucester, and Servants with torches.

Glou. Now, Edmund, where's the villain?

Edm. Here stood he in the dark, his sharp sword out,

Mumbling of wicked charms, conjuring the moon

To stand 's auspicious mistress.

Glou. But where is he?

Edm. Look, sir, I bleed.

Glou. Where is the villain, Edmund?

Edm. Fled this way, sir. When by no means he could-

Glou. Pursue him, ho! Go after. [Exeunt some Servants].

By no means what?

Edm. Persuade me to the murther of your lordship;

But that I told him the revenging gods

'Gainst parricides did all their thunders bend;

Spoke with how manifold and strong a bond

The child was bound to th' father- sir, in fine,

Seeing how loathly opposite I stood

To his unnatural purpose, in fell motion
With his prepared sword he charges home
My unprovided body, lanch'd mine arm;
But when he saw my best alarum'd spirits,
Bold in the quarrel's right, rous'd to th' encounter,
Or whether gasted by the noise I made,
Full suddenly he fled.
Glou. Let him fly far.
Not in this land shall he remain uncaught;
And found- dispatch. The noble Duke my master,
My worthy arch and patron, comes to-night.
By his authority I will proclaim it
That he which find, him shall deserve our thanks,
Bringing the murderous caitiff to the stake;
He that conceals him, death.
Edm. When I dissuaded him from his intent
And found him pight to do it, with curst speech
I threaten'd to discover him. He replied,
'Thou unpossessing bastard, dost thou think,
If I would stand against thee, would the reposal
Of any trust, virtue, or worth in thee
Make thy words faith'd? No. What I should deny
(As this I would; ay, though thou didst produce
My very character), I'ld turn it all
To thy suggestion, plot, and damned practice;
And thou must make a dullard of the world,
If they not thought the profits of my death
Were very pregnant and potential spurs
To make thee seek it.'
Glou. Strong and fast'ned villain!

Would he deny his letter? I never got him.
Tucket within.
Hark, the Duke's trumpets! I know not why he comes.
All ports I'll bar; the villain shall not scape;
The Duke must grant me that. Besides, his picture
I will send far and near, that all the kingdom
May have due note of him, and of my land,
Loyal and natural boy, I'll work the means
To make thee capable.

Enter Cornwall, Regan, and Attendants.

Corn. How now, my noble friend? Since I came hither (Which I can call but now) I have heard strange news.

Reg. If it be true, all vengeance comes too short
Which can pursue th' offender. How dost, my lord?
Glou. O madam, my old heart is crack'd, it's crack'd!
Reg. What, did my father's godson seek your life?
He whom my father nam'd? Your Edgar?
Glou. O lady, lady, shame would have it hid!
Reg. Was he not companion with the riotous knights
That tend upon my father?
Glou. I know not, madam. 'Tis too bad, too bad!
Edm. Yes, madam, he was of that consort.
Reg. No marvel then though he were ill affected.
'Tis they have put him on the old man's death,
To have th' expense and waste of his revenues.
I have this present evening from my sister
Been well inform'd of them, and with such cautions
That, if they come to sojourn at my house,
I'll not be there.
Corn. Nor I, assure thee, Regan.

Edmund, I hear that you have shown your father
A childlike office.
Edm. 'Twas my duty, sir.
Glou. He did bewray his practice, and receiv'd
This hurt you see, striving to apprehend him.
Corn. Is he pursued?
Glou. Ay, my good lord.
Corn. If he be taken, he shall never more
Be fear'd of doing harm. Make your own purpose,
How in my strength you please. For you, Edmund,
Whose virtue and obedience doth this instant
So much commend itself, you shall be ours.
Natures of such deep trust we shall much need;
You we first seize on.
Edm. I shall serve you, sir,
Truly, however else.
Glou. For him I thank your Grace.
Corn. You know not why we came to visit you-
Reg. Thus out of season, threading dark-ey'd night.
Occasions, noble Gloucester, of some poise,
Wherein we must have use of your advice.
Our father he hath writ, so hath our sister,
Of differences, which I best thought it fit
To answer from our home. The several messengers
From hence attend dispatch. Our good old friend,
Lay comforts to your bosom, and bestow
Your needful counsel to our business,
Which craves the instant use.
Glou. I serve you, madam.
Your Graces are right welcome.

Exeunt. Flourish.

SCENE II.: BEFORE GLOUCESTER'S CASTLE.

Enter Kent and [Oswald the] Steward, Severally.

Osw. Good dawning to thee, friend. Art of this house?

Kent. Ay.

Osw. Where may we set our horses?

Kent. I' th' mire.

Osw. Prithee, if thou lov'st me, tell me.

Kent. I love thee not.

Osw. Why then, I care not for thee.

Kent. If I had thee in Lipsbury Pinfold, I would make thee care for me.

Osw. Why dost thou use me thus? I know thee not.

Kent. Fellow, I know thee.

Osw. What dost thou know me for?

Kent. A knave; a rascal; an eater of broken meats; a base, proud, shallow, beggarly, three-suited, hundred-pound, filthy, worsted-stocking knave; a lily-liver'd, action-taking, whoreson, glass-gazing, superserviceable, finical rogue; one-trunk-inheriting slave; one that wouldst be a bawd in way of good service, and art nothing but the composition of a knave, beggar, coward, pander, and the son and heir of a mongrel bitch; one whom I will beat into clamorous whining, if thou deny the least syllable of thy addition.

Osw. Why, what a monstrous fellow art thou, thus to rail on one that's neither known of thee nor knows thee!

Kent. What a brazen-fac'd varlet art thou, to deny thou knowest me!

Is it two days ago since I beat thee and tripp'd up thy heels before the King? [Draws his sword.] Draw, you rogue! for, though it be night, yet the moon shines. I'll make a sop o' th' moonshine o' you. Draw, you whoreson cullionly barbermonger! draw!

Osw. Away! I have nothing to do with thee.

Kent. Draw, you rascal! You come with letters against the King, and take Vanity the puppet's part against the royalty of her father.

Draw, you rogue, or I'll so carbonado your shanks! Draw, you rascal! Come your ways!

Osw. Help, ho! murther! help!

Kent. Strike, you slave! Stand, rogue! Stand, you neat slave!

Strike! [Beats him.]

Osw. Help, ho! murther! murther!

Enter Edmund, with his rapier drawn, Gloucester, Cornwall, Regan, Servants.

Edm. How now? What's the matter? Parts [them].

Kent. With you, goodman boy, an you please! Come, I'll flesh ye!

Come on, young master!

Glou. Weapons? arms? What's the matter here?

Corn. Keep peace, upon your lives!

He dies that strikes again. What is the matter?

Reg. The messengers from our sister and the King

Corn. What is your difference? Speak.

Osw. I am scarce in breath, my lord.

Kent. No marvel, you have so bestirr'd your valour. You cowardly rascal, nature disclaims in thee; a tailor made thee.

Corn. Thou art a strange fellow. A tailor make a man?

Kent. Ay, a tailor, sir. A stonecutter or a painter could not have made him so ill, though he had been but two hours at the trade.

Corn. Speak yet, how grew your quarrel?

Osw. This ancient ruffian, sir, whose life I have spar'd

At suit of his grey beard-

Kent. Thou whoreson zed! thou unnecessary letter! My lord, if you'll give me leave, I will tread this unbolted villain into mortar and daub the walls of a jakes with him. 'Spare my grey beard,' you wagtail?

Corn. Peace, sirrah!
You beastly knave, know you no reverence?
Kent. Yes, sir, but anger hath a privilege.
Corn. Why art thou angry?
Kent. That such a slave as this should wear a sword,
Who wears no honesty. Such smiling rogues as these,
Like rats, oft bite the holy cords atwain
Which are too intrinse t' unloose; smooth every passion
That in the natures of their lords rebel,
Bring oil to fire, snow to their colder moods;
Renege, affirm, and turn their halcyon beaks
With every gale and vary of their masters,
Knowing naught (like dogs) but following.
A plague upon your epileptic visage!
Smile you my speeches, as I were a fool?
Goose, an I had you upon Sarum Plain,
I'ld drive ye cackling home to Camelot.
Corn. What, art thou mad, old fellow?
Glou. How fell you out? Say that.
Kent. No contraries hold more antipathy
Than I and such a knave.
Corn. Why dost thou call him knave? What is his fault?
Kent. His countenance likes me not.
Corn. No more perchance does mine, or his, or hers.
Kent. Sir, 'tis my occupation to be plain.
I have seen better faces in my time
Than stands on any shoulder that I see
Before me at this instant.

Corn. This is some fellow
Who, having been prais'd for bluntness, doth affect
A saucy roughness, and constrains the garb
Quite from his nature. He cannot flatter, he!
An honest mind and plain- he must speak truth!
An they will take it, so; if not, he's plain.
These kind of knaves I know which in this plainness
Harbour more craft and more corrupter ends
Than twenty silly-ducking observants
That stretch their duties nicely.
Kent. Sir, in good faith, in sincere verity,
Under th' allowance of your great aspect,
Whose influence, like the wreath of radiant fire
On flickering Phoebus' front-
Corn. What mean'st by this?

Kent. To go out of my dialect, which you discommend so much. I know, sir, I am no flatterer. He that beguil'd you in a plain accent was a plain knave, which, for my part, I will not be, though I should win your displeasure to entreat me to't.

Corn. What was th' offence you gave him?
Osw. I never gave him any.
It pleas'd the King his master very late
To strike at me, upon his misconstruction;
When he, conjunct, and flattering his displeasure,
Tripp'd me behind; being down, insulted, rail'd
And put upon him such a deal of man
That worthied him, got praises of the King
For him attempting who was self-subdu'd;
And, in the fleshment of this dread exploit,
Drew on me here again.

Kent. None of these rogues and cowards
But Ajax is their fool.
Corn. Fetch forth the stocks!
You stubborn ancient knave, you reverent braggart,
We'll teach you-
Kent. Sir, I am too old to learn.
Call not your stocks for me. I serve the King;
On whose employment I was sent to you.
You shall do small respect, show too bold malice
Against the grace and person of my master,
Stocking his messenger.
Corn. Fetch forth the stocks! As I have life and honour,
There shall he sit till noon.
Reg. Till noon? Till night, my lord, and all night too!
Kent. Why, madam, if I were your father's dog,
You should not use me so.
Reg. Sir, being his knave, I will.
Corn. This is a fellow of the selfsame colour
Our sister speaks of. Come, bring away the stocks!
Stocks brought out.
Glou. Let me beseech your Grace not to do so.
His fault is much, and the good King his master
Will check him for't. Your purpos'd low correction
Is such as basest and contemn'dest wretches
For pilf'rings and most common trespasses
Are punish'd with. The King must take it ill
That he, so slightly valued in his messenger,
Should have him thus restrain'd.
Corn. I'll answer that.

Reg. My sister may receive it much more worse,
To have her gentleman abus'd, assaulted,
For following her affairs. Put in his legs.-
[Kent is put in the stocks.]
Come, my good lord, away.
Exeunt [all but Gloucester and Kent].
Glou. I am sorry for thee, friend. 'Tis the Duke's pleasure,
Whose disposition, all the world well knows,
Will not be rubb'd nor stopp'd. I'll entreat for thee.
Kent. Pray do not, sir. I have watch'd and travell'd hard.
Some time I shall sleep out, the rest I'll whistle.
A good man's fortune may grow out at heels.
Give you good morrow!
Glou. The Duke 's to blame in this; 'twill be ill taken.
Exit.
Kent. Good King, that must approve the common saw,
Thou out of heaven's benediction com'st
To the warm sun!
Approach, thou beacon to this under globe,
That by thy comfortable beams I may
Peruse this letter. Nothing almost sees miracles
But misery. I know 'tis from Cordelia,
Who hath most fortunately been inform'd
Of my obscured course- and [reads] 'shall find time
From this enormous state, seeking to give
Losses their remedies'- All weary and o'erwatch'd,
Take vantage, heavy eyes, not to behold
This shameful lodging.
Fortune, good night; smile once more, turn thy wheel.
Sleeps.

SCENE III.: THE OPEN COUNTRY.

Enter Edgar.

Edg. I heard myself proclaim'd,
And by the happy hollow of a tree
Escap'd the hunt. No port is free, no place
That guard and most unusual vigilance
Does not attend my taking. Whiles I may scape,
I will preserve myself; and am bethought
To take the basest and most poorest shape
That ever penury, in contempt of man,
Brought near to beast. My face I'll grime with filth,
Blanket my loins, elf all my hair in knots,
And with presented nakedness outface
The winds and persecutions of the sky.
The country gives me proof and precedent
Of Bedlam beggars, who, with roaring voices,
Strike in their numb'd and mortified bare arms
Pins, wooden pricks, nails, sprigs of rosemary;
And with this horrible object, from low farms,
Poor pelting villages, sheepcotes, and mills,
Sometime with lunatic bans, sometime with prayers,
Enforce their charity. 'Poor Turlygod! poor Tom!'
That's something yet! Edgar I nothing am.
Exit.

SCENE IV.: BEFORE GLOUCESTER'S CASTLE; KENT IN THE STOCKS.

Enter Lear, Fool, and Gentleman.

Lear. 'Tis strange that they should so depart from home,
And not send back my messenger.
Gent. As I learn'd,

The night before there was no purpose in them
Of this remove.
Kent. Hail to thee, noble master!
Lear. Ha!
Mak'st thou this shame thy pastime?
Kent. No, my lord.

Fool. Ha, ha! look! he wears cruel garters. Horses are tied by the head, dogs and bears by th' neck, monkeys by th' loins, and men by th' legs. When a man's over-lusty at legs, then he wears wooden nether-stocks.

Lear. What's he that hath so much thy place mistook
To set thee here?
Kent. It is both he and she-
Your son and daughter.
Lear. No.
Kent. Yes.
Lear. No, I say.
Kent. I say yea.
Lear. No, no, they would not!
Kent. Yes, they have.
Lear. By Jupiter, I swear no!
Kent. By Juno, I swear ay!
Lear. They durst not do't;
They would not, could not do't. 'Tis worse than murther
To do upon respect such violent outrage.
Resolve me with all modest haste which way
Thou mightst deserve or they impose this usage,
Coming from us.
Kent. My lord, when at their home
I did commend your Highness' letters to them,

Ere I was risen from the place that show'd
My duty kneeling, came there a reeking post,
Stew'd in his haste, half breathless, panting forth
From Goneril his mistress salutations;
Deliver'd letters, spite of intermission,
Which presently they read; on whose contents,
They summon'd up their meiny, straight took horse,
Commanded me to follow and attend
The leisure of their answer, gave me cold looks,
And meeting here the other messenger,
Whose welcome I perceiv'd had poison'd mine-
Being the very fellow which of late
Display'd so saucily against your Highness-
Having more man than wit about me, drew.
He rais'd the house with loud and coward cries.
Your son and daughter found this trespass worth
The shame which here it suffers.
Fool. Winter's not gone yet, if the wild geese fly that way.
Fathers that wear rags
Do make their children blind;
But fathers that bear bags
Shall see their children kind.
Fortune, that arrant whore,
Ne'er turns the key to th' poor.
But for all this, thou shalt have as many dolours for thy daughters as thou canst tell in a year.
Lear. O, how this mother swells up toward my heart!
Hysterica passio! Down, thou climbing sorrow!
Thy element's below! Where is this daughter?
Kent. With the Earl, sir, here within.

Lear. Follow me not;

Stay here.

Exit.

Gent Made you no more offence but what you speak of?

Kent. None.

How chance the King comes with so small a number?

Fool. An thou hadst been set i' th' stocks for that question,

thou'dst well deserv'd it.

Kent. Why, fool?

Fool. We'll set thee to school to an ant, to teach thee there's no labouring i' th' winter. All that follow their noses are led by their eyes but blind men, and there's not a nose among twenty but can smell him that's stinking. Let go thy hold when a great wheel runs down a hill, lest it break thy neck with following it; but the great one that goes upward, let him draw thee after.

When a wise man gives thee better counsel, give me mine again. I would have none but knaves follow it, since a fool gives it.

That sir which serves and seeks for gain,

And follows but for form,

Will pack when it begins to rain

And leave thee in the storm.

But I will tarry; the fool will stay,

And let the wise man fly.

The knave turns fool that runs away;

The fool no knave, perdy.

Kent. Where learn'd you this, fool?

Fool. Not i' th' stocks, fool.

Enter Lear and Gloucester

Lear. Deny to speak with me? They are sick? they are weary?

They have travell'd all the night? Mere fetches-

The images of revolt and flying off!

Fetch me a better answer.
Glou. My dear lord,
You know the fiery quality of the Duke,
How unremovable and fix'd he is
In his own course.
Lear. Vengeance! plague! death! confusion!
Fiery? What quality? Why, Gloucester, Gloucester,
I'ld speak with the Duke of Cornwall and his wife.
Glou. Well, my good lord, I have inform'd them so.
Lear. Inform'd them? Dost thou understand me, man?
Glou. Ay, my good lord.
Lear. The King would speak with Cornwall; the dear father
Would with his daughter speak, commands her service.
Are they inform'd of this? My breath and blood!
Fiery? the fiery Duke? Tell the hot Duke that-
No, but not yet! May be he is not well.
Infirmity doth still neglect all office
Whereto our health is bound. We are not ourselves
When nature, being oppress'd, commands the mind
To suffer with the body. I'll forbear;
And am fallen out with my more headier will,
To take the indispos'd and sickly fit
For the sound man.- Death on my state! Wherefore
Should be sit here? This act persuades me
That this remotion of the Duke and her
Is practice only. Give me my servant forth.
Go tell the Duke and 's wife I'ld speak with them-
Now, presently. Bid them come forth and hear me,
Or at their chamber door I'll beat the drum
Till it cry sleep to death.

Glou. I would have all well betwixt you.

Exit.

Lear. O me, my heart, my rising heart! But down!

Fool. Cry to it, nuncle, as the cockney did to the eels when she put 'em i' th' paste alive. She knapp'd 'em o' th' coxcombs with a stick and cried 'Down, wantons, down!' 'Twas her brother that, in pure kindness to his horse, buttered his hay.

Enter Cornwall, Regan, Gloucester, Servants.

Lear. Good morrow to you both.

Corn. Hail to your Grace!

Kent here set at liberty.

Reg. I am glad to see your Highness.

Lear. Regan, I think you are; I know what reason
I have to think so. If thou shouldst not be glad,
I would divorce me from thy mother's tomb,
Sepulchring an adultress. [To Kent] O, are you free?
Some other time for that.- Beloved Regan,
Thy sister's naught. O Regan, she hath tied
Sharp-tooth'd unkindness, like a vulture, here!
[Lays his hand on his heart.]
I can scarce speak to thee. Thou'lt not believe
With how deprav'd a quality- O Regan!

Reg. I pray you, sir, take patience. I have hope
You less know how to value her desert
Than she to scant her duty.

Lear. Say, how is that?

Reg. I cannot think my sister in the least
Would fail her obligation. If, sir, perchance
She have restrain'd the riots of your followers,
'Tis on such ground, and to such wholesome end,

As clears her from all blame.
Lear. My curses on her!
Reg. O, sir, you are old!
Nature in you stands on the very verge
Of her confine. You should be rul'd, and led
By some discretion that discerns your state
Better than you yourself. Therefore I pray you
That to our sister you do make return;
Say you have wrong'd her, sir.
Lear. Ask her forgiveness?
Do you but mark how this becomes the house:
'Dear daughter, I confess that I am old. [Kneels.]
Age is unnecessary. On my knees I beg
That you'll vouchsafe me raiment, bed, and food.'
Reg. Good sir, no more! These are unsightly tricks.
Return you to my sister.
Lear. [rises] Never, Regan!
She hath abated me of half my train;
Look'd black upon me; struck me with her tongue,
Most serpent-like, upon the very heart.
All the stor'd vengeances of heaven fall
On her ingrateful top! Strike her young bones,
You taking airs, with lameness!
Corn. Fie, sir, fie!
Lear. You nimble lightnings, dart your blinding flames
Into her scornful eyes! Infect her beauty,
You fen-suck'd fogs, drawn by the pow'rful sun,
To fall and blast her pride!
Reg. O the blest gods! so will you wish on me
When the rash mood is on.

Lear. No, Regan, thou shalt never have my curse.
Thy tender-hefted nature shall not give
Thee o'er to harshness. Her eyes are fierce; but thine
Do comfort, and not burn. 'Tis not in thee
To grudge my pleasures, to cut off my train,
To bandy hasty words, to scant my sizes,
And, in conclusion, to oppose the bolt
Against my coming in. Thou better know'st
The offices of nature, bond of childhood,
Effects of courtesy, dues of gratitude.
Thy half o' th' kingdom hast thou not forgot,
Wherein I thee endow'd.
Reg. Good sir, to th' purpose.
Tucket within.
Lear. Who put my man i' th' stocks?
Corn. What trumpet's that?
Reg. I know't- my sister's. This approves her letter,
That she would soon be here.

Enter [Oswald the] Steward.

Is your lady come?
Lear. This is a slave, whose easy-borrowed pride
Dwells in the fickle grace of her he follows.
Out, varlet, from my sight!
Corn. What means your Grace?

Enter Goneril.

Lear. Who stock'd my servant? Regan, I have good hope
Thou didst not know on't.- Who comes here? O heavens!
If you do love old men, if your sweet sway
Allow obedience- if yourselves are old,

Make it your cause! Send down, and take my part!
[To Goneril] Art not asham'd to look upon this beard?-
O Regan, wilt thou take her by the hand?
Gon. Why not by th' hand, sir? How have I offended?
All's not offence that indiscretion finds
And dotage terms so.
Lear. O sides, you are too tough!
Will you yet hold? How came my man i' th' stocks?
Corn. I set him there, sir; but his own disorders
Deserv'd much less advancement.
Lear. You? Did you?
Reg. I pray you, father, being weak, seem so.
If, till the expiration of your month,
You will return and sojourn with my sister,
Dismissing half your train, come then to me.
I am now from home, and out of that provision
Which shall be needful for your entertainment.
Lear. Return to her, and fifty men dismiss'd?
No, rather I abjure all roofs, and choose
To wage against the enmity o' th' air,
To be a comrade with the wolf and owl-
Necessity's sharp pinch! Return with her?
Why, the hot-blooded France, that dowerless took
Our youngest born, I could as well be brought
To knee his throne, and, squire-like, pension beg
To keep base life afoot. Return with her?
Persuade me rather to be slave and sumpter
To this detested groom. [Points at Oswald.]
Gon. At your choice, sir.
Lear. I prithee, daughter, do not make me mad.

I will not trouble thee, my child; farewell.
We'll no more meet, no more see one another.
But yet thou art my flesh, my blood, my daughter;
Or rather a disease that's in my flesh,
Which I must needs call mine. Thou art a boil,
A plague sore, an embossed carbuncle
In my corrupted blood. But I'll not chide thee.
Let shame come when it will, I do not call it.
I do not bid the Thunder-bearer shoot
Nor tell tales of thee to high-judging Jove.
Mend when thou canst; be better at thy leisure;
I can be patient, I can stay with Regan,
I and my hundred knights.
Reg. Not altogether so.
I look'd not for you yet, nor am provided
For your fit welcome. Give ear, sir, to my sister;
For those that mingle reason with your passion
Must be content to think you old, and so-
But she knows what she does.
Lear. Is this well spoken?
Reg. I dare avouch it, sir. What, fifty followers?
Is it not well? What should you need of more?
Yea, or so many, sith that both charge and danger
Speak 'gainst so great a number? How in one house
Should many people, under two commands,
Hold amity? 'Tis hard; almost impossible.
Gon. Why might not you, my lord, receive attendance
From those that she calls servants, or from mine?
Reg. Why not, my lord? If then they chanc'd to slack ye,
We could control them. If you will come to me

(For now I spy a danger), I entreat you
To bring but five-and-twenty. To no more
Will I give place or notice.
Lear. I gave you all-
Reg. And in good time you gave it!
Lear. Made you my guardians, my depositaries;
But kept a reservation to be followed
With such a number. What, must I come to you
With five-and-twenty, Regan? Said you so?
Reg. And speak't again my lord. No more with me.
Lear. Those wicked creatures yet do look well-favour'd
When others are more wicked; not being the worst
Stands in some rank of praise. [To Goneril] I'll go with thee.
Thy fifty yet doth double five-and-twenty,
And thou art twice her love.
Gon. Hear, me, my lord.
What need you five-and-twenty, ten, or five,
To follow in a house where twice so many
Have a command to tend you?
Reg. What need one?
Lear. O, reason not the need! Our basest beggars
Are in the poorest thing superfluous.
Allow not nature more than nature needs,
Man's life is cheap as beast's. Thou art a lady:
If only to go warm were gorgeous,
Why, nature needs not what thou gorgeous wear'st
Which scarcely keeps thee warm. But, for true need-
You heavens, give me that patience, patience I need!
You see me here, you gods, a poor old man,
As full of grief as age; wretched in both.

If it be you that stirs these daughters' hearts
Against their father, fool me not so much
To bear it tamely; touch me with noble anger,
And let not women's weapons, water drops,
Stain my man's cheeks! No, you unnatural hags!
I will have such revenges on you both
That all the world shall- I will do such things-
What they are yet, I know not; but they shall be
The terrors of the earth! You think I'll weep.
No, I'll not weep.
I have full cause of weeping, but this heart
Shall break into a hundred thousand flaws
Or ere I'll weep. O fool, I shall go mad!
Exeunt Lear, Gloucester, Kent, and Fool. Storm and tempest.
Corn. Let us withdraw; 'twill be a storm.
Reg. This house is little; the old man and 's people
Cannot be well bestow'd.
Gon. 'Tis his own blame; hath put himself from rest
And must needs taste his folly.
Reg. For his particular, I'll receive him gladly,
But not one follower.
Gon. So am I purpos'd.
Where is my Lord of Gloucester?
Corn. Followed the old man forth.

Enter Gloucester.

He is return'd.
Glou. The King is in high rage.
Corn. Whither is he going?
Glou. He calls to horse, but will I know not whither.

Corn. 'Tis best to give him way; he leads himself.
Gon. My lord, entreat him by no means to stay.
Glou. Alack, the night comes on, and the bleak winds
Do sorely ruffle. For many miles about
There's scarce a bush.
Reg. O, sir, to wilful men
The injuries that they themselves procure
Must be their schoolmasters. Shut up your doors.
He is attended with a desperate train,
And what they may incense him to, being apt
To have his ear abus'd, wisdom bids fear.
Corn. Shut up your doors, my lord: 'tis a wild night.
My Regan counsels well. Come out o' th' storm. [Exeunt.]

ACT III. SCENE I.

A heath.

Storm still. Enter Kent and a Gentleman at several doors.

Kent. Who's there, besides foul weather?
Gent. One minded like the weather, most unquietly.
Kent. I know you. Where's the King?
Gent. Contending with the fretful elements;
Bids the wind blow the earth into the sea,
Or swell the curled waters 'bove the main,
That things might change or cease; tears his white hair,
Which the impetuous blasts, with eyeless rage,
Catch in their fury and make nothing of;
Strives in his little world of man to outscorn
The to-and-fro-conflicting wind and rain.
This night, wherein the cub-drawn bear would couch,
The lion and the belly-pinched wolf

Keep their fur dry, unbonneted he runs,
And bids what will take all.
Kent. But who is with him?
Gent. None but the fool, who labours to outjest
His heart-struck injuries.
Kent. Sir, I do know you,
And dare upon the warrant of my note
Commend a dear thing to you. There is division
(Although as yet the face of it be cover'd
With mutual cunning) 'twixt Albany and Cornwall;
Who have (as who have not, that their great stars
Thron'd and set high?) servants, who seem no less,
Which are to France the spies and speculations
Intelligent of our state. What hath been seen,
Either in snuffs and packings of the Dukes,
Or the hard rein which both of them have borne
Against the old kind King, or something deeper,
Whereof, perchance, these are but furnishings-
But, true it is, from France there comes a power
Into this scattered kingdom, who already,
Wise in our negligence, have secret feet
In some of our best ports and are at point
To show their open banner. Now to you:
If on my credit you dare build so far
To make your speed to Dover, you shall find
Some that will thank you, making just report
Of how unnatural and bemadding sorrow
The King hath cause to plain.
I am a gentleman of blood and breeding,
And from some knowledge and assurance offer

This office to you.
Gent. I will talk further with you.
Kent. No, do not.
For confirmation that I am much more
Than my out-wall, open this purse and take
What it contains. If you shall see Cordelia
(As fear not but you shall), show her this ring,
And she will tell you who your fellow is
That yet you do not know. Fie on this storm!
I will go seek the King.
Gent. Give me your hand. Have you no more to say?
Kent. Few words, but, to effect, more than all yet:
That, when we have found the King (in which your pain
That way, I'll this), he that first lights on him
Holla the other.
Exeunt [severally].

SCENE II. : ANOTHER PART OF THE HEATH.

Storm still. Enter Lear and Fool.

Lear. Blow, winds, and crack your cheeks! rage! blow!
You cataracts and hurricanoes, spout
Till you have drench'd our steeples, drown'd the cocks!
You sulph'rous and thought-executing fires,
Vaunt-couriers to oak-cleaving thunderbolts,
Singe my white head! And thou, all-shaking thunder,
Strike flat the thick rotundity o' th' world,
Crack Nature's moulds, all germains spill at once,
That makes ingrateful man!

Fool. O nuncle, court holy water in a dry house is better than this rain water out o' door. Good nuncle, in, and ask thy daughters blessing! Here's a night pities nether wise men nor fools.

Lear. Rumble thy bellyful! Spit, fire! spout, rain!
Nor rain, wind, thunder, fire are my daughters.
I tax not you, you elements, with unkindness.
I never gave you kingdom, call'd you children,
You owe me no subscription. Then let fall
Your horrible pleasure. Here I stand your slave,
A poor, infirm, weak, and despis'd old man.
But yet I call you servile ministers,
That will with two pernicious daughters join
Your high-engender'd battles 'gainst a head
So old and white as this! O! O! 'tis foul!

Fool. He that has a house to put 's head in has a good head-piece.

The codpiece that will house
Before the head has any,
The head and he shall louse:
So beggars marry many.
The man that makes his toe
What he his heart should make
Shall of a corn cry woe,
And turn his sleep to wake.

For there was never yet fair woman but she made mouths in a glass.

Enter Kent.

Lear. No, I will be the pattern of all patience;
I will say nothing.

Kent. Who's there?

Fool. Marry, here's grace and a codpiece; that's a wise man and a fool.

Kent. Alas, sir, arc you here? Things that love night
Love not such nights as these. The wrathful skies
Gallow the very wanderers of the dark
And make them keep their caves. Since I was man,
Such sheets of fire, such bursts of horrid thunder,
Such groans of roaring wind and rain, I never
Remember to have heard. Man's nature cannot carry
Th' affliction nor the fear.
Lear. Let the great gods,
That keep this dreadful pudder o'er our heads,
Find out their enemies now. Tremble, thou wretch,
That hast within thee undivulged crimes
Unwhipp'd of justice. Hide thee, thou bloody hand;
Thou perjur'd, and thou simular man of virtue
That art incestuous. Caitiff, in pieces shake
That under covert and convenient seeming
Hast practis'd on man's life. Close pent-up guilts,
Rive your concealing continents, and cry
These dreadful summoners grace. I am a man
More sinn'd against than sinning.
Kent. Alack, bareheaded?
Gracious my lord, hard by here is a hovel;
Some friendship will it lend you 'gainst the tempest.
Repose you there, whilst I to this hard house
(More harder than the stones whereof 'tis rais'd,
Which even but now, demanding after you,
Denied me to come in) return, and force
Their scanted courtesy.
Lear. My wits begin to turn.

Come on, my boy. How dost, my boy? Art cold?
I am cold myself. Where is this straw, my fellow?
The art of our necessities is strange,
That can make vile things precious. Come, your hovel.
Poor fool and knave, I have one part in my heart
That's sorry yet for thee.
Fool. [sings]
He that has and a little tiny wit-
With hey, ho, the wind and the rain-
Must make content with his fortunes fit,
For the rain it raineth every day.
Lear. True, my good boy. Come, bring us to this hovel.
Exeunt [Lear and Kent].

Fool. This is a brave night to cool a courtesan. I'll speak a prophecy ere I go:

When priests are more in word than matter;
When brewers mar their malt with water;
When nobles are their tailors' tutors,
No heretics burn'd, but wenches' suitors;
When every case in law is right,
No squire in debt nor no poor knight;
When slanders do not live in tongues,
Nor cutpurses come not to throngs;
When usurers tell their gold i' th' field,
And bawds and whores do churches build:
Then shall the realm of Albion
Come to great confusion.
Then comes the time, who lives to see't,
That going shall be us'd with feet.
This prophecy Merlin shall make, for I live before his time.
Exit.

SCENE III.: GLOUCESTER'S CASTLE.

Enter Gloucester and Edmund.

Glou. Alack, alack, Edmund, I like not this unnatural dealing! When I desir'd their leave that I might pity him, they took from me the use of mine own house, charg'd me on pain of perpetual displeasure neither to speak of him, entreat for him, nor any way sustain him.

Edm. Most savage and unnatural!

Glou. Go to; say you nothing. There is division betwixt the Dukes, and a worse matter than that. I have received a letter this night- 'tis dangerous to be spoken- I have lock'd the letter in my closet. These injuries the King now bears will be revenged home; there's part of a power already footed; we must incline to the King. I will seek him and privily relieve him. Go you and maintain talk with the Duke, that my charity be not of him perceived. If he ask for me, I am ill and gone to bed. Though I die for't, as no less is threat'ned me, the King my old master must be relieved. There is some strange thing toward, Edmund.

Pray you be careful.

Exit.

Edm. This courtesy, forbid thee, shall the Duke

Instantly know, and of that letter too.

This seems a fair deserving, and must draw me

That which my father loses- no less than all.

The younger rises when the old doth fall.

Exit.

SCENE IV.: THE HEATH. BEFORE A HOVEL.

Storm still. Enter Lear, Kent, and Fool.

Kent. Here is the place, my lord. Good my lord, enter.

The tyranny of the open night 's too rough

For nature to endure.

Lear. Let me alone.

Kent. Good my lord, enter here.
Lear. Wilt break my heart?
Kent. I had rather break mine own. Good my lord, enter.
Lear. Thou think'st 'tis much that this contentious storm
Invades us to the skin. So 'tis to thee;
But where the greater malady is fix'd,
The lesser is scarce felt. Thou'dst shun a bear;
But if thy flight lay toward the raging sea,
Thou'dst meet the bear i' th' mouth. When the mind's free,
The body's delicate. The tempest in my mind
Doth from my senses take all feeling else
Save what beats there. Filial ingratitude!
Is it not as this mouth should tear this hand
For lifting food to't? But I will punish home!
No, I will weep no more. In such a night
To shut me out! Pour on; I will endure.
In such a night as this! O Regan, Goneril!
Your old kind father, whose frank heart gave all!
O, that way madness lies; let me shun that!
No more of that.
Kent. Good my lord, enter here.
Lear. Prithee go in thyself; seek thine own ease.
This tempest will not give me leave to ponder
On things would hurt me more. But I'll go in.
[To the Fool] In, boy; go first.- You houseless poverty-
Nay, get thee in. I'll pray, and then I'll sleep.
Exit [Fool].
Poor naked wretches, wheresoe'er you are,
That bide the pelting of this pitiless storm,
How shall your houseless heads and unfed sides,

Your loop'd and window'd raggedness, defend you
From seasons such as these? O, I have ta'en
Too little care of this! Take physic, pomp;
Expose thyself to feel what wretches feel,
That thou mayst shake the superflux to them
And show the heavens more just.

Edg. [within] Fathom and half, fathom and half! Poor Tom!

Enter Fool [from the hovel].

Fool. Come not in here, nuncle, here's a spirit. Help me, help me!

Kent. Give me thy hand. Who's there?

Fool. A spirit, a spirit! He says his name's poor Tom.

Kent. What art thou that dost grumble there i' th' straw?
Come forth.

Enter Edgar [disguised as a madman].

Edg. Away! the foul fiend follows me! Through the sharp hawthorn blows the cold wind. Humh! go to thy cold bed, and warm thee.

Lear. Hast thou given all to thy two daughters, and art thou come to this?

Edg. Who gives anything to poor Tom? whom the foul fiend hath led through fire and through flame, through ford and whirlpool, o'er bog and quagmire; that hath laid knives under his pillow and halters in his pew, set ratsbane by his porridge, made him proud of heart, to ride on a bay trotting horse over four-inch'd bridges, to course his own shadow for a traitor. Bless thy five wits! Tom 's acold. O, do de, do de, do de. Bless thee from whirlwinds, star-blasting, and taking! Do poor Tom some charity, whom the foul fiend vexes. There could I have him now- and there- and there again- and there!

Storm still.

Lear. What, have his daughters brought him to this pass?

Couldst thou save nothing? Didst thou give 'em all?
Fool. Nay, he reserv'd a blanket, else we had been all sham'd.
Lear. Now all the plagues that in the pendulous air
Hang fated o'er men's faults light on thy daughters!
Kent. He hath no daughters, sir.
Lear. Death, traitor! nothing could have subdu'd nature
To such a lowness but his unkind daughters.
Is it the fashion that discarded fathers
Should have thus little mercy on their flesh?
Judicious punishment! 'Twas this flesh begot
Those pelican daughters.
Edg. Pillicock sat on Pillicock's Hill. 'Allow, 'allow, loo, loo!
Fool. This cold night will turn us all to fools and madmen.

Edg. Take heed o' th' foul fiend; obey thy parents: keep thy word justly; swear not; commit not with man's sworn spouse; set not thy sweet heart on proud array. Tom 's acold.

Lear. What hast thou been?

Edg. A servingman, proud in heart and mind; that curl'd my hair, wore gloves in my cap; serv'd the lust of my mistress' heart and did the act of darkness with her; swore as many oaths as I spake words, and broke them in the sweet face of heaven; one that slept in the contriving of lust, and wak'd to do it. Wine lov'd I deeply, dice dearly; and in woman out-paramour'd the Turk.

False of heart, light of ear, bloody of hand; hog in sloth, fox in stealth, wolf in greediness, dog in madness, lion in prey.

Let not the creaking of shoes nor the rustling of silks betray thy poor heart to woman. Keep thy foot out of brothel, thy hand out of placket, thy pen from lender's book, and defy the foul fiend. Still through the hawthorn blows the cold wind; says suum, mun, hey, no, nonny. Dolphin my boy, my boy, sessa! let him trot by.

Storm still.

Lear. Why, thou wert better in thy grave than to answer with thy uncover'd body this extremity of the skies. Is man no more than this? Consider him well. Thou ow'st the worm no silk, the beast no hide, the sheep no wool, the cat no perfume. Ha! Here's three on's are sophisticated! Thou art the thing itself; unaccommodated man is no more but such a poor, bare, forked animal as thou art. Off, off, you lendings! Come, unbutton here.

[Tears at his clothes.]

Fool. Prithee, nuncle, be contented! 'Tis a naughty night to swim in. Now a little fire in a wild field were like an old lecher's heart-a small spark, all the rest on's body cold. Look, here comes a walking fire.

Enter Gloucester with a torch.

Edg. This is the foul fiend Flibbertigibbet. He begins at curfew, and walks till the first cock. He gives the web and the pin, squints the eye, and makes the harelip; mildews the white wheat, and hurts the poor creature of earth. Saint Withold footed thrice the 'old;

He met the nightmare, and her nine fold;

Bid her alight

And her troth plight,

And aroint thee, witch, aroint thee!

Kent. How fares your Grace?

Lear. What's he?

Kent. Who's there? What is't you seek?

Glou. What are you there? Your names?

Edg. Poor Tom, that eats the swimming frog, the toad, the todpole, the wall-newt and the water; that in the fury of his heart, when the foul fiend rages, eats cow-dung for sallets, swallows the old rat and the ditch-dog, drinks the green mantle of the standing pool; who is whipp'd from tithing to tithing, and stock-punish'd and imprison'd; who hath had three suits to his back, six shirts to his body, horse to ride, and weapons to wear; But mice and rats, and such small deer,

Have been Tom's food for seven long year.
Beware my follower. Peace, Smulkin! peace, thou fiend!
Glou. What, hath your Grace no better company?
Edg. The prince of darkness is a gentleman!
Modo he's call'd, and Mahu.
Glou. Our flesh and blood is grown so vile, my lord,
That it doth hate what gets it.
Edg. Poor Tom 's acold.
Glou. Go in with me. My duty cannot suffer
T' obey in all your daughters' hard commands.
Though their injunction be to bar my doors
And let this tyrannous night take hold upon you,
Yet have I ventur'd to come seek you out
And bring you where both fire and food is ready.
Lear. First let me talk with this philosopher.
What is the cause of thunder?
Kent. Good my lord, take his offer; go into th' house.
Lear. I'll talk a word with this same learned Theban.
What is your study?
Edg. How to prevent the fiend and to kill vermin.
Lear. Let me ask you one word in private.
Kent. Importune him once more to go, my lord.
His wits begin t' unsettle.
Glou. Canst thou blame him?
Storm still.
His daughters seek his death. Ah, that good Kent!
He said it would be thus- poor banish'd man!
Thou say'st the King grows mad: I'll tell thee, friend,

I am almost mad myself. I had a son,
Now outlaw'd from my blood. He sought my life
But lately, very late. I lov'd him, friend-
No father his son dearer. True to tell thee,
The grief hath craz'd my wits. What a night 's this!
I do beseech your Grace-
Lear. O, cry you mercy, sir.
Noble philosopher, your company.
Edg. Tom's acold.
Glou. In, fellow, there, into th' hovel; keep thee warm.
Lear. Come, let's in all.
Kent. This way, my lord.
Lear. With him!
I will keep still with my philosopher.
Kent. Good my lord, soothe him; let him take the fellow.
Glou. Take him you on.
Kent. Sirrah, come on; go along with us.
Lear. Come, good Athenian.
Glou. No words, no words! hush.
Edg. Child Rowland to the dark tower came;
His word was still
Fie, foh, and fum!
I smell the blood of a British man.
Exeunt.

SCENE V.: GLOUCESTER'S CASTLE.

Enter Cornwall and Edmund.

Corn. I will have my revenge ere I depart his house.

Edm. How, my lord, I may be censured, that nature thus gives way to loyalty, something fears me to think of.

Corn. I now perceive it was not altogether your brother's evil disposition made him seek his death; but a provoking merit, set awork by a reproveable badness in himself.

Edm. How malicious is my fortune that I must repent to be just!

This is the letter he spoke of, which approves him an intelligent party to the advantages of France. O heavens! that this treason were not- or not I the detector!

Corn. Go with me to the Duchess.

Edm. If the matter of this paper be certain, you have mighty business in hand.

Corn. True or false, it hath made thee Earl of Gloucester.

Seek out where thy father is, that he may be ready for our apprehension.

Edm. [aside] If I find him comforting the King, it will stuff his suspicion more fully.- I will persever in my course of loyalty, though the conflict be sore between that and my blood.

Corn. I will lay trust upon thee, and thou shalt find a dearer father in my love.

Exeunt.

SCENE VI.: A FARMHOUSE NEAR GLOUCESTER'S CASTLE.

Enter Gloucester, Lear, Kent, Fool, and Edgar.

Glou. Here is better than the open air; take it thankfully. I will piece out the comfort with what addition I can. I will not be long from you.

Kent. All the power of his wits have given way to his impatience.

The gods reward your kindness!

Exit [Gloucester].

Edg. Frateretto calls me, and tells me Nero is an angler in the lake of darkness. Pray, innocent, and beware the foul fiend.

Fool. Prithee, nuncle, tell me whether a madman be a gentleman or a yeoman.

Lear. A king, a king!

Fool. No, he's a yeoman that has a gentleman to his son; for he's a mad yeoman that sees his son a gentleman before him.

Lear. To have a thousand with red burning spits

Come hizzing in upon 'em-

Edg. The foul fiend bites my back.

Fool. He's mad that trusts in the tameness of a wolf, a horse's health, a boy's love, or a whore's oath.

Lear. It shall be done; I will arraign them straight.

[To Edgar] Come, sit thou here, most learned justicer.

[To the Fool] Thou, sapient sir, sit here. Now, you she-foxes!

Edg. Look, where he stands and glares! Want'st thou eyes at trial, madam?

Come o'er the bourn, Bessy, to me.

Fool. Her boat hath a leak,

And she must not speak

Why she dares not come over to thee.

Edg. The foul fiend haunts poor Tom in the voice of a nightingale.

Hoppedance cries in Tom's belly for two white herring. Croak not, black angel; I have no food for thee.

Kent. How do you, sir? Stand you not so amaz'd.

Will you lie down and rest upon the cushions?

Lear. I'll see their trial first. Bring in their evidence.

[To Edgar] Thou, robed man of justice, take thy place.

[To the Fool] And thou, his yokefellow of equity,

Bench by his side. [To Kent] You are o' th' commission,

Sit you too.

Edg. Let us deal justly.

Sleepest or wakest thou, jolly shepherd?
Thy sheep be in the corn;
And for one blast of thy minikin mouth
Thy sheep shall take no harm.
Purr! the cat is gray.
Lear. Arraign her first. 'Tis Goneril. I here take my oath before this honourable assembly, she kicked the poor King her father.
Fool. Come hither, mistress. Is your name Goneril?
Lear. She cannot deny it.
Fool. Cry you mercy, I took you for a joint-stool.
Lear. And here's another, whose warp'd looks proclaim
What store her heart is made on. Stop her there!
Arms, arms! sword! fire! Corruption in the place!
False justicer, why hast thou let her scape?
Edg. Bless thy five wits!
Kent. O pity! Sir, where is the patience now
That you so oft have boasted to retain?
Edg. [aside] My tears begin to take his part so much
They'll mar my counterfeiting.
Lear. The little dogs and all,
Tray, Blanch, and Sweetheart, see, they bark at me.
Edg. Tom will throw his head at them. Avaunt, you curs!
Be thy mouth or black or white,
Tooth that poisons if it bite;
Mastiff, greyhound, mongrel grim,
Hound or spaniel, brach or lym,
Bobtail tyke or trundle-tall-
Tom will make them weep and wail;
For, with throwing thus my head,
Dogs leap the hatch, and all are fled.

Do de, de, de. Sessa! Come, march to wakes and fairs and market towns. Poor Tom, thy horn is dry.

Lear. Then let them anatomize Regan. See what breeds about her

heart. Is there any cause in nature that makes these hard hearts? [To Edgar] You, sir- I entertain you for one of my hundred; only I do not like the fashion of your garments. You'll say they are Persian attire; but let them be chang'd.

Kent. Now, good my lord, lie here and rest awhile.

Lear. Make no noise, make no noise; draw the curtains.

So, so, so. We'll go to supper i' th' morning. So, so, so.

Fool. And I'll go to bed at noon.

Enter Gloucester.

Glou. Come hither, friend. Where is the King my master?

Kent. Here, sir; but trouble him not; his wits are gone.

Glou. Good friend, I prithee take him in thy arms.

I have o'erheard a plot of death upon him.

There is a litter ready; lay him in't

And drive towards Dover, friend, where thou shalt meet

Both welcome and protection. Take up thy master.

If thou shouldst dally half an hour, his life,

With thine, and all that offer to defend him,

Stand in assured loss. Take up, take up!

And follow me, that will to some provision

Give thee quick conduct.

Kent. Oppressed nature sleeps.

This rest might yet have balm'd thy broken senses,

Which, if convenience will not allow,

Stand in hard cure. [To the Fool] Come, help to bear thy master.

Thou must not stay behind.

Glou. Come, come, away!

Exeunt [all but Edgar].

Edg. When we our betters see bearing our woes,
We scarcely think our miseries our foes.
Who alone suffers suffers most i' th' mind,
Leaving free things and happy shows behind;
But then the mind much sufferance doth o'erskip
When grief hath mates, and bearing fellowship.
How light and portable my pain seems now,
When that which makes me bend makes the King bow,
He childed as I fathered! Tom, away!
Mark the high noises, and thyself bewray
When false opinion, whose wrong thought defiles thee,
In thy just proof repeals and reconciles thee.
What will hap more to-night, safe scape the King!
Lurk, lurk. [Exit.]

SCENE VII.: GLOUCESTER'S CASTLE.

Enter Cornwall, Regan, Goneril, [Edmund the] Bastard, and Servants.

Corn. [to Goneril] Post speedily to my lord your husband, show him this letter. The army of France is landed.- Seek out the traitor Gloucester.

[Exeunt some of the Servants.]

Reg. Hang him instantly.

Gon. Pluck out his eyes.

Corn. Leave him to my displeasure. Edmund, keep you our sister company. The revenges we are bound to take upon your traitorous father are not fit for your beholding. Advise the Duke where you are going, to a most festinate preparation. We are bound to the like. Our posts shall be swift and intelligent betwixt us.

Farewell, dear sister; farewell, my Lord of Gloucester.

Enter [Oswald the] Steward.

How now? Where's the King?
Osw. My Lord of Gloucester hath convey'd him hence.
Some five or six and thirty of his knights,
Hot questrists after him, met him at gate;
Who, with some other of the lord's dependants,
Are gone with him towards Dover, where they boast
To have well-armed friends.
Corn. Get horses for your mistress.
Gon. Farewell, sweet lord, and sister.
Corn. Edmund, farewell.
Exeunt Goneril, [Edmund, and Oswald].
Go seek the traitor Gloucester,
Pinion him like a thief, bring him before us.
[Exeunt other Servants.]
Though well we may not pass upon his life
Without the form of justice, yet our power
Shall do a court'sy to our wrath, which men
May blame, but not control.

Enter Gloucester, brought in by two or three.

Who's there? the traitor?
Reg. Ingrateful fox! 'tis he.
Corn. Bind fast his corky arms.
Glou. What mean, your Graces? Good my friends, consider
You are my guests. Do me no foul play, friends.
Corn. Bind him, I say.
[Servants bind him.]
Reg. Hard, hard. O filthy traitor!

Glou. Unmerciful lady as you are, I am none.
Corn. To this chair bind him. Villain, thou shalt find-
[Regan plucks his beard.]
Glou. By the kind gods, 'tis most ignobly done
To pluck me by the beard.
Reg. So white, and such a traitor!
Glou. Naughty lady,
These hairs which thou dost ravish from my chin
Will quicken, and accuse thee. I am your host.
With robber's hands my hospitable favours
You should not ruffle thus. What will you do?
Corn. Come, sir, what letters had you late from France?
Reg. Be simple-answer'd, for we know the truth.
Corn. And what confederacy have you with the traitors
Late footed in the kingdom?
Reg. To whose hands have you sent the lunatic King?
Speak.
Glou. I have a letter guessingly set down,
Which came from one that's of a neutral heart,
And not from one oppos'd.
Corn. Cunning.
Reg. And false.
Corn. Where hast thou sent the King?
Glou. To Dover.
Reg. Wherefore to Dover? Wast thou not charg'd at peril-
Corn. Wherefore to Dover? Let him first answer that.
Glou. I am tied to th' stake, and I must stand the course.
Reg. Wherefore to Dover, sir?
Glou. Because I would not see thy cruel nails
Pluck out his poor old eyes; nor thy fierce sister

In his anointed flesh stick boarish fangs.
The sea, with such a storm as his bare head
In hell-black night endur'd, would have buoy'd up
And quench'd the steeled fires.
Yet, poor old heart, he holp the heavens to rain.
If wolves had at thy gate howl'd that stern time,
Thou shouldst have said, 'Good porter, turn the key.'
All cruels else subscrib'd. But I shall see
The winged vengeance overtake such children.
Corn. See't shalt thou never. Fellows, hold the chair.
Upon these eyes of thine I'll set my foot.
Glou. He that will think to live till he be old,
Give me some help!- O cruel! O ye gods!
Reg. One side will mock another. Th' other too!
Corn. If you see vengeance-
1. Serv. Hold your hand, my lord!
I have serv'd you ever since I was a child;
But better service have I never done you
Than now to bid you hold.
Reg. How now, you dog?
1. Serv. If you did wear a beard upon your chin,
I'ld shake it on this quarrel.
Reg. What do you mean?
Corn. My villain! Draw and fight.
1. Serv. Nay, then, come on, and take the chance of anger.
Reg. Give me thy sword. A peasant stand up thus?
She takes a sword and runs at him behind.
1. Serv. O, I am slain! My lord, you have one eye left
To see some mischief on him. O! He dies.
Corn. Lest it see more, prevent it. Out, vile jelly!

Where is thy lustre now?
Glou. All dark and comfortless! Where's my son Edmund?
Edmund, enkindle all the sparks of nature
To quit this horrid act.
Reg. Out, treacherous villain!
Thou call'st on him that hates thee. It was he
That made the overture of thy treasons to us;
Who is too good to pity thee.
Glou. O my follies! Then Edgar was abus'd.
Kind gods, forgive me that, and prosper him!
Reg. Go thrust him out at gates, and let him smell
His way to Dover.
Exit [one] with Gloucester.
How is't, my lord? How look you?
Corn. I have receiv'd a hurt. Follow me, lady.
Turn out that eyeless villain. Throw this slave
Upon the dunghill. Regan, I bleed apace.
Untimely comes this hurt. Give me your arm.
Exit [Cornwall, led by Regan].
2. Serv. I'll never care what wickedness I do,
If this man come to good.
3. Serv. If she live long,
And in the end meet the old course of death,
Women will all turn monsters.
2. Serv. Let's follow the old Earl, and get the bedlam
To lead him where he would. His roguish madness
Allows itself to anything.
3. Serv. Go thou. I'll fetch some flax and whites of eggs
To apply to his bleeding face. Now heaven help him!
Exeunt.

ACT IV. SCENE I.: THE HEATH.

Enter Edgar.

Edg. Yet better thus, and known to be contemn'd,
Than still contemn'd and flatter'd. To be worst,
The lowest and most dejected thing of fortune,
Stands still in esperance, lives not in fear.
The lamentable change is from the best;
The worst returns to laughter. Welcome then,
Thou unsubstantial air that I embrace!
The wretch that thou hast blown unto the worst
Owes nothing to thy blasts.

Enter Gloucester, led by an Old Man.

But who comes here?
My father, poorly led? World, world, O world!
But that thy strange mutations make us hate thee,
Life would not yield to age.
Old Man. O my good lord,
I have been your tenant, and your father's tenant,
These fourscore years.
Glou. Away, get thee away! Good friend, be gone.
Thy comforts can do me no good at all;
Thee they may hurt.
Old Man. You cannot see your way.
Glou. I have no way, and therefore want no eyes;
I stumbled when I saw. Full oft 'tis seen
Our means secure us, and our mere defects
Prove our commodities. Ah dear son Edgar,
The food of thy abused father's wrath!
Might I but live to see thee in my touch,

I'ld say I had eyes again!
Old Man. How now? Who's there?
Edg. [aside] O gods! Who is't can say 'I am at the worst'?
I am worse than e'er I was.
Old Man. 'Tis poor mad Tom.
Edg. [aside] And worse I may be yet. The worst is not
So long as we can say 'This is the worst.'
Old Man. Fellow, where goest?
Glou. Is it a beggarman?
Old Man. Madman and beggar too.
Glou. He has some reason, else he could not beg.
I' th' last night's storm I such a fellow saw,
Which made me think a man a worm. My son
Came then into my mind, and yet my mind
Was then scarce friends with him. I have heard more since.
As flies to wanton boys are we to th' gods.
They kill us for their sport.
Edg. [aside] How should this be?
Bad is the trade that must play fool to sorrow,
Ang'ring itself and others.- Bless thee, master!
Glou. Is that the naked fellow?
Old Man. Ay, my lord.
Glou. Then prithee get thee gone. If for my sake
Thou wilt o'ertake us hence a mile or twain
I' th' way toward Dover, do it for ancient love;
And bring some covering for this naked soul,
Who I'll entreat to lead me.
Old Man. Alack, sir, he is mad!
Glou. 'Tis the time's plague when madmen lead the blind.
Do as I bid thee, or rather do thy pleasure.

Above the rest, be gone.

Old Man. I'll bring him the best 'parel that I have,

Come on't what will.

Exit.

Glou. Sirrah naked fellow-

Edg. Poor Tom's acold. [Aside] I cannot daub it further.

Glou. Come hither, fellow.

Edg. [aside] And yet I must.- Bless thy sweet eyes, they bleed.

Glou. Know'st thou the way to Dover?

Edg. Both stile and gate, horseway and footpath. Poor Tom hath been scar'd out of his good wits. Bless thee, good man's son, from the foul fiend! Five fiends have been in poor Tom at once: of lust, as Obidicut; Hobbididence, prince of dumbness; Mahu, of stealing; Modo, of murder; Flibbertigibbet, of mopping and mowing, who since possesses chambermaids and waiting women. So, bless thee, master!

Glou. Here, take this Purse, thou whom the heavens' plagues
Have humbled to all strokes. That I am wretched
Makes thee the happier. Heavens, deal so still!
Let the superfluous and lust-dieted man,
That slaves your ordinance, that will not see
Because he does not feel, feel your pow'r quickly;
So distribution should undo excess,
And each man have enough. Dost thou know Dover?

Edg. Ay, master.

Glou. There is a cliff, whose high and bending head
Looks fearfully in the confined deep.
Bring me but to the very brim of it,
And I'll repair the misery thou dost bear
With something rich about me. From that place
I shall no leading need.

Edg. Give me thy arm.
Poor Tom shall lead thee.
Exeunt.

SCENE II.: BEFORE THE DUKE OF ALBANY'S PALACE.

Enter Goneril and [Edmund the] Bastard.

Gon. Welcome, my lord. I marvel our mild husband
Not met us on the way.

Enter [Oswald the] Steward.

Now, where's your master?
Osw. Madam, within, but never man so chang'd.
I told him of the army that was landed:
He smil'd at it. I told him you were coming:
His answer was, 'The worse.' Of Gloucester's treachery
And of the loyal service of his son
When I inform'd him, then he call'd me sot
And told me I had turn'd the wrong side out.
What most he should dislike seems pleasant to him;
What like, offensive.
Gon. [to Edmund] Then shall you go no further.
It is the cowish terror of his spirit,
That dares not undertake. He'll not feel wrongs
Which tie him to an answer. Our wishes on the way
May prove effects. Back, Edmund, to my brother.
Hasten his musters and conduct his pow'rs.
I must change arms at home and give the distaff
Into my husband's hands. This trusty servant
Shall pass between us. Ere long you are like to hear
(If you dare venture in your own behalf)
A mistress's command. Wear this. [Gives a favour.]

Spare speech.

Decline your head. This kiss, if it durst speak,

Would stretch thy spirits up into the air.

Conceive, and fare thee well.

Edm. Yours in the ranks of death!

Exit.

Gon. My most dear Gloucester!

O, the difference of man and man!

To thee a woman's services are due;

My fool usurps my body.

Osw. Madam, here comes my lord.

Exit.

Enter Albany.

Gon. I have been worth the whistle.

Alb. O Goneril,

You are not worth the dust which the rude wind

Blows in your face! I fear your disposition.

That nature which contemns it origin

Cannot be bordered certain in itself.

She that herself will sliver and disbranch

From her material sap, perforce must wither

And come to deadly use.

Gon. No more! The text is foolish.

Alb. Wisdom and goodness to the vile seem vile;

Filths savour but themselves. What have you done?

Tigers, not daughters, what have you perform'd?

A father, and a gracious aged man,

Whose reverence even the head-lugg'd bear would lick,

Most barbarous, most degenerate, have you madded.

Could my good brother suffer you to do it?

A man, a prince, by him so benefited!
If that the heavens do not their visible spirits
Send quickly down to tame these vile offences,
It will come,
Humanity must perforce prey on itself,
Like monsters of the deep.
Gon. Milk-liver'd man!
That bear'st a cheek for blows, a head for wrongs;
Who hast not in thy brows an eye discerning
Thine honour from thy suffering; that not know'st
Fools do those villains pity who are punish'd
Ere they have done their mischief. Where's thy drum?
France spreads his banners in our noiseless land,
With plumed helm thy state begins to threat,
Whiles thou, a moral fool, sit'st still, and criest
'Alack, why does he so?'
Alb. See thyself, devil!
Proper deformity seems not in the fiend
So horrid as in woman.
Gon. O vain fool!
Alb. Thou changed and self-cover'd thing, for shame!
Bemonster not thy feature! Were't my fitness
To let these hands obey my blood,
They are apt enough to dislocate and tear
Thy flesh and bones. Howe'er thou art a fiend,
A woman's shape doth shield thee.
Gon. Marry, your manhood mew!

Enter a Gentleman.

Alb. What news?
Gent. O, my good lord, the Duke of Cornwall 's dead,

Slain by his servant, going to put out
The other eye of Gloucester.
Alb. Gloucester's eyes?
Gent. A servant that he bred, thrill'd with remorse,
Oppos'd against the act, bending his sword
To his great master; who, thereat enrag'd,
Flew on him, and amongst them fell'd him dead;
But not without that harmful stroke which since
Hath pluck'd him after.
Alb. This shows you are above,
You justicers, that these our nether crimes
So speedily can venge! But O poor Gloucester!
Lose he his other eye?
Gent. Both, both, my lord.
This letter, madam, craves a speedy answer.
'Tis from your sister.
Gon. [aside] One way I like this well;
But being widow, and my Gloucester with her,
May all the building in my fancy pluck
Upon my hateful life. Another way
The news is not so tart.- I'll read, and answer.
Exit.
Alb. Where was his son when they did take his eyes?
Gent. Come with my lady hither.
Alb. He is not here.
Gent. No, my good lord; I met him back again.
Alb. Knows he the wickedness?
Gent. Ay, my good lord. 'Twas he inform'd against him,
And quit the house on purpose, that their punishment
Might have the freer course.

Alb. Gloucester, I live
To thank thee for the love thou show'dst the King,
And to revenge thine eyes. Come hither, friend.
Tell me what more thou know'st.
Exeunt.

SCENE III.: THE FRENCH CAMP NEAR DOVER.

Enter Kent and a Gentleman.

Kent. Why the King of France is so suddenly gone back know you the reason?

Gent. Something he left imperfect in the state, which since his coming forth is thought of, which imports to the kingdom so much fear and danger that his personal return was most required and necessary.

Kent. Who hath he left behind him general?

Gent. The Marshal of France, Monsieur La Far.

Kent. Did your letters pierce the Queen to any demonstration of grief?

Gent. Ay, sir. She took them, read them in my presence,
And now and then an ample tear trill'd down
Her delicate cheek. It seem'd she was a queen
Over her passion, who, most rebel-like,
Sought to be king o'er her.

Kent. O, then it mov'd her?

Gent. Not to a rage. Patience and sorrow strove
Who should express her goodliest. You have seen
Sunshine and rain at once: her smiles and tears
Were like, a better way. Those happy smilets
That play'd on her ripe lip seem'd not to know
What guests were in her eyes, which parted thence
As pearls from diamonds dropp'd. In brief,

Sorrow would be a rarity most belov'd,
If all could so become it.
Kent. Made she no verbal question?
Gent. Faith, once or twice she heav'd the name of father
Pantingly forth, as if it press'd her heart;
Cried 'Sisters, sisters! Shame of ladies! Sisters!
Kent! father! sisters! What, i' th' storm? i' th' night?
Let pity not be believ'd!' There she shook
The holy water from her heavenly eyes,
And clamour moisten'd. Then away she started
To deal with grief alone.
Kent. It is the stars,
The stars above us, govern our conditions;
Else one self mate and mate could not beget
Such different issues. You spoke not with her since?
Gent. No.
Kent. Was this before the King return'd?
Gent. No, since.
Kent. Well, sir, the poor distressed Lear's i' th' town;
Who sometime, in his better tune, remembers
What we are come about, and by no means
Will yield to see his daughter.
Gent. Why, good sir?
Kent. A sovereign shame so elbows him; his own unkindness,
That stripp'd her from his benediction, turn'd her
To foreign casualties, gave her dear rights
To his dog-hearted daughters- these things sting
His mind so venomously that burning shame
Detains him from Cordelia.
Gent. Alack, poor gentleman!

Kent. Of Albany's and Cornwall's powers you heard not?
Gent. 'Tis so; they are afoot.
Kent. Well, sir, I'll bring you to our master Lear
And leave you to attend him. Some dear cause
Will in concealment wrap me up awhile.
When I am known aright, you shall not grieve
Lending me this acquaintance. I pray you go
Along with me. Exeunt.

SCENE IV.: THE FRENCH CAMP.

Enter, with Drum and Colours, Cordelia, Doctor, and Soldiers.
Cor. Alack, 'tis he! Why, he was met even now
As mad as the vex'd sea, singing aloud,
Crown'd with rank fumiter and furrow weeds,
With hardocks, hemlock, nettles, cuckoo flow'rs,
Darnel, and all the idle weeds that grow
In our sustaining corn. A century send forth.
Search every acre in the high-grown field
And bring him to our eye. [Exit an Officer.] What can man's wisdom
In the restoring his bereaved sense?
He that helps him take all my outward worth.
Doct. There is means, madam.
Our foster nurse of nature is repose,
The which he lacks. That to provoke in him
Are many simples operative, whose power
Will close the eye of anguish.
Cor. All blest secrets,
All you unpublish'd virtues of the earth,
Spring with my tears! be aidant and remediate
In the good man's distress! Seek, seek for him!

Lest his ungovern'd rage dissolve the life
That wants the means to lead it.

Enter Messenger.

Mess. News, madam.
The British pow'rs are marching hitherward.
Cor. 'Tis known before. Our preparation stands
In expectation of them. O dear father,
It is thy business that I go about.
Therefore great France
My mourning and important tears hath pitied.
No blown ambition doth our arms incite,
But love, dear love, and our ag'd father's right.
Soon may I hear and see him!
Exeunt.

SCENE V.: GLOUCESTER'S CASTLE.

Enter Regan and [Oswald the] Steward.

Reg. But are my brother's pow'rs set forth?
Osw. Ay, madam.
Reg. Himself in person there?
Osw. Madam, with much ado.
Your sister is the better soldier.
Reg. Lord Edmund spake not with your lord at home?
Osw. No, madam.
Reg. What might import my sister's letter to him?
Osw. I know not, lady.
Reg. Faith, he is posted hence on serious matter.
It was great ignorance, Gloucester's eyes being out,
To let him live. Where he arrives he moves
All hearts against us. Edmund, I think, is gone,

In pity of his misery, to dispatch
His nighted life; moreover, to descry
The strength o' th' enemy.
Osw. I must needs after him, madam, with my letter.
Reg. Our troops set forth to-morrow. Stay with us.
The ways are dangerous.
Osw. I may not, madam.
My lady charg'd my duty in this business.
Reg. Why should she write to Edmund? Might not you
Transport her purposes by word? Belike,
Something- I know not what- I'll love thee much-
Let me unseal the letter.
Osw. Madam, I had rather-
Reg. I know your lady does not love her husband;
I am sure of that; and at her late being here
She gave strange eliads and most speaking looks
To noble Edmund. I know you are of her bosom.
Osw. I, madam?
Reg. I speak in understanding. Y'are! I know't.
Therefore I do advise you take this note.
My lord is dead; Edmund and I have talk'd,
And more convenient is he for my hand
Than for your lady's. You may gather more.
If you do find him, pray you give him this;
And when your mistress hears thus much from you,
I pray desire her call her wisdom to her.
So farewell.
If you do chance to hear of that blind traitor,
Preferment falls on him that cuts him off.
Osw. Would I could meet him, madam! I should show

What party I do follow.

Reg. Fare thee well. Exeunt.

SCENE VI.: THE COUNTRY NEAR DOVER.

Enter Gloucester, and Edgar [like a Peasant].

Glou. When shall I come to th' top of that same hill?
Edg. You do climb up it now. Look how we labour.
Glou. Methinks the ground is even.
Edg. Horrible steep.
Hark, do you hear the sea?
Glou. No, truly.
Edg. Why, then, your other senses grow imperfect
By your eyes' anguish.
Glou. So may it be indeed.
Methinks thy voice is alter'd, and thou speak'st
In better phrase and matter than thou didst.
Edg. Y'are much deceiv'd. In nothing am I chang'd
But in my garments.
Glou. Methinks y'are better spoken.
Edg. Come on, sir; here's the place. Stand still. How fearful
And dizzy 'tis to cast one's eyes so low!
The crows and choughs that wing the midway air
Show scarce so gross as beetles. Halfway down
Hangs one that gathers sampire- dreadful trade!
Methinks he seems no bigger than his head.
The fishermen that walk upon the beach
Appear like mice; and yond tall anchoring bark,
Diminish'd to her cock; her cock, a buoy
Almost too small for sight. The murmuring surge
That on th' unnumb'red idle pebble chafes

Cannot be heard so high. I'll look no more,
Lest my brain turn, and the deficient sight
Topple down headlong.
Glou. Set me where you stand.
Edg. Give me your hand. You are now within a foot
Of th' extreme verge. For all beneath the moon
Would I not leap upright.
Glou. Let go my hand.
Here, friend, is another purse; in it a jewel
Well worth a poor man's taking. Fairies and gods
Prosper it with thee! Go thou further off;
Bid me farewell, and let me hear thee going.
Edg. Now fare ye well, good sir.
Glou. With all my heart.
Edg. [aside]. Why I do trifle thus with his despair
Is done to cure it.
Glou. O you mighty gods! He kneels.
This world I do renounce, and, in your sights,
Shake patiently my great affliction off.
If I could bear it longer and not fall
To quarrel with your great opposeless wills,
My snuff and loathed part of nature should
Burn itself out. If Edgar live, O, bless him!
Now, fellow, fare thee well.
He falls [forward and swoons].
Edg. Gone, sir, farewell.-
And yet I know not how conceit may rob
The treasury of life when life itself
Yields to the theft. Had he been where he thought,
By this had thought been past.- Alive or dead?

Ho you, sir! friend! Hear you, sir? Speak!-
Thus might he pass indeed. Yet he revives.
What are you, sir?
Glou. Away, and let me die.
Edg. Hadst thou been aught but gossamer, feathers, air,
So many fadom down precipitating,
Thou'dst shiver'd like an egg; but thou dost breathe;
Hast heavy substance; bleed'st not; speak'st; art sound.
Ten masts at each make not the altitude
Which thou hast perpendicularly fell.
Thy life is a miracle. Speak yet again.
Glou. But have I fall'n, or no?
Edg. From the dread summit of this chalky bourn.
Look up a-height. The shrill-gorg'd lark so far
Cannot be seen or heard. Do but look up.
Glou. Alack, I have no eyes!
Is wretchedness depriv'd that benefit
To end itself by death? 'Twas yet some comfort
When misery could beguile the tyrant's rage
And frustrate his proud will.
Edg. Give me your arm.
Up- so. How is't? Feel you your legs? You stand.
Glou. Too well, too well.
Edg. This is above all strangeness.
Upon the crown o' th' cliff what thing was that
Which parted from you?
Glou. A poor unfortunate beggar.
Edg. As I stood here below, methought his eyes
Were two full moons; he had a thousand noses,
Horns whelk'd and wav'd like the enridged sea.

It was some fiend. Therefore, thou happy father,
Think that the clearest gods, who make them honours
Of men's impossibility, have preserv'd thee.
Glou. I do remember now. Henceforth I'll bear
Affliction till it do cry out itself
'Enough, enough,' and die. That thing you speak of,
I took it for a man. Often 'twould say
'The fiend, the fiend'- he led me to that place.
Edg. Bear free and patient thoughts.

Enter Lear, mad, [fantastically dressed with weeds].

But who comes here?
The safer sense will ne'er accommodate
His master thus.
Lear. No, they cannot touch me for coming;
I am the King himself.
Edg. O thou side-piercing sight!
Lear. Nature 's above art in that respect. There's your press
money. That fellow handles his bow like a crow-keeper. Draw
me
a clothier's yard. Look, look, a mouse! Peace, peace; this piece
of toasted cheese will do't. There's my gauntlet; I'll prove it
on a giant. Bring up the brown bills. O, well flown, bird! i'
th' clout, i' th' clout! Hewgh! Give the word.
Edg. Sweet marjoram.
Lear. Pass.
Glou. I know that voice.

Lear. Ha! Goneril with a white beard? They flatter'd me like a dog, and told me I had white hairs in my beard ere the black ones were there. To say 'ay' and 'no' to everything I said! 'Ay' and 'no' too was no good divinity. When the rain came to wet me once, and the wind to make me chatter; when the thunder would not peace at my bidding; there I found 'em, there I smelt 'em out. Go to, they are not men o' their words! They told me I was everything. 'Tis a lie- I am not ague-proof.

Glou. The trick of that voice I do well remember.
Is't not the King?
Lear. Ay, every inch a king!
When I do stare, see how the subject quakes.
I pardon that man's life. What was thy cause?
Adultery?
Thou shalt not die. Die for adultery? No.
The wren goes to't, and the small gilded fly
Does lecher in my sight.
Let copulation thrive; for Gloucester's bastard son
Was kinder to his father than my daughters
Got 'tween the lawful sheets.
To't, luxury, pell-mell! for I lack soldiers.
Behold yond simp'ring dame,
Whose face between her forks presageth snow,
That minces virtue, and does shake the head
To hear of pleasure's name.
The fitchew nor the soiled horse goes to't
With a more riotous appetite.
Down from the waist they are Centaurs,
Though women all above.
But to the girdle do the gods inherit,
Beneath is all the fiend's.

There's hell, there's darkness, there's the sulphurous pit; burning, scalding, stench, consumption. Fie, fie, fie! pah, pah!

Give me an ounce of civet, good apothecary, to sweeten my imagination. There's money for thee.

Glou. O, let me kiss that hand!

Lear. Let me wipe it first; it smells of mortality.

Glou. O ruin'd piece of nature! This great world

Shall so wear out to naught. Dost thou know me?

Lear. I remember thine eyes well enough. Dost thou squiny at me?

No, do thy worst, blind Cupid! I'll not love. Read thou this

challenge; mark but the penning of it.

Glou. Were all the letters suns, I could not see one.

Edg. [aside] I would not take this from report. It is,

And my heart breaks at it.

Lear. Read.

Glou. What, with the case of eyes?

Lear. O, ho, are you there with me? No eyes in your head, nor no

money in your purse? Your eyes are in a heavy case, your purse

in a light. Yet you see how this world goes.

Glou. I see it feelingly.

Lear. What, art mad? A man may see how the world goes with no eyes.

Look with thine ears. See how yond justice rails upon yond simple thief. Hark in thine ear. Change places and, handy-dandy, which is the justice, which is the thief? Thou hast seen a farmer's dog bark at a beggar?

Glou. Ay, sir.

Lear. And the creature run from the cur? There thou mightst behold the great image of authority: a dog's obeyed in office.

Thou rascal beadle, hold thy bloody hand!

Why dost thou lash that whore? Strip thine own back.

Thou hotly lusts to use her in that kind

For which thou whip'st her. The usurer hangs the cozener.

Through tatter'd clothes small vices do appear;
Robes and furr'd gowns hide all. Plate sin with gold,
And the strong lance of justice hurtless breaks;
Arm it in rags, a pygmy's straw does pierce it.
None does offend, none- I say none! I'll able 'em.
Take that of me, my friend, who have the power
To seal th' accuser's lips. Get thee glass eyes
And, like a scurvy politician, seem
To see the things thou dost not. Now, now, now, now!
Pull off my boots. Harder, harder! So.
Edg. O, matter and impertinency mix'd!
Reason, in madness!
Lear. If thou wilt weep my fortunes, take my eyes.
I know thee well enough; thy name is Gloucester.
Thou must be patient. We came crying hither;
Thou know'st, the first time that we smell the air
We wawl and cry. I will preach to thee. Mark.
Glou. Alack, alack the day!
Lear. When we are born, we cry that we are come
To this great stage of fools. This' a good block.
It were a delicate stratagem to shoe
A troop of horse with felt. I'll put't in proof,
And when I have stol'n upon these sons-in-law,
Then kill, kill, kill, kill, kill, kill!

Enter a Gentleman [with Attendants].

Gent. O, here he is! Lay hand upon him.- Sir,
Your most dear daughter-
Lear. No rescue? What, a prisoner? I am even
The natural fool of fortune. Use me well;

You shall have ransom. Let me have a surgeon;
I am cut to th' brains.
Gent. You shall have anything.
Lear. No seconds? All myself?
Why, this would make a man a man of salt,
To use his eyes for garden waterpots,
Ay, and laying autumn's dust.
Gent. Good sir-
Lear. I will die bravely, like a smug bridegroom. What!
I will be jovial. Come, come, I am a king;
My masters, know you that?
Gent. You are a royal one, and we obey you.

Lear. Then there's life in't. Nay, an you get it, you shall get it by running. Sa, sa, sa, sa!

Exit running. [Attendants follow.]
Gent. A sight most pitiful in the meanest wretch,
Past speaking of in a king! Thou hast one daughter
Who redeems nature from the general curse
Which twain have brought her to.
Edg. Hail, gentle sir.
Gent. Sir, speed you. What's your will?
Edg. Do you hear aught, sir, of a battle toward?
Gent. Most sure and vulgar. Every one hears that
Which can distinguish sound.
Edg. But, by your favour,
How near's the other army?
Gent. Near and on speedy foot. The main descry
Stands on the hourly thought.
Edg. I thank you sir. That's all.
Gent. Though that the Queen on special cause is here,

Her army is mov'd on.
Edg. I thank you, sir
Exit [Gentleman].
Glou. You ever-gentle gods, take my breath from me;
Let not my worser spirit tempt me again
To die before you please!
Edg. Well pray you, father.
Glou. Now, good sir, what are you?
Edg. A most poor man, made tame to fortune's blows,
Who, by the art of known and feeling sorrows,
Am pregnant to good pity. Give me your hand;
I'll lead you to some biding.
Glou. Hearty thanks.
The bounty and the benison of heaven
To boot, and boot!

Enter [Oswald the] Steward.

Osw. A proclaim'd prize! Most happy!
That eyeless head of thine was first fram'd flesh
To raise my fortunes. Thou old unhappy traitor,
Briefly thyself remember. The sword is out
That must destroy thee.
Glou. Now let thy friendly hand
Put strength enough to't.
[Edgar interposes.]
Osw. Wherefore, bold peasant,
Dar'st thou support a publish'd traitor? Hence!
Lest that th' infection of his fortune take
Like hold on thee. Let go his arm.
Edg. Chill not let go, zir, without vurther 'cagion.

Osw. Let go, slave, or thou diest!

Edg. Good gentleman, go your gait, and let poor voke pass. An chud ha' bin zwagger'd out of my life, 'twould not ha' bin zo long as 'tis by a vortnight. Nay, come not near th' old man. Keep out, che vore ye, or Ise try whether your costard or my ballow be the harder. Chill be plain with you.

Osw. Out, dunghill!

They fight.

Edg. Chill pick your teeth, zir. Come! No matter vor your foins.

[Oswald falls.]

Osw. Slave, thou hast slain me. Villain, take my purse.
If ever thou wilt thrive, bury my body,
And give the letters which thou find'st about me
To Edmund Earl of Gloucester. Seek him out
Upon the British party. O, untimely death! Death!

He dies.

Edg. I know thee well. A serviceable villain,
As duteous to the vices of thy mistress
As badness would desire.

Glou. What, is he dead?

Edg. Sit you down, father; rest you.
Let's see his pockets; these letters that he speaks of
May be my friends. He's dead. I am only sorry
He had no other deathsman. Let us see.
Leave, gentle wax; and, manners, blame us not.
To know our enemies' minds, we'ld rip their hearts;
Their papers, is more lawful. Reads the letter.

'Let our reciprocal vows be rememb'red. You have many opportunities to cut him off. If your will want not, time and place will be fruitfully offer'd. There is nothing done, if he return the conqueror. Then am I the prisoner, and his bed my jail; from the loathed warmth whereof deliver me, and supply the place for your labour.

'Your (wife, so I would say) affectionate servant,
'Goneril.'
O indistinguish'd space of woman's will!
A plot upon her virtuous husband's life,
And the exchange my brother! Here in the sands
Thee I'll rake up, the post unsanctified
Of murtherous lechers; and in the mature time
With this ungracious paper strike the sight
Of the death-practis'd Duke, For him 'tis well
That of thy death and business I can tell.
Glou. The King is mad. How stiff is my vile sense,
That I stand up, and have ingenious feeling
Of my huge sorrows! Better I were distract.
So should my thoughts be sever'd from my griefs,
And woes by wrong imaginations lose
The knowledge of themselves.
A drum afar off.
Edg. Give me your hand.
Far off methinks I hear the beaten drum.
Come, father, I'll bestow you with a friend. Exeunt.

SCENE VII.: A TENT IN THE FRENCH CAMP.

Enter Cordelia, Kent, Doctor, and Gentleman.

Cor. O thou good Kent, how shall I live and work
To match thy goodness? My life will be too short
And every measure fail me.
Kent. To be acknowledg'd, madam, is o'erpaid.
All my reports go with the modest truth;

Nor more nor clipp'd, but so.

Cor. Be better suited.

These weeds are memories of those worser hours.

I prithee put them off.

Kent. Pardon, dear madam.

Yet to be known shortens my made intent.

My boon I make it that you know me not

Till time and I think meet.

Cor. Then be't so, my good lord. [To the Doctor] How, does the King?

Doct. Madam, sleeps still.

Cor. O you kind gods,

Cure this great breach in his abused nature!

Th' untun'd and jarring senses, O, wind up

Of this child-changed father!

Doct. So please your Majesty

That we may wake the King? He hath slept long.

Cor. Be govern'd by your knowledge, and proceed

I' th' sway of your own will. Is he array'd?

Enter Lear in a chair carried by Servants.

Gent. Ay, madam. In the heaviness of sleep

We put fresh garments on him.

Doct. Be by, good madam, when we do awake him.

I doubt not of his temperance.

Cor. Very well.

Music.

Doct. Please you draw near. Louder the music there!

Cor. O my dear father, restoration hang

Thy medicine on my lips, and let this kiss

Repair those violent harms that my two sisters

Have in thy reverence made!
Kent. Kind and dear princess!
Cor. Had you not been their father, these white flakes
Had challeng'd pity of them. Was this a face
To be oppos'd against the warring winds?
To stand against the deep dread-bolted thunder?
In the most terrible and nimble stroke
Of quick cross lightning? to watch- poor perdu!-
With this thin helm? Mine enemy's dog,
Though he had bit me, should have stood that night
Against my fire; and wast thou fain, poor father,
To hovel thee with swine and rogues forlorn,
In short and musty straw? Alack, alack!
'Tis wonder that thy life and wits at once
Had not concluded all.- He wakes. Speak to him.
Doct. Madam, do you; 'tis fittest.
Cor. How does my royal lord? How fares your Majesty?
Lear. You do me wrong to take me out o' th' grave.
Thou art a soul in bliss; but I am bound
Upon a wheel of fire, that mine own tears
Do scald like molten lead.
Cor. Sir, do you know me?
Lear. You are a spirit, I know. When did you die?
Cor. Still, still, far wide!
Doct. He's scarce awake. Let him alone awhile.
Lear. Where have I been? Where am I? Fair daylight,
I am mightily abus'd. I should e'en die with pity,
To see another thus. I know not what to say.
I will not swear these are my hands. Let's see.
I feel this pin prick. Would I were assur'd

Of my condition!
Cor. O, look upon me, sir,
And hold your hands in benediction o'er me.
No, sir, you must not kneel.
Lear. Pray, do not mock me.
I am a very foolish fond old man,
Fourscore and upward, not an hour more nor less;
And, to deal plainly,
I fear I am not in my perfect mind.
Methinks I should know you, and know this man;
Yet I am doubtful; for I am mainly ignorant
What place this is; and all the skill I have
Remembers not these garments; nor I know not
Where I did lodge last night. Do not laugh at me;
For (as I am a man) I think this lady
To be my child Cordelia.
Cor. And so I am! I am!
Lear. Be your tears wet? Yes, faith. I pray weep not.
If you have poison for me, I will drink it.
I know you do not love me; for your sisters
Have, as I do remember, done me wrong.
You have some cause, they have not.
Cor. No cause, no cause.
Lear. Am I in France?
Kent. In your own kingdom, sir.
Lear. Do not abuse me.
Doct. Be comforted, good madam. The great rage
You see is kill'd in him; and yet it is danger
To make him even o'er the time he has lost.
Desire him to go in. Trouble him no more

Till further settling.

Cor. Will't please your Highness walk?

Lear. You must bear with me.

Pray you now, forget and forgive. I am old and foolish.

Exeunt. Manent Kent and Gentleman.

Gent. Holds it true, sir, that the Duke of Cornwall was so slain?

Kent. Most certain, sir.

Gent. Who is conductor of his people?

Kent. As 'tis said, the bastard son of Gloucester.

Gent. They say Edgar, his banish'd son, is with the Earl of Kent in Germany.

Kent. Report is changeable. 'Tis time to look about; the powers of the kingdom approach apace.

Gent. The arbitrement is like to be bloody.

Fare you well, sir. [Exit.]

Kent. My point and period will be throughly wrought,

Or well or ill, as this day's battle's fought.

Exit.

ACT V. SCENE I.

The British camp near Dover.

Enter, with Drum and Colours, Edmund, Regan, Gentleman, and Soldiers.

Edm. Know of the Duke if his last purpose hold,

Or whether since he is advis'd by aught

To change the course. He's full of alteration

And self-reproving. Bring his constant pleasure.

[Exit an Officer.]

Reg. Our sister's man is certainly miscarried.

Edm. Tis to be doubted, madam.

Reg. Now, sweet lord,

You know the goodness I intend upon you.
Tell me- but truly- but then speak the truth-
Do you not love my sister?
Edm. In honour'd love.
Reg. But have you never found my brother's way
To the forfended place?
Edm. That thought abuses you.
Reg. I am doubtful that you have been conjunct
And bosom'd with her, as far as we call hers.
Edm. No, by mine honour, madam.
Reg. I never shall endure her. Dear my lord,
Be not familiar with her.
Edm. Fear me not.
She and the Duke her husband!
Enter, with Drum and Colours, Albany, Goneril, Soldiers.
Gon. [aside] I had rather lose the battle than that sister
Should loosen him and me.
Alb. Our very loving sister, well bemet.
Sir, this I hear: the King is come to his daughter,
With others whom the rigour of our state
Forc'd to cry out. Where I could not be honest,
I never yet was valiant. For this business,
It toucheth us as France invades our land,
Not bolds the King, with others whom, I fear,
Most just and heavy causes make oppose.
Edm. Sir, you speak nobly.
Reg. Why is this reason'd?
Gon. Combine together 'gainst the enemy;
For these domestic and particular broils
Are not the question here.

Alb. Let's then determine
With th' ancient of war on our proceeding.
Edm. I shall attend you presently at your tent.
Reg. Sister, you'll go with us?
Gon. No.
Reg. 'Tis most convenient. Pray you go with us.
Gon. [aside] O, ho, I know the riddle.- I will go.
[As they are going out,] enter Edgar [disguised].
Edg. If e'er your Grace had speech with man so poor,
Hear me one word.
Alb. I'll overtake you.- Speak.
Exeunt [all but Albany and Edgar].
Edg. Before you fight the battle, ope this letter.
If you have victory, let the trumpet sound
For him that brought it. Wretched though I seem,
I can produce a champion that will prove
What is avouched there. If you miscarry,
Your business of the world hath so an end,
And machination ceases. Fortune love you!
Alb. Stay till I have read the letter.
Edg. I was forbid it.
When time shall serve, let but the herald cry,
And I'll appear again.
Alb. Why, fare thee well. I will o'erlook thy paper.
Exit [Edgar].

Enter Edmund.

Edm. The enemy 's in view; draw up your powers.
Here is the guess of their true strength and forces
By diligent discovery; but your haste
Is now urg'd on you.

Alb. We will greet the time.

Exit.

Edm. To both these sisters have I sworn my love;
Each jealous of the other, as the stung
Are of the adder. Which of them shall I take?
Both? one? or neither? Neither can be enjoy'd,
If both remain alive. To take the widow
Exasperates, makes mad her sister Goneril;
And hardly shall I carry out my side,
Her husband being alive. Now then, we'll use
His countenance for the battle, which being done,
Let her who would be rid of him devise
His speedy taking off. As for the mercy
Which he intends to Lear and to Cordelia-
The battle done, and they within our power,
Shall never see his pardon; for my state
Stands on me to defend, not to debate.

Exit.

SCENE II.: A FIELD BETWEEN THE TWO CAMPS.

Alarum within. Enter, with Drum and Colours, the Powers of France over the stage, Cordelia with her Father in her hand, and exeunt.

Enter Edgar and Gloucester.

Edg. Here, father, take the shadow of this tree
For your good host. Pray that the right may thrive.
If ever I return to you again,
I'll bring you comfort.

Glou. Grace go with you, sir!

Exit [Edgar].

Alarum and retreat within. Enter Edgar,
Edg. Away, old man! give me thy hand! away!
King Lear hath lost, he and his daughter ta'en.
Give me thy hand! come on!
Glou. No further, sir. A man may rot even here.
Edg. What, in ill thoughts again? Men must endure
Their going hence, even as their coming hither;
Ripeness is all. Come on.
Glou. And that's true too. Exeunt.

SCENE III.: THE BRITISH CAMP, NEAR DOVER.

Enter, in conquest, with Drum and Colours, Edmund; Lear and Cordelia as prisoners; Soldiers, Captain.

Edm. Some officers take them away. Good guard
Until their greater pleasures first be known
That are to censure them.
Cor. We are not the first
Who with best meaning have incurr'd the worst.
For thee, oppressed king, am I cast down;
Myself could else outfrown false Fortune's frown.
Shall we not see these daughters and these sisters?
Lear. No, no, no, no! Come, let's away to prison.
We two alone will sing like birds i' th' cage.
When thou dost ask me blessing, I'll kneel down
And ask of thee forgiveness. So we'll live,
And pray, and sing, and tell old tales, and laugh
At gilded butterflies, and hear poor rogues
Talk of court news; and we'll talk with them too-
Who loses and who wins; who's in, who's out-
And take upon 's the mystery of things,
As if we were God's spies; and we'll wear out,

In a wall'd prison, packs and sects of great ones
That ebb and flow by th' moon.
Edm. Take them away.
Lear. Upon such sacrifices, my Cordelia,
The gods themselves throw incense. Have I caught thee?
He that parts us shall bring a brand from heaven
And fire us hence like foxes. Wipe thine eyes.
The goodyears shall devour 'em, flesh and fell,
Ere they shall make us weep! We'll see 'em starv'd first.
Come. Exeunt [Lear and Cordelia, guarded].
Edm. Come hither, Captain; hark.
Take thou this note [gives a paper]. Go follow them to prison.
One step I have advanc'd thee. If thou dost
As this instructs thee, thou dost make thy way
To noble fortunes. Know thou this, that men
Are as the time is. To be tender-minded
Does not become a sword. Thy great employment
Will not bear question. Either say thou'lt do't,
Or thrive by other means.
Capt. I'll do't, my lord.
Edm. About it! and write happy when th' hast done.
Mark- I say, instantly; and carry it so
As I have set it down.
Capt. I cannot draw a cart, nor eat dried oats;
If it be man's work, I'll do't.
Exit.

Flourish. Enter Albany, Goneril, Regan, Soldiers.

Alb. Sir, you have show'd to-day your valiant strain,
And fortune led you well. You have the captives
Who were the opposites of this day's strife.

We do require them of you, so to use them
As we shall find their merits and our safety
May equally determine.
Edm. Sir, I thought it fit
To send the old and miserable King
To some retention and appointed guard;
Whose age has charms in it, whose title more,
To pluck the common bosom on his side
And turn our impress'd lances in our eyes
Which do command them. With him I sent the Queen,
My reason all the same; and they are ready
To-morrow, or at further space, t' appear
Where you shall hold your session. At this time
We sweat and bleed: the friend hath lost his friend;
And the best quarrels, in the heat, are curs'd
By those that feel their sharpness.
The question of Cordelia and her father
Requires a fitter place.
Alb. Sir, by your patience,
I hold you but a subject of this war,
Not as a brother.
Reg. That's as we list to grace him.
Methinks our pleasure might have been demanded
Ere you had spoke so far. He led our powers,
Bore the commission of my place and person,
The which immediacy may well stand up
And call itself your brother.
Gon. Not so hot!
In his own grace he doth exalt himself
More than in your addition.

Reg. In my rights
By me invested, he compeers the best.
Gon. That were the most if he should husband you.
Reg. Jesters do oft prove prophets.
Gon. Holla, holla!
That eye that told you so look'd but asquint.
Reg. Lady, I am not well; else I should answer
From a full-flowing stomach. General,
Take thou my soldiers, prisoners, patrimony;
Dispose of them, of me; the walls are thine.
Witness the world that I create thee here
My lord and master.
Gon. Mean you to enjoy him?
Alb. The let-alone lies not in your good will.
Edm. Nor in thine, lord.
Alb. Half-blooded fellow, yes.
Reg. [to Edmund] Let the drum strike, and prove my title thine.
Alb. Stay yet; hear reason. Edmund, I arrest thee
On capital treason; and, in thine attaint,
This gilded serpent [points to Goneril]. For your claim, fair sister,
I bar it in the interest of my wife.
'Tis she is subcontracted to this lord,
And I, her husband, contradict your banes.
If you will marry, make your loves to me;
My lady is bespoke.
Gon. An interlude!
Alb. Thou art arm'd, Gloucester. Let the trumpet sound.
If none appear to prove upon thy person
Thy heinous, manifest, and many treasons,

There is my pledge [throws down a glove]! I'll prove it on thy heart,

Ere I taste bread, thou art in nothing less

Than I have here proclaim'd thee.

Reg. Sick, O, sick!

Gon. [aside] If not, I'll ne'er trust medicine.

Edm. There's my exchange [throws down a glove]. What in the world he is

That names me traitor, villain-like he lies.

Call by thy trumpet. He that dares approach,

On him, on you, who not? I will maintain

My truth and honour firmly.

Alb. A herald, ho!

Edm. A herald, ho, a herald!

Alb. Trust to thy single virtue; for thy soldiers,

All levied in my name, have in my name

Took their discharge.

Reg. My sickness grows upon me.

Alb. She is not well. Convey her to my tent.

[Exit Regan, led.]

Enter a Herald.

Come hither, herald. Let the trumpet sound,

And read out this.

Capt. Sound, trumpet! A trumpet sounds.

Her. (reads) 'If any man of quality or degree within the lists of the army will maintain upon Edmund, supposed Earl of Gloucester, that he is a manifold traitor, let him appear by the third sound of the trumpet. He is bold in his defence.'

Edm. Sound! First trumpet.

Her. Again! Second trumpet.

Her. Again! Third trumpet.

Trumpet answers within.

Enter Edgar, armed, at the third sound, a Trumpet before him.

Alb. Ask him his purposes, why he appears
Upon this call o' th' trumpet.
Her. What are you?
Your name, your quality? and why you answer
This present summons?
Edg. Know my name is lost;
By treason's tooth bare-gnawn and canker-bit.
Yet am I noble as the adversary
I come to cope.
Alb. Which is that adversary?
Edg. What's he that speaks for Edmund Earl of Gloucester?
Edm. Himself. What say'st thou to him?
Edg. Draw thy sword,
That, if my speech offend a noble heart,
Thy arm may do thee justice. Here is mine.
Behold, it is the privilege of mine honours,
My oath, and my profession. I protest-
Maugre thy strength, youth, place, and eminence,
Despite thy victor sword and fire-new fortune,
Thy valour and thy heart- thou art a traitor;
False to thy gods, thy brother, and thy father;
Conspirant 'gainst this high illustrious prince;
And from th' extremest upward of thy head
To the descent and dust beneath thy foot,
A most toad-spotted traitor. Say thou 'no,'
This sword, this arm, and my best spirits are bent
To prove upon thy heart, whereto I speak,

Thou liest.
Edm. In wisdom I should ask thy name;
But since thy outside looks so fair and warlike,
And that thy tongue some say of breeding breathes,
What safe and nicely I might well delay
By rule of knighthood, I disdain and spurn.
Back do I toss those treasons to thy head;
With the hell-hated lie o'erwhelm thy heart;
Which- for they yet glance by and scarcely bruise-
This sword of mine shall give them instant way
Where they shall rest for ever. Trumpets, speak!
Alarums. Fight. [Edmund falls.]
Alb. Save him, save him!
Gon. This is mere practice, Gloucester.
By th' law of arms thou wast not bound to answer
An unknown opposite. Thou art not vanquish'd,
But cozen'd and beguil'd.
Alb. Shut your mouth, dame,
Or with this paper shall I stop it. [Shows her her letter to Edmund.]- [To Edmund]. Hold, sir.
[To Goneril] Thou worse than any name, read thine own evil.
No tearing, lady! I perceive you know it.
Gon. Say if I do- the laws are mine, not thine.
Who can arraign me for't?
Alb. Most monstrous!
Know'st thou this paper?
Gon. Ask me not what I know.
Exit.
Alb. Go after her. She's desperate; govern her.
[Exit an Officer.]

Edm. What, you have charg'd me with, that have I done,
And more, much more. The time will bring it out.
'Tis past, and so am I.- But what art thou
That hast this fortune on me? If thou'rt noble,
I do forgive thee.
Edg. Let's exchange charity.
I am no less in blood than thou art, Edmund;
If more, the more th' hast wrong'd me.
My name is Edgar and thy father's son.
The gods are just, and of our pleasant vices
Make instruments to scourge us.
The dark and vicious place where thee he got
Cost him his eyes.
Edm. Th' hast spoken right; 'tis true.
The wheel is come full circle; I am here.
Alb. Methought thy very gait did prophesy
A royal nobleness. I must embrace thee.
Let sorrow split my heart if ever I
Did hate thee, or thy father!
Edg. Worthy prince, I know't.
Alb. Where have you hid yourself?
How have you known the miseries of your father?
Edg. By nursing them, my lord. List a brief tale;
And when 'tis told, O that my heart would burst!
The bloody proclamation to escape
That follow'd me so near (O, our lives' sweetness!
That with the pain of death would hourly die
Rather than die at once!) taught me to shift
Into a madman's rags, t' assume a semblance
That very dogs disdain'd; and in this habit

Met I my father with his bleeding rings,
Their precious stones new lost; became his guide,
Led him, begg'd for him, sav'd him from despair;
Never (O fault!) reveal'd myself unto him
Until some half hour past, when I was arm'd,
Not sure, though hoping of this good success,
I ask'd his blessing, and from first to last
Told him my pilgrimage. But his flaw'd heart
(Alack, too weak the conflict to support!)
'Twixt two extremes of passion, joy and grief,
Burst smilingly.
Edm. This speech of yours hath mov'd me,
And shall perchance do good; but speak you on;
You look as you had something more to say.
Alb. If there be more, more woful, hold it in;
For I am almost ready to dissolve,
Hearing of this.
Edg. This would have seem'd a period
To such as love not sorrow; but another,
To amplify too much, would make much more,
And top extremity.
Whilst I was big in clamour, came there a man,
Who, having seen me in my worst estate,
Shunn'd my abhorr'd society; but then, finding
Who 'twas that so endur'd, with his strong arms
He fastened on my neck, and bellowed out
As he'd burst heaven; threw him on my father;
Told the most piteous tale of Lear and him
That ever ear receiv'd; which in recounting
His grief grew puissant, and the strings of life

Began to crack. Twice then the trumpets sounded,
And there I left him tranc'd.
Alb. But who was this?
Edg. Kent, sir, the banish'd Kent; who in disguise
Followed his enemy king and did him service
Improper for a slave.

Enter a Gentleman with a bloody knife.

Gent. Help, help! O, help!
Edg. What kind of help?
Alb. Speak, man.
Edg. What means that bloody knife?
Gent. 'Tis hot, it smokes.
It came even from the heart of- O! she's dead!
Alb. Who dead? Speak, man.
Gent. Your lady, sir, your lady! and her sister
By her is poisoned; she hath confess'd it.
Edm. I was contracted to them both. All three
Now marry in an instant.

Enter Kent.

Edg. Here comes Kent.
Alb. Produce their bodies, be they alive or dead.
[Exit Gentleman.]
This judgement of the heavens, that makes us tremble
Touches us not with pity. O, is this he?
The time will not allow the compliment
That very manners urges.
Kent. I am come
To bid my king and master aye good night.
Is he not here?

Alb. Great thing of us forgot!
Speak, Edmund, where's the King? and where's Cordelia?
The bodies of Goneril and Regan are brought in.
Seest thou this object, Kent?
Kent. Alack, why thus?
Edm. Yet Edmund was belov'd.
The one the other poisoned for my sake,
And after slew herself.
Alb. Even so. Cover their faces.
Edm. I pant for life. Some good I mean to do,
Despite of mine own nature. Quickly send
(Be brief in't) to the castle; for my writ
Is on the life of Lear and on Cordelia.
Nay, send in time.
Alb. Run, run, O, run!
Edg. To who, my lord? Who has the office? Send
Thy token of reprieve.
Edm. Well thought on. Take my sword;
Give it the Captain.
Alb. Haste thee for thy life. [Exit Edgar.]
Edm. He hath commission from thy wife and me
To hang Cordelia in the prison and
To lay the blame upon her own despair
That she fordid herself.
Alb. The gods defend her! Bear him hence awhile.
[Edmund is borne off.]
Enter Lear, with Cordelia [dead] in his arms, [Edgar, Captain, and others following].
Lear. Howl, howl, howl, howl! O, you are men of stone.

Had I your tongues and eyes, I'ld use them so
That heaven's vault should crack. She's gone for ever!
I know when one is dead, and when one lives.
She's dead as earth. Lend me a looking glass.
If that her breath will mist or stain the stone,
Why, then she lives.
Kent. Is this the promis'd end?
Edg. Or image of that horror?
Alb. Fall and cease!
Lear. This feather stirs; she lives! If it be so,
It is a chance which does redeem all sorrows
That ever I have felt.
Kent. O my good master!
Lear. Prithee away!
Edg. 'Tis noble Kent, your friend.
Lear. A plague upon you, murderers, traitors all!
I might have sav'd her; now she's gone for ever!
Cordelia, Cordelia! stay a little. Ha!
THE END

Bibliography

Douglas, B.: *English Literature in the Earlier Seventeenth Century, 1600-1660*, Oxford, Clarendon Press, 1962.

Edmund, Kerchever: *English Literature at the Close of the Middle Ages*, New York: Oxford University Press, 1947.

Florette, Henri: *Kings Mountain*, Garden City, Doubleday, 1950.

Garrison, Webb: *Great Stories of the American Revolution*, Nashville, Rutledge Hill Press, 1990.

Glynne, William Gladstone: *Early English Stages, 1300 to 1660*, London, Routledge and Paul; 1959.

James, Runcieman: *English Literature of the Late Seventeenth Century*, New York, Oxford University Press, 1969.

John, S.: *This Destructive War: The British Campaign in the Carolinas, 1780-1782*, University of Alabama Press, 1985.

Laver, J.: *Principles of Phonetics*, Cambridge, Cambridge University Press, 1994.

Logan, P.: *The Later Jacobean and Caroline Dramatists*, Lincoln, University of Nebraska Press, 1978.

Matricardi, Paolo: *Complete Book of World War II Combat Aircraft*, NY, Military Press, 1988

Rahilly, J.: *Phonetics: The Science of Speech*, London, Arnold, 1999.

Roberta, G.: *Deadly Fashion: the Rise and Fall of Cigurette Smoking in North America*, New York, Garland, 1989.

Royle, Trevor: *The Macmillan Companion to Scottish Literature*, London, MacMillan Reference Books, 1983.

Seidlhofer, B.: *Pronunciation, Oxford*, Oxford University Press, 1994.

Stevenson, Lionel: *Victorian Fiction: a Guide to Research*, Cambridge, Harvard University Press, 1966.

Sydney, J.: *Brands, Consumers, Symbols and Research*, Thousand Oaks, Sage Publications, 1999.

Thorpe, Ernest: *Principles of Textual Criticism*, San Marino, Huntington Library, 1972.

Underhill, A.: *Sound Foundations*, London, Heineman, 1994.

Wearing, J. P.: *The London Stage, 1890-1899: a Calendar of Plays and Players*, NJ, Scarecrow Press, 1976.

Wickham, Gladstone: *Early English Stages, 1300 to 1660*, London, Routledge and Paul; 1959.

William, John: *A History of English Poetry*, London, MacMillan and Co., 1903.

Index

A

Account, 90.
Albany, 89, 90, 91, 94, 99, 114, 119, 120, 142, 166, 188, 189, 193.
Alexander, 264, 285, 286.
Armado, 205, 211, 212, 214, 215, 216, 217, 218, 219, 220, 230, 231, 232, 233, 234, 239, 240, 242, 245.

B

Blackamoors, 270, 275.
Boyet, 222, 223, 226, 227, 228, 229, 230, 236, 237.
Brutus, 12, 13, 19, 20, 21, 22, 23, 25, 26, 27, 28, 29, 30, 31, 35, 36, 39, 40, 41, 42, 43, 44, 45, 46, 47.

C

Citizens, 13, 49, 58.
Commission, 155, 193, 201.
Composition, 101, 124.
Court, 91, 113, 117, 119, 144, 192, 206, 207, 210, 211, 221, 223, 224, 229, 240.

D

Dreams, 26, 34.

E

Evidence, 155.

F

Flourish, 3, 4, 6, 8, 38, 96, 99, 124, 193, 221, 256.
Forbidden, 221.

G

Goneril, 89, 91, 92, 96, 105, 112, 114, 115, 116, 132, 137, 139, 148, 155, 158, 159, 165, 166, 177, 183, 188, 190, 193, 194, 197, 201.

H

Hercules, 217, 253, 259, 264, 285, 287.
Holofernes, 205, 242, 243, 244, 245, 246, 247.

I

Influence, 104, 127, 295.
Instruments, 16, 22, 198.
Intelligence, 120.
Invention, 101, 246, 247.

J

Judgement, 24, 52, 200.
Julius Caesar, 1, 83.
Justice, 64, 145, 155, 159, 179, 196, 260.

K

King, 21, 89, 90, 91, 94, 95, 96, 97, 99, 101, 103, 105, 108, 112, 126, 129, 130, 134, 135, 142, 143, 144, 148, 154, 157, 158.

L

Language, 271.
Law, 40, 90, 100, 146, 180, 197, 210, 260, 280.
Liberty, 41, 42, 43, 91, 135, 234.
Lucius, 19, 20, 21, 22, 27, 30, 36, 38, 61, 63, 68, 69, 72, 73, 74, 75.

M

Majesty, 93, 94, 95, 96, 97, 184, 185, 203, 210, 225, 255.

P

Philosophy, 69, 79, 207.
Pilgrimage, 199.
Poetry, 247.
Poverty, 148, 275, 279.
Power, 17, 20, 56, 70, 82, 94, 95, 102, 115, 142, 147, 154, 159, 171, 179, 190, 203, 222, 249.
Punishment, 150, 169, 214.

R

Regan, 89, 91, 92, 96, 119, 120, 122, 123, 125, 135, 136, 137, 138, 139, 141, 148, 156,

S

Sonnets, 248.

T

Titinius, 7, 61, 63, 68, 69, 72, 76, 80, 81, 82, 83, 84.

V

Victory, 83, 189, 239.

W

Wisdom, 33, 45, 50, 103, 109, 113, 117, 141, 167.